Henry VIII
and the
Conforming Catholics

by

Paul O'Grady

A Michael Glazier Book
THE LITURGICAL PRESS
Collegeville, Minnesota

A Michael Glazier Book
published by
THE LITURGICAL PRESS

Cover design by David Manahan, O.S.B. This detail from the title-page illustration of the Great Bible, also called Cranmer's Bible (1540), is from Holbein's woodcut depicting Henry VIII seated while Archbishop Cranmer and Thomas Cromwell distribute copies to the people.

Typography by Brenda Belizzone, Mary Brown, Phyllis Boyd LeVane.

1	2	3	4	5	6	7	8	9	10

Library of Congress Cataloging-in-Publication Data
O'Grady, Paul.
    Henry VIII and the conforming Catholics / by Paul O'Grady.
        p.   cm.
    "A Michael Glazier book."
    Includes bibliographical references and indexes.
    ISBN 0-8146-5781-8
    1. Catholics—England—History—16th century. 2. Church of England—History—16th century. 3. England—Church history—16th century. 4. Reformation—England. 5. Anglican Communion—England--History—16th century. 6. Catholic Church—England—History—16th century. I. Title. II. Title: Henry 8th and the conforming Catholics.
BX1492.047 1990
282'.42'09031—dc20   89-7635
                                          CIP

Contents

Dedicated With Love

to
My Mother, Amy O'Grady Ceitlin
My Aunt, Nathlie Koelling Ernman
Ronnie and Jean Koelling
and
In Loving Memory
of
Margaret Fortune Fay

Introduction

The present book offers a general study of Henrician Catholic apologetics. A great part of its evidence rests upon published English language tracts written by conforming Catholics during and after the schism with Rome. These writings offer a rationale for the new settlement, defending it from the imputations of Papist and Reformer alike. Some few of these works are well known; most are not. In either case, with relatively few exceptions, they seem to have been inadequately examined with reference to content and import. I have eschewed detailed consideration of the official formulae of Henrician religion. These have been exhaustively analyzed by pens more competent than mine; moreover, it is a cardinal principle of this book that the official and Catholic positions ought not to be confused even when, as is the case with the "King's Book", they appear to be almost identical.

Plainly then, what follows is a treatise in the history of ideas. Its author's assumption is that intellectual systems, once generated, have a logic of their own, partially autonomous from those circumstances which bring them to birth, cosset them, or thrust them aside. Nevertheless, I am keenly aware that any school of thought is conditioned by historical factors extraneous to it, and I hope not to have fallen too frequently into what Prof. G.R. Elton so aptly describes as the "pitfall of intellectual history . . . its uncertainty as to what actually happened."

On the other hand, I offer no apology for concentrating on ideas themselves. Mental activity is history too. Sixteenth century man interpreted his world in theological terms. To some degree this terminology is alien to us today; nevertheless, a trap awaits those who would attempt to force Henrician thought into categories foreign to it. In his otherwise seminal study, *Tudor Prelates and Politics*, Dr. L.B. Smith tags the conforming Catholics as apostles of "worldly prudence" and their Protestant antagonists as "idealists". Such terms are reminiscent of American political theory of four decades ago, and one may doubt their appositeness when applied to Tudor religious rivalries. If—to cite but one obvious objection—the conforming Catholic leadership was marked by "worldly prudence", why, even as the weightier party, did they so badly bungle the transition to the next reign? and why were many of the same leaders so inflexible as to then suffer imprisonment for their convictions?

It was precisely this sort of question that led me to the present subject. Years of reading in Tudor history had left me increasingly puzzled about the Catholic leadership who subscribed to the settlement. Did simple *timor mori* explain all? In light of the real hardships undergone by many of them in the reign of Edward VI, and again in that of Elizabeth, when conformity would indeed have been the prudent course, I could not bring myself to believe that mere timidity or opportunism offered a sufficient rationale for their position. Yet the fact remained that few historians had a good word to say for the Henrician Catholics, and more importantly, little effort had been expended to make their position intelligible. Conforming Catholicism became and has remained the neglected stepchild of the Tudor revolution.

This neglect of Henrician Catholicism has deep roots in Tudor historiography. The earliest Reformation historians (and no small number of their successors) were men of ardent religious conviction. Their histories were polemical reenactments of the original struggles. And, albeit for separate reasons, Roman Catholic and Protestant historians alike were predisposed to look upon the Catholic conformists with aversion. In the first case, the increasingly prevalent role of the papacy in post-Tridentine Catholicism made it difficult for historians of the Roman persuasion to grasp that for many (possibly most) Tudor Catholics, the primacy was a peripheral doctrine, or even an expediency, rather than a central article of faith. And had not the schism produced notable martyrs in the persons of Fisher, More and the Carthusians? That the surviving conformists submitted to Rome with something like avidity under Mary served to clinch the matter:

for the Roman historian, conforming Catholicism could be written off as a lamentable defection of fortitude.

Arriving from the opposite direction, Protestant historians reached a similar if harsher verdict. For the Protestant, there was little more to Henrician Catholicism than the duplicity of its adherents. Wanting the boldness of a More or Fisher, and bent to pliancy by a masterful King, these craven-spirited men were compelled to dissemble their covert popery until the accession of Queen Mary. Then indeed, their cankered consciences revealed themselves to exact an awesome vengeance.

More peculiar, at first sight, is the reluctance of the 19th century Anglo-Catholic school to lay claim to their forbearers. No doubt these hesitations are rooted in their predecessors ready submission to Rome, and the role played by many of them in the Marian persecutions. It must be conceded that "wily Winchester" and "Bloody Bonner" were hardly promising prototypes for a fresh doctrinal and devotional revival. In quest of a more reputable pedigree, a number of the High-Church party embarked upon the unrewarding task of demonstrating that Cranmer and Ridley were misunderstood Catholics!

But what of more recent historians, unencumbered by sectarian *parti pris*, or perhaps, by any religious interest at all? These, too, have tended to gloss over the conforming Catholics. Perhaps here we may detect the subtle influence of the prevailing *zeitgeist*, whether progressive or Marxist, which works to diminish our interest in those who have gone under in a given historical contest. And certainly the Henrician Catholic party did collapse, and with a finality that might have occasioned more astonishment than it has. Yet analysis of this very failure can serve to illuminate previously obscure areas of the Tudor crisis.

•　•　•

A word about the limitations of this study. As suggested before, I have restricted my investigation of primary sources to domestic propaganda written in English: sermons, tracts, and apologetics having a polemical thrust. (Where a tract—such as Richard Sampson's *Oratio*—was written in Latin and later translated, I have used the translation, but never without first referring to the original. The translations are invariably made by men more "evangelically" minded than the authors.) Against good advice, I have decided not to extend this study beyond the middle of the reign of Edward VI. (The few Marian

referred to are used as "controls".) I hope instead, to show that the
the years 1533 - 1550 are an integral and coherent unit of study. After
1550, the nature of the challenges confronting English Catholicism
change radically. Quite simply, the Act of Uniformity (1549) mandated
a Protestant Prayer Book while simultaneously outlawing the practice
of Catholicism in England. During the last three years of Edward VI's
reign, still more radical reforms were introduced. From 1550 onward,
it was clear that Catholic survival would be wholly dependent on
continental succor. The price to be paid for this was submission to
Rome. Nor could there by any doubt that from the moment of her
accession to the throne, the Princess Mary would settle for anything
less than recognition of the Roman primacy.

I must alert the reader to my failure to take account of two disparate
factors. The first, and to my mind more negligible, is the indebtedness
of Henrician Catholic polemicists to earlier English writers such as
Fisher and More, or to continental papists such as Cochlaeus or Eck.
Of course, the Henrician Catholics did not confess their borrowings: it
would have been dangerous for them to have done so; in any case, it
was Tudor practice to give scant recognition to contemporary sources.
Aside from certain commonplace Catholic arguments, I have not
attempted to identify specific sources. Consequently, I may have
attributed greater originality to certain writers than may be properly
claimed for them.

More serious is the book's failure to take account of the waning of
Catholic devotional life. Here was one feature of the Henrician Reformation by no means abridged by the fall of Thomas Cromwell, and it
may be argued that no other factor played so great a role in the
enervation of English Catholicism than the progressive curtailment
during Henry's reign of the public festivals and private devotions which
characterized the old faith. Trained theologians might espy sinister
portents in the lacunae of the *Ten Articles*; for the populace at large
such distinctions signified little or nothing. Far more important was
the war of attrition waged against centuries of parochial custom,
against the private and public rites of veneration. Bishop and dogmatic
theologian, pinched by the requirements of political accommodation
or mesmerized by Erasmian minimalism might settle for a stubborn
modicum of orthodoxy: behind them, the great masses shifted imper-
ceptibly from their moorings. Exactly when and how this shift took
place is yet impossible to say:[1] suffice to for the present that at some

point within the quarter of a century discussed in this book, Catholicism came to represent a sect rather than a consensus.

The withering of traditional Catholic piety proved an impossible theme to integrate into this book, for it is a large issue, belonging more to social than intellectual history. Still, I beg the reader to keep it in mind as an essential, contributing factor to the fortunes of Henrician Catholicism.

I cannot claim to have contributed much that is original in my consideration of two great Henrician Catholics, Stephen Gardiner and John Longland. The first, particularly, has been the subject of biography of James Muller, the editor of a splendid edition of the Bishop's letters. I am deeply indebted to both books, and of course to Pierre Janelle's edition of Gardiner's three early tracts.

More recently, M. Bowker has offered some penetrating remarks on the theology of John Longland, bishop of Lincoln—particularly with regard to Longland's attack on simony.[2] We are in agreement over the Bishop's unique understanding of the Supremacy as a reinforcement of episcopal autarchy.

The reader will note that I have devoted considerable attention to the religious thought of Thomas Starkey: here, for better or worse, I can claim to offer a thoroughgoing revision. In the case of other prominent conforming Catholics: Cuthbert Tunstall, Richard Sampson, John Stokesley, Simon Mathew, Edward Lee, John Standish, William Peryn, and, above all, Richard Smith, I hope to have been able to bring fresh insights into the character of their thought. Want of space and fear of redundancy have impelled me to give short shrift to others such as Roger Edgeworth and John Clerk, while any balanced treatment of the issues demanded fresh consideration of Bishops Gardiner and Longland.

One final observation. In a number of instances, I have taken issue with some eminent scholars. I hope these occasional nips will be understood within their context—as ungracious acknowledgements of debts too enormous to repay.

As to the structure of the book: an introductory chapter attempts to place conforming Catholicism within the frame of the reign itself. Three subsequent chapters discuss the antecedents of Henrician Catholicism: those factors lodged in medieval and Renaissance thought which allowed the conformists to construct a vindication of their position within traditional precedents. Finally, the concluding chapters offer a survey of Catholic polemics, and some explanation for the failure to achieve cohesion among themselves and to carry the day against the Reformers.

1

Henry VIII and Conforming Catholicism

"That Henricianism was merely 'Catholicism without the pope' will not do" writes Dr. Scarisbrick in his magisterial study of Henry VIII: in that judgment the present writer wholly concurs.[1] The Henrician "settlement" was achieved, late in 1534, with the Act of Supremacy. From that date, until the decisive lurch leftward in 1549, Henrician religion embraced two distinct factions, the avowed goal of which was the elimination of the other. To be sure, at the time of the schism, the supporters of the old religion were the overwhelming majority, but by 1536, the balance had been somewhat righted by the government's insinuation of reform-minded clerics into certain key bishoprics of southern convocation. From the onset, the struggle between Catholic and Reformer was without quarter, yet no less strictly manipulated by the government. But may we speak of a discernible government policy? In taking account of the maze of starts, feints, retractions and contradictions which comprised government procedure between 1529 and 1549, the very term "settlement" seems ludicrously inapposite: flux, not fixity, is the hallmark of Henricianism.

To grasp the situation, we must, once and for all, discard the legend of a king who stoutly maintained all of Catholicism save the papal primacy. The facts do not support the legend. As early as October 1529, we find Henry startling the Imperial ambassador with a measured critique of Luther,[2] remarkable surely from the reputed author of the *Assertio*. Nor was this all: the new permissiveness was corroborated in the same year by the papal legate who remarked upon the free circulation of heretical books at the court, apparently with the King's connivance.[3] The diplomatic accounts in their turn lend credibility to other, and less verifiable anecdotes of Henry's receptivity to the Reformation at this early date: his kindness to the widow of Simon Fish, and (more revealing in this suppositious Catholic) his receptivity to William Tyndale's *Obedience of a Christian Man*. According to John Foxe, in 1529 Cardinal Wolsey gave instructions to confiscate all heretical books, and Richard Sampson, then Dean of Windsor, had snatched the offending volume from the hands of a young man in the Boleyn circle. Anne had vowed to make the Cardinal pay for his temerity, and presented the book to Henry, who after perusing it remarked that "this book is for me and all kings to read."[4]

Those who would make a dogma of Henry's orthodoxy often explain these and similar discrepancies by alluding to one or another temporarily prevailing influence with the King. In the above story, for instance, Foxe attributes the royal favor toward Tyndale to the suasions of "the lady Anne":

> ... and in a little time the King, by the help of this virtuous lady ... had his eyes opened to the truth, to advance God's religion and glory, to abhor the pope's doctrine ... and to deliver his subjects of the Egyptian darkness ... [5]

Now, however, one may choose to credit this tale, it has the defect of assuming a theological passivity in Henry not borne out by the primary documents. While Anne certainly was a patroness of prominent Reformers,[6] one may doubt the future queen "opened" Henry's eyes to the truth. For one thing, Anne's Protestantism appears more politique than profound: under sentence of death, she asked for the sacrament to be reserved in her chamber.[7] Moreover, it is clear that Anne, whatever her endowments, lacked the skill to sway Henry's theological opinions: a king who showed small inclination to retreat when confronted with the learned arguments of Cranmer or Tunstall was hardly likely to submit himself to the casuistry of the "lady Anne". One may hazard that the gloss on this story is little more than the attempt of an Elizabethan polemicist to enhance the great Queen's pedigree through presenting her mother as a patroness of the Gospel. It is to the same category, perhaps, that we should consign Foxe's cloying tale of Anne's evangelical mission to the refractory nuns of Syon.[8]

Somewhat more convincing are the arguments made for the influence of Thomas Cromwell. Certainly this energetic and ubiquitous minister gave focus to Henry's previously diffuse efforts to grapple with the Church. It was he who synchronized the government's campaign to reform, reduce and mulct the ecclesiastical estate, and it is to his genius that we must ascribe the coordination of the propaganda campaign, and the recruitment of those talented polemicists, Richard Morison and Thomas Starkey, from Pole's nest of scholars in Padua.[9] Nevertheless, it is unlikely that Cromwell either moved the King's religious opinions or, as the attainder against him charged, subverted the settlement by conspiring to advance a religious policy repugnant to Henry.

Though the matter is both too tangential and too complicated to be thoroughly discussed here, we may urge the following three considerations with reference to Cromwell's influence: (1) Henry's receptivity to theological innovation preceded by three years at least the ascendancy of his first minister; (2) the King had a lively amateur's interest- and competence—in theology. Cromwell, even if one holds with Prof. Elton's verdict on the minister's sincere Protestantism,[10] evinces no like flair. His voluminous correspondence reveals only the conventional religious platitudes of the day, and a probably genuine, if pragmatic, interest in advancing "Reform"; (3) finally, after the execution of Cromwell in July 1540, the King continued the policy of temporizing in religious questions as before, in spite of the fact that the Six Articles, supposedly a mirror of the King's Catholic theology—and passed during the ascendancy of Cromwell—were enacted to secure a retrenchment.

Indeed after the Six Articles, and concurrent with Cromwell's fall, we note a most extraordinary example of Henry's propensity to unsettle his own settlement. This is a seventeen-part questionnaire, drafted by Cranmer, clearly with the King's connivance, and sent to a number of bishops and theologians. In effect, the questionnaire (on the sacraments) reopens in the most provocative way the very issues closed to inquiry by the Six Articles a year previously. Nothing could make more clear the provisional nature of those articles, at least so far as the King was concerned.[11]

Still more astonishing (if it is to be believed) is the proposal, reported by Cranmer's secretary Morice, that the King made to a visiting French emissary in 1546: that Henry and Francis jointly abolish the mass in their respective domains, and seize the property of the chantries.[12] Perhaps the proposal reflects no more than Henry's hope of seducing Francis from the forthcoming Council of Trent,[13] though there is compelling evidence that Henry was dissuaded from further innovations at this time by bishop Gardiner's frank threat that these would wreck the Anglo-Imperial alliance.[14] In any event, the project, whether seriously mooted or not, is scarcely the speculation of a man who is still a "good Catholic": rather it is evidence of the erosion of his earlier beliefs.

One is aware, of course, that Henry could and did strike intermittently at Protestant factions. But these were invariably sacramentaries, or, in the case of Cromwell and Barnes, this was the (quite implausible) indictment drawn against them. Still, no one would attempt to deny that in certain matters, e.g., the Real Presence in the sacrament* and the celibacy of the clergy, Henry held fast to convictions best described as conservative. But a *melange* of incoherent prejudices is very far from a firm Catholic theology, antipapal or not.

All this is quite germane to our subject, for if we are to grasp the position of Henrician Catholics, it is essential to understand that Henry VIII was scarcely more a Catholic than a Protestant. He was no Catholic because, as we shall see, he adamantly refused to define, or allow to be defined, the corporate nature of a visible, teaching Church. To put it plainly, he would not abdicate his recently acquired spiritual authority to a pope, councils or tradition. Insofar as the King posited any spiritual arbiter in matters of faith, this was scripture, as interpreted by the Supreme Head himself. He did not, to be sure, claim direct inspiration from the Holy Spirit, but he certainly approached the notion of a sacerdotal monarchy where all priestly power issued from his own person.[15]

Significantly, Henry found sole support for this view among the Reformers, particularly Cranmer and Barlow, the two most "advanced" bishops on the bench (after the resignations of Latimer and Shaxton in 1539). In the above mentioned questionnaire, there appears the query, whether bishops or *anyone else* may make a priest?[16] the implication, made explicit two questions further on, being whether a king may make a priest. To this, Cranmer and Barlow replied affirmatively: " ... so may princes and governors also .... "[17] The bid, however, was disallowed by the Catholic majority whose opinion was trenchantly expressed by Edward Lee, Archbishop of York: " ... that any other than bishops ... may make a priest, we neither find in scripture nor out of scripture."[18] In the face of massive disapproval, the King and his southern primate, neither wanting in prudence, backed down, and sacerdotal monarchy passed into the limbo of bizarre theologies.

As mentioned before, Henry appears to have approximated a belief in *sola scriptura*. Earlier Protestant historians of the reign have appreciated this more than their successors, and consequently have been prepared to take the King's "Protestantism" more seriously. For Hall, Foxe, and Strype, Henry was not merely the prince who opened the portals to the Reformation; he was prepared to stride a considerable distance through them. On reflection, this view has something to commend it. The entire affair of the divorce turned on an appeal to scripture against the authority of pope and canon law. Inculcated in this school, the King does not appear to have forgotten his lessons. As early as 1530, before a conference of bishops and doctors, the King promised to have the New Testament "purely translated into the English tongue."[19] In fact, the project would be deferred until the ascendancy of Cromwell, when it was carried out in fits and starts, until the publication of the *Great Bible* in 1539. But before this, at the convocation which drew up the Ten Articles (1536) or shortly thereafter, during the preliminary meetings which issued in the *Bishops' Book*, Henry, through his Vicar-general, instructed his assembled clergy to "determine all things by Scripture and not by custom or unwritten verities."[20] The royal proclivity toward *sola scriptura* stood as one effective impediment to the working out of a specifically antipapal Catholic theology by his more conservative theologians.

Some historians have expressed amazement at the persistent harmony between the King and his southern primate, but closer investigation does much to dissolve the assumed dichotomy of their opinions. On such matters as *sola scriptura* and the sacerdotal monarchy they shared an accord best described as solitary. It is difficult to agree with those surprised at the boldness of Cranmer's letter of 1536 to his prince, advising him toward further reformation.[21] In good part, the Archbishop's words are no more than an echo of the King's sentiments. On the contrary, it would appear that Cranmer was closer to the King on certain theological matters than were Catholics like Gardiner, Stokesley, and Lee, with whom Henry is usually presumed to have had a greater religious affinity. And seen from this point of view, Henry's unfailing loyalty to his primate is somewhat less mysterious.

But this said, it must be added that Cranmer, no more than the Catholic prelates, had decisive influence with the King. Very early, the primate showed himself willing to entertain the distinctively Lutheran doctrine of *sola fide* and to advertise the same to Henry.[22] But the King refused the bait. Professor Scarisbrick has clearly delineated Henry's stubborn commitment to "pelagianism".[23] Here, Henry must be aligned with Erasmus and the Florentine Platonists, and his convictions flew contrary not only to the Lutherans, but to papists like Pole and Contarini as well as Henrician Catholics such as Longland and Pate. Cranmer did not give up hope of winning the King to the truth, but over and again, Henry would delete or qualify solefidian formulae presented to him for approval. On this point, he remained firm to the end.[24]

What all this amounts to is that Henry remained very much his own theologian, no trivial point in light of the great latitude the new settlement allowed him in imposing his views on the national Church. Nor was the King modest in the exercise of his office as *magister* of *Ecclesia Anglicana*: the royal apologists were confirming the fact of the matter (and more), as well as resuscitating the *imperium*, when they compared Henry to Justinian.[25] One example, among multitudes, of the royal self assurance are Henry's dealings with Cuthbert Tunstall, bishop of Durham. In the judgment of Chapuys, Tunstall was "one of the wisest, most learned and virtuous prelates of this kingdom",[26] a verdict in which Pole and others concurred with no qualifications at all.[27] This did not save the renowned bishop from a magisterial royal rebuke when, during the discussions preceding the formulation of the Six Articles, he attempted to persuade Henry that auricular confession was enjoined by the divine law.[28] The King peppered the bishop's letter with snappy one-liners such as "fallax" and "si praeceptum habaret, non praecipi persuaderet", then took pen in hand himself to refute the bishop, and in terms which hardly encouraged further unsolicited advice.[29] We may add that in the forthcoming articles, Henry's view, which coincided with that of Cranmer, carried the day.

In light of this and similar rebukes and humiliations, one must ask how some Catholics continued to hoodwink themselves about Henry's bed-rock orthodoxy. No doubt, their very subscription to the supremacy inclined many to self-deception, wishful thinking or, at least, the simulation thereof. Nor must one underestimate Henry's skill at playing the role of 'captive prince', bewitched by cunning women and wicked counselors. Time and again, e.g., with the fall of Anne Boleyn and Thomas Cromwell, Catholic hopes were raised, only to be rudely dashed in the aftermath.[30] A like inference, perhaps, lay behind the abortive conspiracies against Cranmer and Catherine Parr. In 1545, Stephen Gardiner, writing to Paget, could assure the latter that Henry's occasional permissiveness to the new sect was founded on no more than guile and diplomatic accommodation.[31]

Yet we may be wary of taking all this too solemnly. English Protestants, no less than Catholics, could take Henry for their protector: Cranmer, no less than Gardiner, could insist that Henry was "deceived" (or deceiving) when he acted in a way antipathetic to the "truth".[32] One wonders indeed how so many, contemporaries as well as later historians, have found it in themselves to credit this image of Henry the Gullible, the easily-put-upon, bambozzled in turn by Wolsey, Cromwell, Gardiner, Cranmer, his wives, whoever. Surely a more viable picture emerges of Henry the Lion-tamer, possessed in full measure of his second daughter's genius for keeping potentially disruptive factions in dynamic equilibrium.

That Henry himself presided over the contending parties, favoring first one side, then the other, and again, taking his own very personal course; this must be grasped if we are to put Henrician Catholicism in its proper perspective. At times, particularly when the two continental powers seemed on the verge of alliance against England, it behooved the King to posture as a traditionalist. Domestic disturbances too, such as the risings of 1536, might signal a more effective application of the bit to Protestant radicals. But never, after 1534, were Catholics to be in undisputed control of policy making. Even the triumphs of 1539, 1540 and 1543 proved illusory, and more brief than any might have anticipated. After the Six Articles, we have seen Henry stirring (or urging Cranmer to stir) the same waters he seemed so anxious to still but a year before. The second Catholic triumph, accompanied by the Catherine Howard marriage and the "King's Book", also ended darkly with the young Queen's execution, and the backfiring of the Prebendaries' Plot. From 1544 onward, the Catholic position steadily deteriorated until the fall of Norfolk and the exclusion of Gardiner from the Council led to the ultimate debacle of a Protestant regency.

• • •

If the foregoing outline be accepted (and much of the evidence is yet to be sketched in), it becomes apparent that the Catholic position from

1534 to 1549 was never less than precarious. A similar insecurity continually beset those Catholics who sought to defend the old religion within the terms of the new settlement. From the inception of the break with Rome, the Catholic apologist had to repel the charge of bad faith, and this on two fronts. Papists explained (or condoned) his surrender to the Royal Supremacy as a consequence of timidity or crass time serving. So the bishop of Faenza, papal nuncio in Paris, described Stephen Gardiner, royal apologist *par excellence* to his Roman correspondent:

> The bishop of Winton [Winchester] is most desirous of returning to the right road, and he made his book *De Vera Obedientia* under compulsion, not having the strength to suffer death patiently . . . [33]

Less charitable was Reginald Pole who accused Richard Sampson, first of the Henrician Catholics into the field with an apologia, as a "Judas" who sold himself for the prospect of becoming heir to the rich diocese of Norwich.[34]

Papist fire was the more deadly since its premises were shared by the King, Cromwell, and the Protestant clique; they, too, questioned the sincerity of conforming Catholic leaders, and the government soon pressed them into printed commitment. It is indeed noteworthy that the publicity and polemics of the Supremacy were written largely by those identified with the old religion. In the five years succeeding the Act in Restraint of Appeals, Richard Sampson, Stephen Gardiner, Simon Mathew, John Longland, Thomas Starkey and Cuthbert Tunstall were impressed into the government's propaganda machine. Of the highly placed, prominent men who wrote tracts favoring the new order, only Edward Fox, the diplomatist, was of dubious orthodoxy.[35] That the government used various pressures to procure public conformity cannot be doubted by those familiar with the record. Stephen Gardiner wrote his tract against John Fisher and *De Vera Obedientia* to redeem himself from a precipitous fall from favor which followed his opposition to the King.[36] Simon Mathew found himself in print after justifying the execution of Fisher and More at S. Paul's,[37] while anti-papal diatribes won a book a piece for Longland and Tunstall respectively. Only Bishop Stokesley of London successfully resisted the importunities of Cromwell. Sometime in Lent, 1535, this archconservative delivered himself of a rousing tirade against papal authority, and Cromwell made a memorandum to have the bishop write out and make a book of his sermon.[38] The story then takes a somewhat mysterious turn. Three months later (25 July) Chapuys wrote to Charles V that the King's minister was so enthusiastic over Stokesley's sermon that he would have given £1000 sterling for the Emperor to have heard it. Oddly enough, Chapuys was under the impression that Cromwell had heard the sermon "a few days ago", which raises the speculation that Stokesley had preached the same sermon twice. On this occasion, Cromwell promised to have Stokesley write the sermon out, and asked the ambassador to forward it to his master. Whether this was done is not clear. But when Cromwell called upon the bishop to deliver it to the printer, Stokesley demurred, writing Cromwell that the sermon had been preached *ex tempore*, as was his habit, and further that it was "superfluous" since he had said nothing not already published in the book of Edward Fox. Cromwell was patently annoyed, but further pressure failed to produce a book.[39]

Vigorous antipapal polemics, however, did not absolve Catholics from the suspicion of covertly favoring Rome and a return to the old ways. It was government policy to send only the most impeccably orthodox clergy to convert the recusant inmates of Syon.[40] Yet while Stephen Gardiner was on a mission there to do just that, Henry wrote to Cromwell (23 April 1535) voicing his suspicions of Winchester's "colored doubleness" and ordering his minister to search out evidence for the same.[41] Similar imprecations befell Edward Lee performing a like mission among the Carthusians of Hull and Mountgrace.[42] A battery of questions put to Bishop Fisher, then in the Tower for overt failure to comply with the new laws, reveals that the government entertained similar suspicions of bishops Veysey (Exeter), Sherbourne (Chichester), Clerk (Bath & Wells) and, again, of Edward Lee. Though Fisher's replies apparently exonerated all of these, Lee, in particular, was the subject of increasing suspicion during the late summer and autumn of 1535[43]—altogether an uncomfortable time for the Henrician Catholic leadership. Further evidence will be presented later for this harassment; it will suffice at this point to note that, while in some cases it abated in intensity, it would remain a permanent feature of the reign.

We must now turn to the question of how far the government's suspicions were objectively justified. Was the Catholic leadership covertly papist? And were its professions of loyalty merely specious? Did the examples of Fisher, More and the other martyrs produce a merely surface acquiescence among the rest? Such questions are, of course, impossible to answer with any degree of certitude, since such evidence as we have, seldom carries us to the heart of individual motives. In rare figures such as Richard Pate, ambassador to the Emperor, who absconded to Rome in 1541, we might assume that a suspicion of covert popery was justified, though, turning the question, we may well ask if the government's prior suspicions were not the deciding impetus of his flight? A little surmise might be attached to the case of Richard Smith, a daring Oxford theologian who fled to Louvain. Though suspected of "popery", he did not in fact defect until the following reign, when, hauled before the Council, he was made to undergo the humiliation of *two* public recantations, themselves grotesque parodies of the articles he had originally asserted! At the opposite extreme, there can be little doubt that Thomas Starkey was both a sincere antipapalist and a pragmatic Supremacist; yet even here, government mistrust and a premature death conspire to leave us with lingering doubts. More complicated, yet no less typical, was the case of Cuthbert Tunstall. As late as 1534, there was some doubt as to whether the bishop of Durham might be expected to conform himself at all. Yet conform he did, and apparently with sufficient conviction that twenty-five years later, he remained the one Catholic bishop upon whom the Elizabethan government pinned hopes of a fresh conformity.[44] Enough diversity appears in these few cases to show that no uniform or certain reply to the question of sincerity can be given. Moreover, as the case of Tunstall in particular makes clear, sincerity and conviction might wax or wane in the course of a given career.

By contrast with the domestic evidence, that of foreign ambassadors seems less ambivalent. We have already noted the bishop of Faenza's opinion of Gardiner's real beliefs. (But the nuncio had occasion to retract his earlier—and from his point of view—more generous judgment.)[45] In 1541, we find Gardiner again suspect when the news was leaked (by Cranmer?)[46] of his secret negotiations with a papal agent at the Diet of Ratisbon—secret that is, to everyone but Henry, who, as we know today, was privy to the talks.[47] The correspondence of Chapuys reveals a number of English prelates who were less than enthusiastic about the new order of things, awaiting (in the words of bishop Tunstall rebutting the same charge) a "new mutation", and one bishop, Kite of Carlisle, involved in outright treason.[48] Yet tempting as they are, the diplomatic reports must be regarded with some scepticism.

True, it is quite probable that a timorous prelate might speak his mind freely only to a sympathetic, frankly papist foreigner like Chapuys. But equally, we cannot dismiss the likelihood that papist diplomats in England sought out religious conservatives, and were frequently told what they wanted to hear. In the case of English ambassadors abroad, those dispatched to Roman Catholic courts were usually men of the old religion, sent with the intention of reminding Paris or Ratisbon that, however schismatical, Henry yet belonged to the Catholic family of princes. We should not be surprised if these emissaries ingratiated themselves with their hosts through polite deception, and a graceful glossing over of outstanding difficulties. We must conclude then, that the diplomatic evidence, though valuable, yields no more certainty than domestic testimony.

Most misleading of all is to judge Henrician Catholicism by its aftermath. Offered the choice between Edwardian Protestantism and popery, Henrician Catholic leadership unhesitatingly chose the latter. The decisive years were those between 1549-1552 when it became clear to Catholics that no option of any sort remained to the old religion within the Supremacy. Simultaneously, they suffered a complete revelation of the ambiguities of Erastianism. They learned their lesson so well that Elizabeth was able to persuade but one of her sister's bishops to conform and retain his see.[49] Nothing could offer a more bold contrast than the easy surrender of the primacy by Henry's bishops, and the adamant refusal of their Marian successors to do likewise. The explanation, I would suggest, is to be found in the Henrician and Edwardian experience of the Marian prelates, and beyond that, in the increasing polarization of theological sentiment which accompanied the rise of Calvinism and Tridentine Catholicism. By 1558, a viable Catholicism could be conceived of only within the structure of the Roman primacy.

Yet it is a grave error to read backward from the situation of 1558 and to argue that Henrician Catholics embarking on the fresh venture of the Royal Supremacy viewed the primacy in the same light as their successors. Doubtless the breach with Rome was not of their making, but once it had been accomplished, a remarkable number of the Catholic leaders seemed happy to accomodate themselves to it, and, what is more, to defend the new regime with surprising ardor. Without denying a considerable element of timeserving in this compliance, it will not do as a comprehensive explanation. Many who made the surrender easily under Henry chose deprivation and imprisonment (and for all they might know, worse) under Edward and Elizabeth. One must conclude that until events compelled them to think otherwise, they held the primacy to be, at best, a convenience: in the words of archbishop Edward Lee, one of the most stalwart of the conforming Catholics, "I have often said these be no causes to die for." Lee's attitude—it was shared by others—should occasion less surprise than it has: an *adiaphorist* position with regard to the primacy had deep roots in recent Catholic tradition which we shall examine in the next chapters: it is one of the constituent factors of Henrician Catholicism.

Another motive for conformity, practical rather than theoretical, and one seldom credited to these men, was the hope that the Royal Supremacy, more effectively than Rome, might conserve an endangered Catholicism. Before we express surprise at what may appear to be a perverse judgment, let us recall that this was the Rome of Pope Clement VII whose eleven year pontificate had seen Scandinavia and the greater part of Germany slip away from papal allegiance into what Catholics regarded as religious and social chaos. No small number of the Henrician Catholic leadership were diplomats who had observed the parochialism and impotence of the papal court at first hand. Edward Lee, Gardiner, Bonner, Stokesley, Sampson and Fox had all been on diplomatic missions to Rome before the schism. From their perspective, a King whose orthodoxy had been a byword (until this time) might seem to offer a more certain shelter against the headwinds of continental heresy than Rome herself. Edward Lee specifically accompanied his subscription to the Supremacy with the comment that he did so to preserve "the unity of the faith" and to have "the Catholic Church saved; for the saving whereof, he perceives the kings Christian and Catholic mind."[50] And two years later, Thomas Starkey wrote to assure Reginald Pole that no Lutheran upheaval was taking place in England.[51]

Another and related theme of Catholic conformists was to deny that any schism had taken place at all:

> ... as for any separation from the vniuersall church, we knowe none, ne euer meanyd any such ...[52]

wrote Stephen Gardiner in an unpublished manuscript destined for the French court in 1535. And in the following year, Cuthbert Tunstall sharply rejected a similar charge made in Pole's book *de Unitate Ecclesiastica*, insisting that Henry had not "swerved from the unity of Christ's church."[53] As the years wore on, and the Protestant party made inroads in the new settlement, inroads manifest in the Ten Articles, the *Bishops' Book* and the *Great Bible*, this stance became more difficult to maintain,[54] though some kept faith to the end. In 1547, Stephen Gardiner, standing amidst the ruins of his fondest hopes, conducted a brilliant exchange of letters with Cranmer, the burden of which was the dead King's presumed orthodoxy.

•   •   •

An analysis of the writings of the Henrician Catholics reveals three distinct preoccupations: rejection of the primacy, defense of the Supremacy and attacks on the new heresies. While these concerns could overlap in time, the first two naturally dominated the earliest years of the settlement when the problems of persuading would-be recusants were still acute. Hostility to heresy, on the other hand, is to some degree evident in nearly all these books; but after 1540, it emerges as nearly the sole preoccupation of Catholic writers. Such references as there are to the primacy and supremacy after 1540 are purely perfunctory.

Our task then, is to some degree simplifed by chronology. The following three chapters will attempt to detail those causes which allowed the Henrician Catholics to constitute themselves, however fleetingly, as a party. The concluding chapters will discuss the anti-Protestant polemic of this school, as well as those factors which explain their failure to achieve internal coherence among themselves, much less to carry the day against the Reformers.

2

Repudiation of Papal Authority—Conciliarism

In November 1534, the five year struggle between Rome and Henry VIII was tersely concluded when Parliament declared the King "the only supreme head in earth of the Church of England", and shortly thereafter buttressed its claim with a new treasons act making it a capital offense to take him for anything less. For the following fifteen years, the only licit Catholicism in England was that which acknowledged the Royal Supremacy.

But how did the overwhelming majority of the Catholic leadership come to accept this?—or, at the very least, to subscribe to it? If the government's judicious use of terror cannot be discounted, neither does it tell the whole story.

It must, first of all, be insisted that the government prepared the ground well. A most striking feature of the five years leading to the break is the official insistence on the orthodoxy of the proceedings: at all times the pretence was maintained that what was being striven after was not a new order at all, but rather a reassertion of the ancient prerogatives of the Crown and the Church. To be sure, the Reformers waited in the wings, yet officially, they were allowed to do nothing. Government inspired documents and explanations of policy remained scrupulously Catholic. As if to underline this, persecution of heretics was expanded after the fall of Wolsey.[1]

As early as 1530, at the King's behest, researchers were being dispersed throughout the libraries and archives of Europe to dredge up support for the King's "Imperial" authority. No less urgent was the search for such documents as might serve to circumscribe papal claims.[2]

A richly diverse arsenal was assembled in which medieval and mythical chronicle jostled with the new criticism of Valla, earlier parliamentary statutes with the tracts of Parisian doctors supporting Philip the Fair, the decrees of fifteenth-century Councils with the letters of Innocent III. Upon this miscellaneous stockpile the King's polemicists were to draw for the next two decades.

As things turned out, the weakest leg of the royal apologetic rested upon those "ancient" chronicles whose authority so quaintly garnishes the Statute in Restraint of Appeals. Already impugned by the sophisticated criticism associated with the names of Valla and Erasmus, this quasi-legendary history would play a diminishing role in the works of subsequent controversialists.

Far more pertinent to Catholics marching with the new order was the appeal to sources admittedly "Catholic": scripture, of course, but as interpreted and formed by tradition: the Church fathers, the ancient Councils, and (in some cases) certain recent ones like Constance and Basle, if these were free of the taint of papal connivance. To these must be added a mainstream of custom or use, and the authority of several late medieval doctors such as Ockham, Gerson and Nicholas of Cusa, of acceptable, if not impeccable, orthodoxy.

It is important to note at this juncture that papal excommunication did not necessarily inhibit a man's reputation for orthodoxy, and that contrary to Fr. Hughes' dictum, a belief in the divine origins of the papacy was *not* a universally accepted criterion of Catholicism at this time.[3] No less a figure than Thomas More confessed that:

> I was myselfe some tyme not of the mynd that the prymatie of that see shold bebygone by thinstitution of God, vntil that redd in that mater those thingis that the Kyngis Highnes had written in his moost famouse boke agaynst the heresyes of Martyn Luther...

and a little on in the same letter, More is willing to grant as a debating point that the

> ...primatie is at least wise instituted by the corps of Christendom, and for a great vrgent cause in avoyding of scysmes ... more than the space of a thowsand yere...[4]

That other celebrated defender of unity, Reginald Pole, appears likewise to have entertained doubts as to whether the primacy was divinely instituted, or merely an acceptable convenience.[5] Nor was it easy to counter the argument that Saint Cyprian, the real founder of Latin ecclesiology (and destined to be liberally cited in the impending polemics), died unrepentantly excommunicated after a dispute with Rome, yet all Catholics recognized both his sanctity and authority.[6] And, to take a less venerable figure, it does not appear that Ockham's prestige was much compromised by his excommunication by pope John XXII. Indeed, even before the Great Schism, many Catholics seem to have become inured to the blasts of anathema. Then, between 1378 and 1415, the entire Catholic world had been excommunicated by one or the other of the contending pontiffs, and it was (and is) yet undetermined as to which of the two (later, three) claimants had retained the true Petrine authority. This absurd situation was bound to breed a certain insouciance toward papal authority, and there is ample evidence that such an attitude remained fairly prevalent into the sixteenth century. In 1511, during a heated quarrel with pope Julius II, Louis XII drew France into a temporary schism, with no appreciable difference to French Catholic life.[7] From one aspect then, papal jurisdiction might be seen to endanger, rather than confirm, Church unity. This insight no doubt lay behind Stephen Gardiner's jibe about the utility of popes: the Council "lest the people sholde want shepherdes made provision for iij sortes..."[8] Schism was an integral part of the Catholic experience in the two hundred years prior to the Reformation.

But if schism were a dubious matter, heresy was not. We find no Henrician Catholic apologist appealing to any authority whom Catholic opinion regarded as a heretic pure and simple. Richard Smith, Regius professor of Divinity at Oxford, speaks for the Henrician Catholic consensus when he rails at "the ungodlye doctrines ... of Waldeses, Johan Wicleph, John Hus and Martyn Luther."[9]

Aside from the classic heresies, e.g., Arianism, abhorred by Catholic and Reformer alike, Henrician Catholics maintained a vigorous detestation of three sorts of heresy which manifested themselves in the late middle ages. These were (1) the appeal to Scripture against the visible teaching Church, (2) the setting of a Church of invisible, predestined elect over against the Church militant, and (3) the denial of the efficacy of good works toward salvation. Catholics also maintained a steadfast belief in the Real Presence in the eucharist, but this would not become a crucial issue until the mid 1540's, when certain of the "established" Reformers, such as Ridley and Cranmer, abandoned Lutheranism for a more "spiritual" or symbolic interpretation of the sacrament. Because of the Erasmian influence among them (an influence which can scarcely be exaggerated), Henrician Catholics could be surprisingly pliant on such matters as purgatory, the invocation of saints, pilgrimages, and the monastic life; but on the previously mentioned positions, they remained unyielding.

The definition of heresy raised the thorniest problem of all: what authority was the ultimate arbiter of orthodoxy? Where did the *magisterium* of the Church reside, if not in Rome? In the consensus of believers? But if so, how was this to be ascertained? The venerable and historical answer of the Church had been: General Councils. But if this were so, consisting of whom, and quite as important, by whom convoked?

This problem of ecclesiology lay at the very center of Henrician Catholicism, and if its proponents failed to solve it, they are not to be much blamed, for in one form or another, it continues to vex Christian Churches to the present day. Provisionally at least, Henrician Catholics and Reformers took refuge behind the Supremacy, as a shield for what each regarded as theological propriety. In the end, of course, religious passion could not be harnessed to political whim and the accident of a reigning monarch: Catholic supremacists gave up the ghost with Edward, their Protestant counterparts with Mary.

Having given a broad outline of the problem, we must now turn to particulars. How did Henrician Catholics justify the abjuration of papal jurisdiction? (There was, of course, no doctrine of infallibility at this time.) Two interlocked and brazen impediments stood against the acceptance of absolute jurisdiction. The first was the authority of General Councils. The second was that three popes at least* were assumed by a large consensus of authorities to have been heretics. A heretic pope, by definition, could not retain the *plenitudo potestatis,* since he was, ipso facto, no member of the Church. In short, there was no doctrine of papal indefectibility. This was grasped by many papists themselves, and Thomas More, who died for the primacy, or more precisely, for the unity of the Church of which the primacy was the visible symbol, found "indubitable" authority in "General Councils lawfully assembled." "Never", More confessed, "thought I the pope above a General Council."[10]

---

* See p. 155

The appeal to a General Council and to conciliar thought was an obvious step in the formative years of the settlement, when the government wished to abridge Roman jurisdiction while retaining the appearance of orthodoxy. As early as 1461, Pope Pius II, aware of the dangerous precedent of the Councils of Constance and Basle, had countered such maneuvers with his bull *Exercribilis,* which denounced all appeals to future councils as heresy. But so self-serving a device did not command the assent of a great part of the Catholic community, where conciliarism remained a treasured legacy.[11]

We have noted the precedent set by Louis XII in 1511. By 1530, with the Reformation raging through Germany, a General Council remained the sole hope for those anxious to restore religious unity. The memory of the fiasco at Basle had been buried beneath the debris of the collapsing Church of central Europe. At no time in the last hundred years had the cry for a Council been so vocal or urgent.

The authority of a General Council had been succinctly described by Jean Gerson, perhaps the most distinguished of the Conciliarists, in a sermon delivered before the Emperor Sigismund:

> A general council holds its power directly from Christ: everyone, whatever his degree or dignity, even if it be papal, is bound to obey it. [12]

This opinion, to be sure, flouted the papal claim to a *plenitudo potestatis,* a claim which found its most redoubtable expression in the words of the bull *Unam Sanctam*: "it is absolutely necessary for every human creature to be subject to the Roman pontiff." It cannot be urged too strongly, however, that ultrapapalism was not the universal consensus of the Roman Catholic world in the sixteenth century—nor for long afterward.*

Theoretical conciliarism was born in the early fourteenth century, an offspring of the collision between Phillip the Fair and pope Boniface VIII. Its first proponent was John of Paris, a Dominican and Thomist, who espoused the French King's cause, and argued that:

> A council, since it represents the whole Church, is above the Pope, and has the power to depose him should he misuse his authority[13]

Starting from the canonist principle that a pope may be deposed for

* See p. 155

heresy, John went on to adduce a number of hypothetical cases where a pontiff might warrant a like fate.

The next development of the theory took place shortly thereafter during the conflict between the popes and Ludwig of Bavaria. Here the alliance of the Spiritual Franciscans with the would-be Emperor added a new dimension to the contest. Ludwig found two able champions in Marsiglio of Padua and William of Ockham. The first had so direct an influence on the Henrician settlement that we must reserve to him a separate chapter. It has been suggested that the condemnation of Marsiglio restricted his influence on all save the most radical proponents of conciliarism,[14] but as a number of his ideas were incorporated into the *Dialogues* of Ockham, he cannot be dismissed as a negligible influence in the mainstream of conciliar thought.

Ockham has been judged to be the most important progenitor of Conciliarism.[15] His *Dialogues* were not condemned by ecclesiastical authority since their hypothetical form did not commit their author to any of their propositions. Nor did Ockham deny—as did Marsiglio—Christ's institution of the primacy. Yet it was he who grasped the nettle of the problem of authority, and asked how the final repository of truth might be ascertained. Characteristically, he gave no firm reply to the question, though he was prepared to consider that, in an extreme case, infallibility might be confined to a remnant of the laity. This astonishing hypothesis was rejected by Jean Gerson, who, however, made Ockham's notion of an "extreme case" his own[16]

An "extreme case" is surely an apposite description of the Great Schism. The thought of the chief conciliarists, Jean Gerson, Pierre D'Ailly and Nicholas of Cusa, was essentially conservative, and evolved only as it became plain that the schism was self-perpetuating: the abortive Council of Pisa (1410) issued in three contending pontiffs. This drove Gerson, in particular, to consider the crucial point of ultimate authority in the Church. The Paris Chancellor was no radical: he never aimed at more than the termination of the schism, and the restoration of unity under a single pope. Yet paradoxically the only way to attain this end was to insist upon an authority above that of the see of Peter, in order to compel the incumbent popes to resign.

In the end, Gerson resorted to John of Paris' dictum and argued that the authority of the whole Church may be thrown against the pope. Spiritual authority exists for the good of the Church, and it may be renounced if "its retention gives rise to scandal."[17] In his effort to legitimate necessity, Gerson drew a sharp distinction between "divine" and "human" law—a distinction revived in the Henrician polemics of Fox, Sampson and Starkey.[18] Like Ockham before him, Gerson entertained a particular animus toward the canon law, contrasting its "iron yoke and heavy burden" with the "light yoke of Christ and the law of liberty,[19] for the canon law had been used to swell the papal prerogative. Canon law, Gerson insists, is not divine law.[20] Amplifying this distinction, he notes that not every scriptural injuction is divine law either: scriptural statements are *de fide* if they are essential to "believe in order to attain the goal of beatitude.[21] Here, over a century before Erasmus, Melancthon or Starkey, is the quintessence of *adiaphorism* .

Gerson further developed his ecclesiology in two late works: *De Auferibilitate Papae ab ecclesia,* and *De Potestate Ecclesia.* In the first, the kernel of the argument is that Christ is the true spouse of the Church—He and the Spirit *alone* never depart from it. The pope indeed is the chief of the Church, and Marsiglio is condemned for asserting that every bishop is a pope in his own diocese. But the pope derives his authority from the constitution of the Church; it does not derive its authority or constitution from him. Normally, the pope should summon a General Council, but in extreme cases the rule of *epikeia* (equity) should prevail. The pope, when all is said, is the sign of the Church's unity, not its actuality.[22]

In *De Potestate Ecclesia*, the above arguments are rounded out: originally, *potestas* was given to all the apostles, and they—or their successors—conferred it upon the see of Rome. Gerson regards this transfer as perfectly legitimate, but it is clearly proximate to Marsiglio's position that Christ never conferred a true primacy on Peter or his successors. The point, as against Marsiglio, is that the Church can, in the interest of unity, ordain a true primacy. No doubt Gerson did not conceive that the primacy should or would be revoked, but it might easily be inferred that if the Church could institute the primacy to conserve unity, a like expediency might be utilized to warrant its abolition. Such was the tack to be taken by Thomas Starkey in his *Exhortation* when, echoing Gerson, he wrote that the primacy

> undoubtedly grewe in amonge us onely as a thinge of conueniency, and . . . of a great helpe and succour to the mayntenace of a certain unitie in Christis churche & not as a thinge of necessitie. . .[23]

Conciliar theology, with its insistence on an authority above that of Rome and canon law, and its corresponding tendency to limit the primacy to an expedient tempered to the good of the whole Church, offered an attractive option to Henrician Catholics. Until 1534, it seemed to provide the underlying structure of the new settlement. As we shall see, this view proved chimerical. The King and the government used Conciliarism as a makeshift span, and then, passing swiftly beyond it, blew up their lines of retreat.

Yet however expedient, Conciliarism was a necessary phase in the making of the settlement. The long and dignified pedigree of the movement served to weaken papalism along the churchmen of cisalpine Europe. The *via moderna*—the school of Ockham—played a lively role at the universities, and therefore in the education of the higher clergy, while the canonists who infested Tudor bishoprics were familiar with the decrees of Constance and Basle. All this served the government well when the breach came. Though we know men like Edward Lee, Tunstall and Gardiner were reluctant to accept the Royal Supremacy, their qualms over the abolition of the primacy were more easily set aside. We have referred earlier to Archbishop Lee's comment; Cuthbert Tunstall was no less explicit when replying to Reginald Pole's long awaited decision not to conform. He suggested that Pole (then in Venice) avail himself of copies "of the said councils in Greek" which would give the lie to the popes' usurpations, and then undertook to defend his own submission:

> . . . and where ye do find a fault with me, that I fainted in my heart and would not die for the bishop of Rome's authority; when this matter was first purposed to me, surely it was no fainting that made me agre thereunto; for I never saw the day since I knew the progress and continuance of Crist's church from the beginning, and read such histories ecclesiastical and ordinances from age to age as do manifestly declare the same, that I ever thought to shed one drop of my blood therefore.[24]

The conciliar reference of this letter is made explicit a few lines further: the Bishop advises Pole to read

> . . . Nicolaum Cusa de Concordia Catholica . . . [because] he should greatly open this matter to you.[25]

It was only an appeal to a future Council which could give at least the specious appearance of orthodoxy to Henry's decision to defy the anticipated papal judgment and to marry Anne. When made, the appeal was accompanied by the denunciation of pope Clement as a heretic. This effectively raised doubts as to Clement's personal jurisdiction a full year before the authority of Rome was explicitly abrogated by the Act of Supremacy. The tactic was no doubt employed to placate informed Catholic opinion at home, as well as abroad, since quite apart from the clergy, the laity of England, as manifest in Parliament, prided itself on its orthodoxy. Though anticlerical, and willing to follow the government's lead as to juristic enactments, the Parliaments of the 1530s showed little taste for doctrinal innovation. In the opinion of Chapuys, it was Parliament—not convocation—which in 1536, proved to be the decisive impediment to a doctrinal accommodation with the German Lutherans.[26] The alacrity with which, three years later, Parliament passed the Six Articles, would seem to confirm the Ambassador's surmise.[27]

The strong headwind of lay opposition to heresy seems to have been intuited by Henry, who seldom lacked acumen in grasping the moods of his subjects. Nevertheless, it is not certain that the King consciously elected to play out the double role which marked the years 1529-33, when he asserted his lapsed "imperial" prerogatives, while threatening the pope with an appeal to a General Council should he render an unfavorable judgment. In reality, these two policies were contradictory. The first implied an autonomous, national settlement under the auspices of a "godly prince", and had obvious affinities with the practice of the Lutheran states; the alternative implied royal and national subordination to the judgment of international Christendom. As early as 1530, Henry was bombarding Rome with this antinomy in an effort to have the divorce revoked to England. He appealed to the authority of "gloriosissimo martyri Cipriano" and "Divus Bernardus" who had also insisted to respective popes that "in eo loco causa terminetur ubi primum nata est."[28] Perhaps, at this early stage, practical requirements obscured logical contrarieties.

But it may be wondered if the King were ever long uncertain as to the course he intended to take. It is one of the great merits of Dr. Scarisbrick's biography of the King to show how early Henry inclined to a national solution, rooted in supposititious prerogative.[29] Henry was balked by a domestic conservatism which made it necessary to proceed *festina lente*, and perhaps, by the lack of a minister with sufficient daring and expertise to carry out a policy frought with risk. With the ascendancy of Cromwell in 1532, the die was cast.[30]

In November 1533, Edmund Bonner sought an audience with pope Clement and made his appeal to a future Council, while in England, a veritable rash of manuscripts and publications appeared vaunting the authority of General Councils and their superiority to "all bishops". Best known of these writings are the *Articles devised by the King's Council*, printed by Berthelet. The theology of the "Articles" is conciliar, and contain not a soupcon of heresy. Of particular interest are articles (2) that Councils forbid a cause from being removed from its locus, (4) A General Council is superior to all bishops, (5) Any man, but especially a prince, may appeal from a bishop to a General Council, and (9) Pope Clement is a bastard and a heretic as well, since flouting the canons of the Councils, he has insisted on revoking the King's cause to Rome.[31]

The reader of the *Letters and Papers of Henry VIII* will note that this Conciliar propaganda reaches its apex about 1534, only to fade rather suddenly and to be replaced by documents which bear a wholly different import. From these, we derive plain evidence that the government was preparing to abandon the conciliar underpinnings of its policy.

According to Chapuys, the King did not wait long to tip his hand. In an illuminating dispatch of late spring, 1534, the Imperial ambassador tells of being summoned before an amplified conventicle of the higher clergy at Westminster. The bishops, he observed, spoke "as if they had studied their parts." During the subsequent discussions, bishop Stokesley remarked that the Pope's sentence against the divorce might be fairly disregarded since the King had appealed his case to a General Council. To this Chapuys replied with some asperity that when he himself had raised the same prospect to Henry, the King had answered that

> ... he would have nothing to do with it ... [and] ... that he would give good order to his kingdom without the aid of a General Council.[32]

which indeed proved to be a precise summary of Henry's present and future stand.

Granted that the divorce was the essential issue in question—as it was, until the birth of Prince Edward—the King had correctly grasped the situation: no conceivable Council would have given judgment in Henry's favor. The composition of any General Council called in these years would be weighted in papist and Imperialist favor. Worse still, the Lutherans were hardly better disposed. When Luther heard of Catherine's death (January 1536), he wrote to a friend that she should have died a queen: her cause—he added somewhat hyperbolically—was defended only "by us poor beggars of divines" here in Wittenberg.[33] Luther may have had old scores to settle with "Junker Heinz", but his opinion was shared by his fellow evangelicals who regarded the English reforms as a shabby pretext for the King's lust and greed.[34] *

The Emperor posed another obstacle to English reliance upon a Council. It was he, in lieu of the Pope, who had the right to convoke a Council, even as the Emperor Sigismund had summoned the Council of Constance. Yet Charles, though he urged a Council upon popes Clement and Paul, had no mind to convoke one on his own authority. For a plethora of reasons ranging from a deeply felt Catholic piety to very practical considerations of Italian policy, he was determined to wait until he could obtain papal compliance. Moreover, a Council summoned by Charles, even in defiance of the Pope, was the last thing Henry wanted, for its successful issue would solve the Emperor's political difficulties. Cromwell, in a moment of frankness, blurted out the truth to Chapuys when he remarked that Henry would never submit to a Council since it would consist mostly of "prestraille" who hated the King for the reform of the Church. The Vicar-General added for good measure that Henry would never consent to a Council called by either the Pope or Charles.[35] To be sure, hardly a month later, Chapuys is writing to his master that Henry will consent to a Council *only* if Charles convokes it. But this, as we have seen, was a safe bet, and Chapuys' sigh is almost audible as he writes that "none of this is to be much regarded."[36]

By autumn 1535, the King and his government were already plunged into their project of preventing a Council by whatever means offered themselves. The new, and far more vigorous pope, Paul III, had begun preparations, and named Mantua as the site. In reply, Cromwell instructed Sir John Wallop and bishop Gardiner, the English envoys in Paris, to persuade the French King to boycott the Council. They were to tell Francis that Henry would agree to a General Council, but

* See p. 155

only in a "safe" and "indifferent" place, and with the prior approval of all the princes. Mantua met none of these stipulations; indeed, it was difficult to imagine a Council that would. Francis, who had even less desire than Henry to becalm the Germanies, did not need much cajoling: the only question, as bishop Fox put it, was the French King's price.[37]

Shortly thereafter, a high-powered delegation consisting of Edward Fox, Nicholas Heath, Edmund Bonner and Robert Barnes was sent off to the Lutheran principalities with the object of presenting a united front against the impending Council. In the instructions given to Fox, much is said about Henry's "zeal for the Gospel" and the Bishop is urged to press for a "free" Council in an "indifferent" place. A separate draft of the same instructions, far more to the print, enjoins him to use every lever to

> ... dissuade them from a general Council when all Christendom meet together and the power of the Emperor, the French King, and the bishop of Rome will be all against them.[38]

—in short, no Council, papal, Imperial, "free", or "indifferent."

If English diplomatic instructions were somewhat ambivalent, the same cannot be said for those given the German negotiators. Quite explicitly they wanted English money and an unequivocal subscription to the Augsburg Confession—otherwise, no alliance.[39] In the end, as Mantua faded into the mists of the future, no bargain was struck. But in the summer of 1536, bishop Fox hurried home to join the newly augmented ranks of the Reformers in convocation. Here, with considerable tact and persuasiveness, he strove to bring the English Church into greater conformity with Lutheranism. His success, as evidenced by the Ten Articles, was only partial.[40] The most conspicuous of Fox's achievements was an omission: four of the sacraments were passed over in silence, and could be construed by those so inclined to be no sacraments at all.[41]

The chief task of the convocation of 1536 was to call a halt to the dangerously rising religious ferment. The previous autumn, archbishop Lee had written to Cromwell warning him of the unsettled state of affairs. Contrary doctrines were being preached

> ... wherwith the people grutche, whiche ooderwise all the kynges commandment heer obeye diligentlie...

As a remedy, the northern primate went on to suggest that a book be drawn up to settle doubtful matters by referring them to "tholie auncient doctours of the Church" whom Melancthon recognized as an authority in disputed matters.[42] That Cromwell took this suggestion, or at least that his mind was working on the same lines, is shown by one of his "remembrances", drawn up at the same time, which admits the urgency of concluding some sort of doctrinal order. Character- istically Erastian, the Vicar-General envisions the King's council or Parliament drawing up a new Church settlement.[43] By 1536 then, the German negotiations and the Pope's summons to a Council gave fresh impetus to the reordering of a "settlement" already imperiled by domestic squabbling. The work of the convocation, and the more informal meetings which issued in the *Bishop's Book* the following year, were no doubt intended to meet this necessity. Yet convocation's "judgment" on General Councils shows with unrivaled clarity how deeply the Church itself was divided, and mirrors the same tensions which run through the Ten Articles and the *Bishop's Book*.

> As concerning General Councils [the bishops write] we ... do per-
> fectly know that there never was, ne is, any thing devised, invented
> or instituted by our forefathers, more expedient or more necessary
> for the establishment of our faith, for the extirpation of heresies, and
> the abolishing of sects and schisms; and finally, for the reducing of
> Christ's people unto one perfect unity and concord in religion...

So far, a perfectly orthodox preamble. The next, more dubious lines are plainly directed at the impending Council of Mantua:

> ... so that the same by lawfully had and congregated in Spiritu
> Sancte, and be also conform, and agreeable ... to the surety and
> indifferency of places...

A somewhat novel introduction of geography, this, into conciliar theology, yet the meaning of the bishops is plain enough: by this standard, Constance and Basle are authentic Councils, convoked under the impeccable guidance of the Holy Spirit. (True, the same rule leaves doubtful the authority of the Lateran Council of 1215, which gave the seal of orthodoxy to the seven sacraments.) But, the bishops continue:

Even so, on the other side, taught by experience we esteem repute and judge that there is, ne can be any thing in the world more pestilent and pernicious to the commonweal of Christendom, or whereby the truth of God's word hath intimes past, or hereafter may be sooner defaced or subverted, or ... may ensue more contention ... discord and other devilish effects, than when such general councils ... be assembled, not Christianly or charitably, but for and upon private malice and ambition, or other wordly carnal ... considerations...

Here, Gregory of Nazianzen is given as an authority for the principle that "omnes conventus episcoporum fugiendes esse" which the bishops helpfully translate as "all general councils to be eschewed"—which by any standard was to stretch the truth somewhat. Convocation then asks that five things be considered: (1) who has the authority to convoke a General Council? (2) whether the causes be deemed weighty enough or "can be otherwise remedied? (3) who ought to be judges there? (4) what order is to be followed, and how are the judgments of the delegates to be ascertained? and (5) what doctrines are to be allowed or defended?

The bishops make an effort to answer only the first of these pertinent questions:

... as to the first point, we think that neither the bishop of Rome, ne any one prince, of what estate ... may be his own authority ... indict any general council, without the express consent ... of the residue of Christian princes, and especially such as have within their realms ... *imperium merum*, that is to say, of such that have the whole, entire and supreme government and authority over all their subjects without knowledging or recognizing any other supreme power or authority...

Their reasons for this would be "overlong and tedious to express." At this point, the document terminates abruptly.[44]

The foregoing "judgment" merits our close attention, for no record of the time so sharply reveals the dilemma of the Henrician Catholics, or shows so plainly the impotence to which the Church had been reduced in three short years. Irreconcilable faction is papered over with incoherence: nothing could be more "necessary" to "perfect unity and concord" than a Council; nor anything more "pestilent and pernicious" or condusive to "discord." Nor does the proviso suggested by S. Gregory improve matters: The Council of Nicaea, whose canons were accepted by Catholic and Reformer alike, was notoriously as contentious and uncharitable as any in the history of the Church: its discords echoed down the last years of antiquity.

In truth, the above "judgment" is an accurate reflection of a deeply riven episcopate. During the three years preceding its formulation, the government had appointed no less than seven Reformers to the bench: henceforth no true consensus might be expected from the upper house.* In fact, it was the government now which took the initiative in giving a reply to the papally summoned Council.

The new drift is exemplified in the so-called "Hatfield manuscripts", conjecturally dated in 1534 by James Gairdner, and more recently placed about 1536 or 1537 by P.A. Sawada.[45] Burnet had originally ascribed them to Cranmer, or an associate of the Archbishop's, but this is certainly an error.[46] The two tracts are quite dissimilar, though both conclude by throwing great dubiety on the authority of Councils.

The author of the first tract was well acquainted with the conciliarists, particularly Gerson, but he insists that

> ... the standard of the Council's defininitions be taken from the scriptures, and not from mens traditions ... Some General Councils have been rejected by others and it is a tender point how much ought to be deferred to a Council.

The author's second point would prove to be a sensitive one to the partisans of a conciliar theology. At the tract's conclusion, the writer confesses to

> much doubting in himself as to General Councils; and ... is persuaded ... that only the word of God was the rule of faith.[47]

The second manuscript found its way to publication in 1538. A most peculiar work, it too purports to deal with General Councils, though these are not touched upon until the fifth chapter. In his preface, the anonymous author assures us that

*See p. 155.

> The Aucteritie and power of generall counsayles ... can not playnely
> be sette forthe ... oneless the power of kynges & princes be fyrste
> knowen and understande.[48]

For kings and princes "haue theyr power immediately of god." The
clergy, a more amphibian order, owe their "mynystration" to "the lawe
of god, and ... the lawe of man."[49] A battery of Old Testament texts
are marshalled to show the kings

> ... iudge the world: that al that be within their dominions are theyr
> subiectes, and owe to obey them, and neyther byshop or priste is not
> excepted in any of these textes.[50]

All that is the familiar, Marsiglian apology for univocal authority over
Church and state. Chapters 1-4 continue to expose the pretensions of
the clergy; scattered throughout are a number of irrelevant, not to say
incoherent observations. The main idea, though, is the importance of
separating men's ordinances from those of God, so the people are no
longer deceived. In the fifth chapter, the author comes somewhat
uncertainly to grips with his professed subject, declaring that

> ... the power of them [councils] standeth moost principally to
> declare the trew catholyke fayth, according to the rules and groundes
> of scripture.

He then turns his own flank with the typical Catholic insistence that
General Councils may also determine "what bokes are to be obeied
and taken as books of scripture."[51] The remaining chapters are devoted
to the task of repelling the Pope's recent summons to the Council at
Vicenza.[52]

One is puzzled that this work ever found its way into print, and
through the government's publisher (Berthelet) at that. Relatively short
in fact, its repetitiveness, digressions, non-sequiturs, and all round
incoherence render it a monument of inconsequential tedium. More
remarkable still, its publication date sandwiches it between two lively
and compact tracts sponsored by the King's Council, and addressed to
the same subject. Nevertheless the *Treatise Concernynge generall
councilles* is unique in one respect: alone of the propaganda works of
this time, it owes its inspiration neither to Catholicism nor the new
heresies, but to Lollardy.[53]

The thrust of both these and other, unpublished tracts, points to a deliberate government campaign to abate the earlier, vaunted authority of Councils, a surmise confirmed by the existence of a memorandum directed toward futher reforms in Church and state. Among these reforms, is the suggestion that "secret" inquiry be made into who may summon, and for what cause, a General Council.[54] It is almost certain that the tracts we have discussed were attempts to grapple with the difficulties raised in the memorandum.

In 1537, there appeared a "protestation" made on behalf of the "kynge of England & his hole counsell and clergie". A trenchant little pamphlet, it was circulated gratis in Germany where it occasioned some embarrassment to the papists.[55] Mantua is a scored as a "feyned" council where the bishop of Rome would assemble his dupes to confirm his fraudulent dealings.[56] In keeping with his earlier pose, the King gives solemn assurance that

> ... we wolde haue a councelle, we desyre it, ye and craue nothynge so oft of god as that we maye haue one ... [but it must be] franke and free where euery man, without fears may say his minde.[57]

Besides, the main issue at any Council must be the pope's authority, and no man may be at once judge and suitor in his own cause.[58] There follows an exhaustive list of reasons the English will not attend: the distance, proximity to Rome, hazards of travel, the present war, and the well-known uncertainty of the pope's "saufe conductes".[59] After further drolleries at the Pope's expense, and at the failure of the Council to convene, the tract concludes on a new note: "They that be wysest doo dispaire of a general councell", and those who are anxious to reform the Church would do well to emulate England, and to summon local assemblies to redress their own wrongs: "Fauour our doinges, O crysten prvncis, your honour and auncient maiestie is restored."[60]

The second tract, issued in 1538 against the summons to Vicenza, purports to be a letter from the King himself, addressed to the Emperor and the German princes.[61] Once more Henry professed his avid desire for a Council, this time in words remarkably evocative of those used previously by convocation.[62] All the arguments of the "protestation" are trotted forth anew; what is novel in this epistle is the strong

emphasis on the sufficiency of scripture, and a corresponding suggestion of the superfluity of Councils. Indeed, Henry does not blush to
ordain the only acceptable agenda for a future gathering:

> ... we woll that suche doctrine, as we following the scripture, do
> professe, ritely be examined, discussed, and to be brought to scrip-
> ture, as to the onely touche stone of true lernynge, we will not suffre
> them [the recent innovations] to be abollyshed.[63]

Plainly the Council conceived of in this epistle is a fantasy assembly,
convoked to to confirm, applaud and emulate the godly doings of the
King of England. By 1538 then, Henry had cast aside even the pretence
of "submitting" himself to a Council.

As things turned out, no Council did assemble at Mantua, nor
again, at Vicenza. It was not until December 1545, a year and a month
before Henry's death, that a papally convoked Council gathered at
Trent. England would be represented by those "traitors", Cardinal
Pole and Richard Pate.

The simple truth is that, whatever his initial intentions, and however
ambivalent his formal declarations, the King, in practice, had opted
for a national reformation under a "godly prince". This option entailed
a repudiation of Conciliarism which was essentially ecumenical and
international. Perhaps this point is obscure in a Western context, but it
becomes clear when we set it against the experience of Eastern
Christendom. Though the Orthodox churches are national, their
autonomy is administrative, not doctrinal. Dogmatically, Orthodoxy
is one, subscribing to the Scripture and Creeds as interpreted by the
eight ecumenical Councils. To undefined points, Orthodoxy extends a
principle of "economy", which is closely akin to the concept of
adiaphorism. In his own lifetime, Henry's caesaro-papism was compared to that of the Emperor Justinian; yet in one sense this comparison is misleading, since the Orthodox princes-including the present
"magistrates" of the Soviet Union—have never brought off a doctrinal
revolution. This is precisely what Henry did accomplish, though the
point has been somewhat obscured by his retention of certain Catholic
beliefs and ceremonies.

It was not merely that Henry had struck out on his own, presuming
upon some future consensus when the rest of the Church should catch
up with him: even more idiosyncratic was his presumption that the

Supremacy granted him not only authority over the administration and discipline of the Church, but over doctrine as well. We have noted the self-assurance which marked his correction of bishop Tunstall in the matter of auricular confession, but it was not only individual theologians who were subject to the royal magisterium: when so moved, Henry could correct or amend the very articles of faith drawn up in convocation. On one occasion, in a circular letter to his bishops, the King claimed that "diverse opinions" in the Church impelled him to "conceive" the Ten Articles approved of in convocation![64] Nor was the point lost on his prelates when, the following years, they presented him with the "Bishops' Book" for approval. Its abject preface, apparently penned by bishop Fox, but certainly subscribed to by his fellow bishops, must represent the low water mark of Henrician religion.[65] After confessing that they have "none auctoritye eyther to assemble our selfes togyther for anye pretence or pourpyse or to publyshe anythinge" without the royal warrant, the bishops "most humbly sybmyt" the book

> ... to the most excellent wysedome & exact judgment of your maiestie, to be recognised, oversene, and *corrected*, if your grace that finde any worde or sentence in it were to be changed, qualified or further expounded ... whereunto *we shall in that case conforme ourselfes*, as to our most bounden duties to god and your highnes apperteineth ... " (italics mine)[66]

It would seem inescapable that if the King may correct, change, qualify or further expound doctrine, and the bishops are "bounden" to conform themselves, then the King may make doctrine *tout court*. To be sure, Henry chose the wiser course of making doctrinal and liturgical formuations *with* his Church and Parliament, but just as assuredly, he kept his hand in these formulations, and often, though not always, the adapted rubric would be his.[67]

In practice then, the English Church was committed by 1536 to a full autonomy. Theoretically, it simply refused to resolve the antinomy of Council or autarchy. The official pronouncements, however inconsistently, maintained both. For its part, the government pushed it claims as far as it prudently could while avoiding any Council that might impose its decrees upon the national settlement. It may be wondered how far Catholics were taken in by this. Two decades later, on the eve of English submission to Rome, John Standish reviewed for the "highe courte of Parliament" the two milestones of national apostasy:

> ... fyrst, forsaking the head of the churche and falling from the unitie thereof: then despising of all generall counselles ...[68]

Protestant opinion of General Councils was never in doubt. Cranmer, by 1537, if not sooner, had come round to the view of Luther. In a letter of that year he asked Henry to consider the

> ... evil ... when in provincial, yea, or yet general councils men have gone about to set forth any thing ... with apparent reasons not infallibly deduced out of the word of God.[69]

In brief, Councils were either mischievous or redundant. Philip Melanchthon in his *Loci Communes* (dedicated to Henry VIII), was even more blunt:

> Neither Pontiffs [he wrote] nor councils nor the universal church have any right to change or decide any matter of faith ... Scripture ... alone is certain to have been produced by the spirit of God [and] to attribute unto councils the authority to create articles of faith is a rash thing ... [Moreover] it is clearer than the noonday sun that councils have often erred and can err.[70]

And the great German theologian went on to challenge even the inerrancy of Nicaea.[71]

After 1534, Catholic opinion varied—at least at first. Neither Gardiner nor Edward Lee, two staunch supporters of the old ways, seem to have set much store by General Councils. Their arguments fell back on a more vaguely defined "tradition" or the consensus of individual Church fathers. On the other hand, many leading Catholics continued to rest their case on the authority of Councils. In a joint letter to Reginald Pole, the bishops of London and Durham insisted that emperors have the authority to summon

> ... universall counseiles of all Countryes in one place, and at one

tyme to assemble, to thentent, all heresies troubling the church, might be there extyrped . . . [72]

The rule of the Church, say Stokesley and Tunstall very firmly, belongs to princes *through* Councils.[73]

Thomas Starkey too, seems to have retained both faith and hope in General Councils. In 1534 or 1535 we find him urging Henry to consult a Council in order to avoid a blot on his reputation.[74] Though a royal chaplain who secured his appointment through Cromwell's intercession, and presumably therefore privy to Henry's and his chief minister's designs, Starkey continued to express opinions embarrassingly at variance from theirs. Sometime after Pole's manifest defection (June 1536), for which he was in part held responsible, Starkey wrote a long letter to the King to reingratiate himself. Amidst reams of unsolicited advice, he tendered this tidbit:

> I trust to see a general counseyl to folow and by your gudnes pryncepally the world restoryd to the old quyetnes, by the wych mean your grace schal not only doo the offyce and dewtye of a veray christian prynce and of a true hede of a chrystian congregation, but also by the consent of all men your hyghnes schalbe iugyd to be worthy of immortal glorye, and wyth him to reyne, who ys the veray hede of al churchys eternally.[75]

This when Henry was endeavoring to forestall a Council of whatever complexion!

For the most part, Catholic leaders remained muted on the subject of Councils until the final year of the reign. No doubt prudence accounted for some of this reticence, but, as we have seen, the authority of Councils raised painful difficulties in ecclesiology. Even Richard Smith, that dogged Conciliarist, recognized only "certyne" Councils as sacrosanct, while Tunstall regarded the decisions of the Greek "eight" as binding. One snag, as Starkey pointed out to the King, was that some General Councils had recognized papal jurisdiction, though, following in the wake of Gerson, he quickly hedged this with the comment that papal authority was a mere "vtylyte" which had outlived its expedience.[76] Still more problematic was the status to be accorded several medieval Councils, clearly convoked by the popes, whose decisions on the sacraments, and particularly the eucharist, were tacitly accepted as binding by Catholics. This second point, however, did not become a live issue until the eucharistic controversies of the 1540s created a renewed upsurge of Conciliarism. Both problems boiled down to the same question: Which Councils, and which of their canons, might be credited with binding authority?

Another insoluble problem was the impracticality of a Council. The councils of Constance and Basle had been quite unable to give effect to their reform programs. Want of "coercive" authority was an inherent weakness in the Conciliarist position: who would hang the bell on the cat? In the second quarter of the sixteenth century this question was anything but theoretical. Faced with the raging brush fire of the Reformation, the Henrician Catholic found himself with sharply curtailed alternatives. He might fall back on a weakened and discredited pope, who at odds with his master, had already proved powerless against the German magistrates and Scandinavian kings; or he might throw his support behind a sovereign resolved in any case to curb Roman jurisdiction, and in so doing, defend the substance of the faith behind the shield of the Supremacy. But how could so novel a solution be squared with the Catholic tradition? The following two chapters will attempt a description of the ideological factors which made accommodation, provisionally at least, possible.

3

Marsiglio & Apologias for the Supremacy

Since the pioneering work of Pierre Janelle five decades ago, historians increasingly have come to recognize the role of Marsiglio of Padua in the forming of the Royal Supremacy.[1] According to Professor A.G. Dickens, it was Marsiglio's doctrine that Cromwell boiled down to the "masterly phrases"[2] which appear in the preamble to the Statute of Appeals:

> ... this realm of England is an Empire ... governed by one Supreme Head and King ... unto whom a body politic ... divided in terms and by names of spirituality and temporality, have been bounded and owen to bear, next to God, a natural and humble obedience[3]

And this statute itself has been adjudged "the most important ... of the sixteenth century ... and perhaps in all our constitutional history."[4] On a less exalted plane, the influence of Marsiglio's *Defensor Pacis* has been detected along the whole range of Tudor antipapal polemics, from the well-known work of Edward Fox, Richard Sampson and Stephen Gardiner to score of lesser known or anonymous pamphleteers.[5]

It is exasperating, but indicative, that so little of the origins of this influence can be directly traced. Marsiglianism appears well before explicit reference is made to its author. In Fox's *de vera defferentia*[6], for instance, Aquinas and Gerson are quoted among the medieval sources, but not Marsiglio. Neither does his name appear in the (admittedly brief) *Oratio* of Richard Sampson—or for that matter in the more exhaustive, and later treatment of the Supremacy in the books of Gardiner. One likely reason for this reticence is Marsiglio's ambivalent reputation. Not an outright heretic like Wycliffe or Hus, he was never accorded the status of a Catholic doctor, as was Gerson, or even Ockham.[7] If we are correct in suggesting that the apologetics of 1530-34 were marked by a scrupulous simulation of orthodoxy, the silence is comprehensible.

Explicit reference to Marsiglio appears in 1534 when William Marshall, translator, publisher and a man of pronouncedly Protestant views,[8] wrote Cromwell begging him for an advance of £20 to publish a translation of the *Defensor*. Marshall's redaction of the work was complete; about one fifth of it, quite unsuitable for the government's designs, had been expunged, and it now awaited publication "these twelve months."[9] We know that Cromwell responded to the prodding, for late in 1536, Marshall wrote the chief minister again, asking him to discharge Marshall and his brother of the debt since the work "though the best in English on the subject of the primacy" had not sold well.[10]

Cromwell's hestitations (if such they were)[11] were justified: the *Defensor* was unmistakably a scholastic treatise, exhaustive, dense, and—to the taste of the day—written in execrable Latin. So Thomas Starkey could commend Marsiglio to Pole (in the original tongue) as being

> ... of a grete judgment & wel to set out thys matter, both by the authortye of scripture & gud reysonys grounded in phylosophy ...

yet complain that "he were in style rude".[12] Indeed, even in its abbreviated and Anglicized form, the *Defensor* was unlikely to commend itself to a public taste mirrored in the racy polemics of Simon Fish or Richard Morison. Yet all this hardly mattered: the men who utilized Marsiglio no doubt read him in the original Latin, then transcribed the essence of his thought in terms appropriate to Henrician reality.

In a short, concluding section of the *Defensor* ("Dicto 3"), the author himself thoughtfully and succinctly summarized his findings, the most pertinent of which follow:

1. For the attainment of eternal beatitude it is necessary to believe only in the truth of ... canonic Scripture ... and the interpretations of it made by the common council of believers ...

3. The evangelic Scripture does not command that anyone be compelled by temporal pain or punishment to observe the commands of divine law.

4. For eternal salvation it is necessary to observe commands of the evangelic law, and their necessary consequences, and the dictates of right reason ...

7. The decretals of the Roman pontiff ... made without the grant of the human legislator, bind no one to temporal punishment.

11. The supreme government in a ... state must be but one in number.

14. A bishop or priest, as such, has no ... coercive jurisdiction over any ... layman, even if the latter be a heretic.

15. Only the ruler ... has coercive jurisdiction over the person and property of every ... person, of whatever status, and of every group of laymen and clergymen.

16. No bishop ... or any group of them is allowed to excommunicate anyone without authorization by the faithful legislator.

17. All bishops are of equal authority immediately through Christ, nor ... is there any superiority or subjection among them in spiritual or temporal affairs.

19. No mortal being can give a dispensation with respect to marriages prohibited by divine law, while those prohibited by human law pertain only to the authority of the human legislator ...

20. Only the faithful legislator has the authority to legitimize illegitimate children so that they may succeed to their inheritance.

21. It pertains only to the ... legislator to exercise coercive judgment with regard to candidates for church orders ... and no ... bishop is allowed to promote anyone ... without his authorization.

23. Only by the authority of the faithful legislator can ... separable church offices be bestowed and taken away, and similarly benefices and other things established for religious purposes.

27. Ecclesiastic temporal goods which remain over and above ... needs, can lawfully, in accordance with divine law, be used ... by the legislator for the common public welfare and defence.

29. ... the ... legislator has the authority to grant exemptions to any group or religious body ...

31. No one who is ... obligated to someone else by lawful oath can be released by any bishop ... without reasonable cause, which is to be judged by the faithful legislator ...

32. Only the general council of all the faithful has the authority to designate a bishop ... or church highest of all, and to deprive ... them from such position.

33. Only the faithful legislator, or ruler by ... authority in the community of believers may assemble through coercive power a general or partial council ...

37. From the coercive jurisdiction granted to a bishop ... a litigant may always appeal to the legislator or ... ruler.[13]

It would be superfluous to comment on the agreement between the above theses and the future Henrician settlement. Moreover, Marsiglio was not content merely to advance the above propositions as the *sine qua non* of tranquility within Christendom, he offers, as well, a devastating judgment of the papal claims. His critique is twofold, consisting of a reinterpretation of the scriptural texts from which the popes derived their claim to *plenitudo potestatis*, and an historical dissection of how the Church of Rome came to assume its hegemony. After a detailed scrutiny of the Petrine claims, Marsiglio concludes to the perennial "equality of the apostles":

> ... the Roman bishop neither has not had immediately from Christ any power or authority over his fellow bishops and priests ... for just as Peter had no power over the other apostles; so too Peter's successors in the episcopal seat at Rome have no power over the successors of the other apostles.[14]

The wealth of detail assembled to prove this provided an arsenal for Henry's apologists.

No less fraught for the future is Marsiglio's treatment of the historical development of the papacy. Having denied its scriptural basis, he seizes upon the Donation of Constantine and turns it against the papacy. Constantine

> ... the faithful legislator ... gave ... the Roman bishop those authorities and powers over all the other bishops and churches which they now claim belong to them from another source.[15]

The Donation, far from reenforcing the papal prerogative, merely serves to show that "this authority to establish headship belongs to the ... legislator or ruler by its authority."[16] Primacy therefore is an expedient of the faithful legislator, to be bestowed or taken away at his pleasure.

According to Marsiglio, this is in keeping with the canonical scripture, for Christ said "my kingdom is not of this world."[17] The same scripture teaches us that Christ willed himself to be subject to the temporal powers:[18] since Our Lord eschewed temporal jurisdiction, it was surely not his intention that his "vicars" should take up what he had laid down.[19]

This leads to the kernel of Marsiglio's argument, that "coercive jurisdiction"—the power to make laws, and, inseparably, to *compel*—belongs to the temporal authority alone: right reason (Aristotle) and Revelation conspire to proclaim this truth. Consequently, the papal claim to *plenitudo potestatis* is a sham, justified by neither divine nor human law.

As may be readily grasped, much of this program was eminently serviceable to the apologists of the Supremacy. Furthermore, Marsiglio was not a crypto-Protestant, not even in the sense in which Wycliffe might be accorded that distinction. His doctrine of scriptural sufficiency, which appears radical to our eyes, was in fact a commonplace among medieval theologians.[20] Fully within the Catholic tradition, he acknowledges the difficulty and obscurity of numerous biblical passages, and he insists that General Councils ought to be summoned "to define or determine doubtful sentences of Holy Scripture",[21] though, to be sure, only the "faithful legislator" has the "coercive jurisdiction" to summon them, or implement their decrees.[22] Like his Henrician Catholic progeny, Marsiglio is orthodox on the matter of the seven sacraments, and he specifically refers to the eucharist as "transubstantiated",[23] while several of his key arguments turn on the sacrament of penance. He certainly laid enormous stress on the fact that Church consisted of all its members, likely no less than clergy,[24] but there is no hint in him of the Reformation doctrines of *sola fide* or the priesthood of all believers.

And startling as his anticipations of the Henrician settlement are, there are concerns in the *Defensor* which neither converge nor coincide with the later English program. Plainly he does not conceive of a particular Church proceeding to legislate without the concordance of the rest. His notion of sovereignty was grounded in the will of the people, a point which his translator, William Marshall, was quick to qualify: "he speaketh not of the rascall multytude but of parlyment."[25] When Marsiglio writes of the "faithful legislator", it is either the emperor or an Italian civil magistrate he has in mind (and for the summoning of Councils, surely the former).[26] Moreover, his radical Aristotelianism led him to favor an elective monarchy—an indiscretion shared by his purest disciple, Starkey.[27] The large section of the *Defensor* given over to the defense of evangelical poverty indicates that what little heterodoxy he entertained was identical with that of the Spiritual Franciscans, who, like himself, had fled to the protection of Ludwig of Bavaria. Finally, for all its scriptural and patristic ballast, the central concerns of the *Defensor* are unmistakably secular. As the title suggests, the book's overriding motif is temporal tranquility. It is the ultimate Ghibbeline retort in the three-century struggle between Papacy and Empire. Not surprisingly then, the *Defensor's* radicalism is less doctrinal than juridicial. Its author cannot conceive of an authority that is not "coercive": in this world, real law is enforceable law. It follows that a dual supreme authority is a monstrosity, a single body governed by two warring heads. Ecclesiastical headship must be extinguished, or made to flow from the temporal, for univocal jurisdiction is the *sine qua non* of temporal tranquility. In the opinion of Janelle, the apologists of the Henrician Supremacy scarcely do more than to provide footnotes or an updating to the arguments of Marsiglio.[28]

The first two apologists of the new settlement were Edward Fox and Richard Sampson.* Both published books in 1534, and since they wrote their respective works before Parliament conferred his new title upon the King, the "Supremacy" to which they refer must necessarily be that qualified one granted by convocation in 1531 and augments by the later Submission of the Clergy and the Act in Restraint of Appeals.[29] Understandably therefore, both writers are more concerned to justify the abrogation of papal jurisdiction than to give precise defini-

*See p. 161.

tion to the Royal Supremacy. Convocation's surrender had been circumscribed the phrase "quantum per Christi legem licet", a tacit admission of continued papal headship. By 1534, it was necessary to get around this, and to show that the "law of Christ" granted the pope nothing like the authority he had once enjoyed in England. To be convincing, the new apologetic had to demonstrate that the Roman primacy had no grounds either in Scripture and the early Church Fathers, and then to establish the means whereby the popes had acquired their illicit authority.

From internal evidence it is clear that Fox's *Opus eximium de Vera Differentia* is the earlier of the two books: the pope is repeatedly accorded his ancient title, and one notes, too, a reluctance on the part of the author to make explicit acknowledgment of the schism to which the argument nonetheless unambiguously tends.[30] The writer, at that time the King's almoner and an active dipolmat, had been for six years a prominent supporter of the divorce.[31] More importantly, as a canvasser of the universities he was especially familiar with the canonical and theological issues involved. At the time he wrote *de Vera Differentia*, Fox was not yet a Reformer, nor was he to be reputed one until his return from an embassy to the Germanies in the summer of 1536.[32] He does, it is true, make one assertion which appears to look forward to his future alignment—that Scripture alone provides certitude, since even the most venerable traditions are full of equivocations.[33] But in fact this work is liberally peppered with appeals not merely to Scripture, but to the authority of Councils, the Fathers, medieval doctors and canonists, and the popes themselves!

The book begins by proposing to make clear the distinction between ecclesiastical and royal power (in that order), and its opening arguments are explicitly Conciliarist. Aeneas Sylvius (Pius II) is rebuked for prohibiting appeals to future Councils, and it is argued that Peter himself was subject to a Council.[34] Gerson's authority is called on to reinforce Marsiglio's (unacknowledged) point that Paul, and not Peter, was unshakably righteous in the matter of the reception of Gentiles into the Church.[35] And this is followed by the no less Marsiglian thesis of the equality of the Apostles.[36] Episcopal quality was roughly maintained throughout the first three centuries of the Church; at Nicaea, "tam sancto concilio", the Roman patriarch was not even present, and so little did this matter that the assembled fathers took no account of his absence.[37] Plainly the onus of these assertions is to show that the present papal claims were unknown to antiquity, and therefore invalid. (We are still long years away from any theory of the "development of dogma".)

Fox then offers to prove that the *plenitudo potestatis* claimed by Rome is a very perversion of Christianity. The instrument of this power is canon law which accords the pope a coercive authority. This Fox rejects in a perfect reiteration of Marsiglio:

> ... in ecclesia autem no coactum sed adquiescentem oportet ad melior conuerti ...[38]

Once again, Fox echoes Gerson when he writes that the canon laws are an intolerable burden, and have left us no better off than Jews. Perhaps the most vigorously argued passages in this book follow as Fox contends that canon law binds no one of necessity, and proceeds to prove his point with examples of unenforced, incoherent or contradictory laws: indeed, the very popes themselves have been ensnared in the continuing proliferation of contrary canons.[39] And, since we are never very far from the divorce in these early works, Fox is particularly insistent that we understand that no canon law can the give the pope the right to dispense from divine law as revealed in Scripture. The point is clinched by reference to the authority of the great Innocent III who asserted that

> ... inter divinas et humanas leges tanta est differentia, quod contra leges diuinas nunquam valeat dispensari ...[40]

In accord with his promise, Fox now takes up the power of "de Regia." Janelle has remarked that the largest portion of this section consists of veritable "avalanche" of citations from the Old Testament, "un simple 'catena' presque sans commentaire".[41] Fox's examples are intended to reveal the authority of the Hebrew kings over the Jewish priesthood. We are invited to ponder the fates of the high priests Achimeliche and Abiathar who met their deaths at the hands of David and Solomon respectively.[42] Perhaps realizing that these examples might not appear germane to those living under the "new dispensation", it is printed out that Christ and the apostles willed themselves to be subject to the civil authority.[43] Nevertheless to Fox (and to his successors) the history of the ante-Nicene Church posed formidable difficulties; not surprisingly, he takes the era at an unseemly gallop. In truth, if papists found much that was awkward in the primitive Church, the supporters of Henry's "imperial" sway were still more discomfited by an age when emperors were pagans, often persecutors, and the Church was left to shape and govern itself. In the Henrician scheme, this state of affairs was viewed as provisional and unnatural: the fully realized Christian society was one where Church and society coincided and were overseen by a Christian magistrate.[44] And it is here we mark most clearly the debt of Henrician Catholic polemic to Marsiglio.

But to continue with Fox—if the ante-Nicene era offered slender pickings, it was quite the opposite with the Christian empire which followed it. Here a series of splendidly assured emperors had given protection and order to the nascent Church, convoked Councils, given authority to their decrees, and repressed heretics (when they were not heretics themselves). Of their number Fox especially singles out Justinian whose omnicompetence is apparent in that

> ... de fide et hereticis, de sacrosactis ecclesiis, de episcopus et clericis, de monachis et nuptiis et omnibus illis causis specialiter statuit.[45]

In spite of its diffuse conclusion, Janelle is surely correct in noting that *de Vera Differentia* is "la source commune a laquelle ont puise divers ecrivains au service du roi."[46] For this reason we have accorded it some attention, though its author was soon to pass into the camp of Reformers.

"Reformer" was the last word to be used by his contemporaries about Richard Sampson who now entered the field with a little book destined for international circulation. We have met him before as the officious Dean of Windsor whose abortive act of censorship brought Tyndale's book into Henry's hands, and we have noted earlier Reginald Pole's scathing comment on his motives for writing the *Oratio*. Yet Sampson's sharp trouncing of the papal hegemony failed to endear him to the Protestants, and Strype came to denounce him as "a secret favorer ... of the Pope, and of such as would not renounce his authority."[47] If ultimately he would find favor with no faction, this was because he would accommodate himself to every ordained change until, having made his peace with Mary, he died in 1554, in possession of his diocese. Yet so far as his meager courage allowed, Sampson was certainly a sustainer of the old ways. At the outset of the schism, the government plainly regarded him with suspicion, but Cromwell attempted to win him over and he was promoted to the see of Chichester in 1536. The new bishop was servile, but not grateful, and in May, 1540 he was arrested and flung in the Tower, the first gambit in a series of dizzying intrigues which led to the minister's fall.

Sampson's book, the *Oratio*,[48] was the first apologia for the new settlement to be deemed worthy of continental distribution. Published in 1534, it was dispatched to Paris, the petty German courts, and to Reginald Pole.[49] It was in response to the *Oratio*, and not to Gardiner's later and more accomplished labors, that Pole cast his denunciation of Henry's recent policies. Simultaneously the *Oratio* was savaged by Cochlaeus, a prominent German polemicist and self-appointed scourge of the Reformation. Sampson replied to neither of these attacks. His silence may lend substance to Pole's charge that he was motivated by ambition. Indeed, in the following year (1535), Sampson was delated to Cromwell for complaining that "there was none promoted but naughty fellows", an unmistakable reference to the known Reformers recently raised to the mitre. He then went on to express the pious hope that "we were not skurged as they were in Almayn, which he feyred shortely shuld com to pass".[50] Though he swiftly sought an interview with Cromwell to explain these remarks away, they would seem to confirm both his conservatism and his inveterate propensity for place seeking. It is very likely that by 1535, the swift advance of the Reformation had dismayed him and dulled his appetite for controversy.

The key to the *Oratio* is the scriptural concept of divinely ordained obedience: "the English nation ... were bound to obey kingly dignity" (Romans, 12; II Peter, 2). Wedded to this injunction is its converse, that no subjection is owed

> ... to the Bishop of Rome, who had no power by any divine right ... (for) ... there was no word in Scripture that attributed power to the Roman province: nor no more mention of the Bishop of Rome in the holy scripture than of the Archbishop of Canterbury.[51]

On the other hand, no person is exempt from secular jurisdiction, and the author in a prescient anticipation of things to come asks us to

> ... marvel not ... if thou see either priest or monk or byshop punished ... than thou dost wonder at the punishment of a lay person ...[52]

Since the prince has his supreme power of God, foolish indeed are those who would deny his title of "Supreme Head" for "Kings are God's vicars, and those who reject their supreme authority utterly cast away God."[53] Having made clear the eminence of princely jurisdiction, Sampson turns to examine the Papal claims to universal authority. Roman pretensions are the obverse of that subjection to "all human ordinance" enjoyed by the apostle Peter himself. Touching the abominations of present day popes, Sampson will say nothing: it would be simpler to "draw all the water from the ocean sea" than to give a complete account of them.[54] He will only pray God that they come to a knowledge of Christ's truth and amend their ways. A good beginning to this amendment would be for the see of Rome to recognize its "own bounds and limits."

As for the primacy, Peter

> ... did never exercise it, because he never had it. For thou shalt find in no place that he at any time did send any of the Apostles, or that he commanded them to do any thing. But we read that he was sent of the Apostles ...[55]

There follow a plethora of arguments against the primacy as exercised by Peter or any of his successors in the see of Rome. Paul, not Peter, had authority over the Gentiles. Paul it was who commissioned Timothy and Titus to their respective churches, and who withstood Peter to his face. When Paul mentions the chief apostles, they are James, Cephas and John, in that order. Peter is "first" only in the sense that he was first to be called, but all the apostles were equal in power. Were this not so, the apostolic Church would have been manifestly in error in failing to recognize a primacy bestowed by Christ himself.

But if the primacy was neither ordained by Christ, nor recognized by the apostles, how did it arise? By the "sufferance of the princes and the people and throw the filthy ambition and pride of the Bishops of that place".[56] It certainly went unrecognized by such eminent fathers as Cyprian and Jerome. Sampson then offers his readers a somewhat lengthy excursus contrasting the arrogance of the popes with apostolic humility. Concluding, he praises Henry VIII, who after patiently bearing these impositions for may years, has abrogated the jurisdiction of the bishop of Rome. Englishmen are bound by the ordinance of God to obey their King: they must follow him in repudiating Roman jurisdiction. Nor have they any cause for uneasiness, for while the power of the pope exists only by virtue of "man law", that of sovereign is rooted in the word of God.[57] Therefore

> ... every true English hearted man is bound to obey his law and ordinance, that ye may especially love the King, supreme head: again, that ye all which are members of this head may heartily love one another as 'I' sayeth Christ, 'have loved you'.[58]

The *Oratio* is a paradigm of those Henrician Catholic tracts which undertook the defense of the King's new prerogatives, for it seeks to justify the supremacy in such a way as to preclude the smallest suggestion of innovation. Henry VIII is, by the law of God, "supreme head"; he has merely resumed a title which he already possesses *de jure divino*. Written before Parliament passed the Act of Supremacy, the *Oratio* never once comes to grips with with the potential difficulties in the title of supreme head of *the Church of England* a reminder, if one is needed, that there is a distinction between being "supreme head" of all Englishmen, and of a *Church*. The latter notion entails theological implications which the Dean of Windsor sidesteps throughout his discourse, there being no reason by law that he should engage them. What interests Sampson are the arguments for a univocal jurisdiction within a single *regnum* . More importantly, his notion of temporal jurisdiction is conceived of in legal and punitive terms: God, through Holy Writ, has commanded us to obey our temporal rulers, the King's title of "supreme head" is only a *de jure* recognition of this: ergo, as Christians, we must obey the King's commands, so long as these do not contradict the divine law. This law tells us unequivocally that the magistrate is put over us by God to correct and punish the wicked, and Sampson will not omit the clergy from this authority, but—there is no whisper of a suggestion that the temporality may order, much less innovate, in doctrinal matters. There is, indeed, no hint of a Reforming proclivity in this work. All of which made the *Oratio* suitable for domestic and foreign consumption in those years the government sought to pose as Catholic and traditionalist.

In the bulk of its argument, the *Oratio* is clearly a distillation of the *Defensor Pacis* to which its owes both its insistence on the univocity of jurisdiction, and the well-worked theme contrasting the scriptual role of Peter with the amplified papal claims of the late middle ages. In essence, Sampson's brief is severely limited to the question of jurisdiction. For this reason, we cannot look to the *Oratio* for a fully developed doctrine of the royal supremacy which had not received its final enactment when the tract was composed.

The case is otherwise with the writings of Stephen Gardiner who contributed two books in support of the King's policy. As both appeared in 1535, the bishop of Winchester could scarcely evade the question of the King's supremacy over the Church as such. But if he could not keep silence on the matter, Gardiner could and did cloud the issue.

Stephen Gardiner is usually reckoned the captain of the Henrician Catholics,[59] but this opinion requires some qualification. With the enactment of the new settlement, his career had gone into eclipse, and he did not regain some measure of royal favor until the summer of 1535. Thereafter, frequent diplomatic missions kept him abroad during much of the 1530's and early 1540's. He himself, in later books and letters, tended to minimize his influence during the first years of the settlement,[60] and it would appear that, until 1539, he played no larger role in defense of the old faith than Stokesley, Tunstall and Edward Lee. With the death of the first and the eclipse of the last two, he would emerge as the ablest and most vigorous of the Catholic controversialists, but this would not be apparent until the very last years of the reign. Then he (and he alone) would discover the tone, racy, inventive, and provocative which gave him unique distinction among the Catholic polemicists, and made him a worthy and feared opponent to the Reformers. But consideration of this aspect of his career must be deferred to a later chapter.

The two tracts presently under consideration—*Si sedes illa and De Vera Obedientia*—were written to redeem their author from the disgrace into which he had fallen after opposing the government in convocation. His opposition to the new policies was well enough known to warrant an explicit retraction of it in the second work.[61] In the preceding year (1534) he had been banished to his diocese, where the extent of his misgivings may be judged from the anxious, conciliatory letters he addressed to both the King and Cromwell. Apparently at the instigation of the latter he was obscurely involved in the government's efforts to obtain the submission of the illustrious but difficult monastery of Syon. But even as he was so engaged, Henry ordered Cromwell to inquire into the sincerity of the Bishop's own conformity, giving vent to his suspicion of Gardiner's "colored doubleness".[62] The subsequent inquiry revealed that the Bishop had told a certain John Mores, the receiver of Syon, that the pope's primacy began with the law of men, and not God, and when Mores had raised the knotty question of certain General Councils which seemed to sustain Roman jurisdiction, Gardiner had replied tht if a General Council conflicts with a law of Parliament, the latter must be obeyed.[63] This surely was ungrudging conformity!

Let us note, in light of the notorious rivalry between Gardiner and Cromwell, that the order for investigation came from Henry, and that its tone is unmistakably that of a master urging a client to an unpalatable task. In any event, by the late summer of 1535 Gardiner was off the hook. It is then we hear mention of both these books which were to be included among the luggage of bishop-elect Edward Fox's mission to the German principalities.[64] In September, Fox wrote Cromwell a curiously elliptical critique of *De Vera Obedientia*[65], and by the end of the same month, Gardiner, restored to royal favor, was on his way to a three year sojourn as Henry's ambassador at the court of Francis I.[66]

Of the two treatises, *Si sedes illa* is much the more slender with regard to both length and subject matter. Moreover, unpublished until 1930, it cannot be numbered among the more important Henrician Catholic tracts. Gardiner's purpose is to offer an apologia for the execution of John Fisher (an act which did nothing to enhance Henry's reputation on the continent), and a refutation of the brief of Pope Paul III, which condemning the same, called upon his Most Christian Majesty to rise in defense of the Apostolic see.[67] In spite of its unhappy occasion, *Si sedes illa* does reveal its author's ripening talent for the pointed thrust and the *tu quoque* argument.

Gardiner begins with an effective barrage against the popes' "pretended holiness", and then swerves neatly to counter Paul III's attempt to drive a wedge between Henry and Francis. Whatever the Pope may have required of the French King

> ... his most Christian maiestie neuer made any desires in this case, nother dyd speke any words of thatt matter, ne euer intermeddled with thatt thyng ...[68]

—a neat maneuver which turns the tables on the Pope, dividing him from Francis, while showing how little weight the voice of Rome carried when caught in the trade winds of diplomatic necessity.

The Bishop then returns to the theme of Roman hypocrisy to pour scorn on

> ... that holynes which hath shakyd the hole worlde with so manye warres, now can nott abyde the lawful deth of one man.[69]

A later thrust augurs his future genius as a polemicist: when Fisher, a great controversialist and scholar, lived quietly in England, no Pope then thought of making him a cardinal; rather "he then lyuyd miserably att home, like a man onknowen and little spoken of" while red hats went to the popes' "children or neuous".[70] In those days, the Roman attitude was "whatt have wee to do with these rude and barbarous ultramontans?"—a lively expression this of cisalpine resentment of Italian arrogance by no means confined to Protestant sensibilities.

Gardiner concludes his argument with the brilliant insinuation that the Pope gave Fisher the red hat in hope of producing a martyr for his derelict and ruined cause, a suggestion which, in part, has found favor with one modern historian.[71] The blood of Fisher then, is on the hands of the Pope, not the king. One understands Henry's reluctance to dispense with Gardiner's services.

Two other concerns play an ancillary role in this tract. There is considerable harping on the matter of the divorce, a recurrent theme of all these polemics until Queen Catherine's death in January 1536. Germane to the issues of that day, it is less so this book, and we shall pass it by. More pertinent is the author's suggestion that the opinion of the universities (canvassed on the legitimacy of the first marriage) is tantamount to the consent of the universal Church. This assertion, derived from Gerson, had already been made by the King in his instructions to Sir John Wallop, Gardiner's predecessor and compere in Paris.[72] The point is made as a prelude to Gardiner's contention that separation from Rome does not constitute a break from the Church universal. With regard to the accusation that the new laws constitute a schism, Gardiner retorts that "we knowe none, ne euer meanyd any suche".[73]

By contrast with its sister tract, *De Vera Obedientia* is more profound and wide-ranging. It also is colored by occasional evangelical turns of phrase unique in the Bishop's writings.[74] This doubtless accounts for its success among the Reformers who managed to use it twice to effect: first, straightforwardly as an attack against Popery, and again, as an instrument to embarrass its author when he was appointed Lord Chancellor at the accession of Mary. Then (1553) the work was republished in an English translation by a radical Protestant, quite possibly, John Bale.

A history of this and the preceding work has been provided by Janelle, and *De Vera Obedientia* in particular has since been discussed at some length by several eminent historians.[75] In this account therefore, we may confine ourselves to a few salient details. Though aimed primarily at the Catholic courts, *De Vera Obedientia* received its first enthusiastic reception at Strasbourg, whither it arrived in the copious train of bishop Fox. Here, Bucer and Capito arranged for a second edition, and the former, in a surge of premature enthusiasm, wrote a preface commending the virtues of the English bishops, contrasting them favorably with their Teutonic counterparts.[76] So far as Gardiner, at least, was concerned, Bucer would shortly have occasion to repent of his generosity: in six years the two men would beome bitter adversaries. In the meantime, the book's success was repeated in Lutheran Hamburg where Edmund Bonner, then on a mission to the Baltic principalities, wrote a preface to a fresh edition which outdid the original in evangelical excess.[77] In Bonner's case, remorse would have some twenty years to mature.

As we have noted, *De Vera Obedientia* begins with an apologia; a *volte* face on the part of Gardiner who, hitherto, had been regarded as a leading opponent of the jurisdictional changes in England. It has taken him long to see the light, but now he, Gardiner, will testify to it. Certain truth is to be found in scripture "the most pure and cleare fountayne itself . . . (and) not in mennes puddles and qualimyres. . . ".[78] To the truth, we owe obedience for "to obeye truly is nothing elles but to obeye unto the truthe".[79] This scholastic sentiment, that one conforms and submits oneself to the truth, is supported with scriptural ballast, e.g., "obedience is better than burnt oferings" (Deut. 11).[80] Our Lord himself gave the example in offering perfect obedience to the Father: "Not as I will, but as thou wilt" (Matt. 6).[81] Now one of God's commandments, constantly reiterated in both Testaments, is that we must submit to our temporal rulers. (Here Gardiner does not repeat the already familiar arguments put forth by Fox and Sampson.)

Having made the point that obedience to the magistrate is a divine commandment, Gardiner takes up the now hackneyed distinction between the divine and human law, insisting that we

> ...kepe surely that marke which is certain and signed with the fyngre of God whereby we may make a distinction between Goddes causes and mannes, that they be not shuffled together...

and that is verified by the words of Christ himself:

> ...in vayne doo you worship me in the commandments of men, seying you have broken my precepts for your own tradition.
>
> (Matt. 15).[82]

By implification, the above skates marvelously close to the Reformers' rejection of tradition. At this point, however, the argument makes a one hundred eighty degree turn revealing, incidentally, the force and subtlety of the Bishop's mind. We must, Gardiner insists, be wary of imagining. In spite of the last quotation, that the New Testament (in most cases) abrogates the Old. Christ, after all, enjoined us to *exceed* the righteousness of the scribes and pharisees, and the Gospel offers no carte blanche for "a light dissolute and filthie maner of life".[83] Here Gardiner is clearly scoring off the evangelical doctrine which derogates good works, while at the same time riding the favorite hobby-horse of Catholic polemicists who represent Luther's "Christian liberty" as antinomianism. Moreover, a second point lurks in the wings: it is essential to understand that

> ...the libertie which is gouen vnto vs by the Gospel and is thought to have abrogated Moses lawe perteineth not ... that we maye forgete the morall preceptes...[84]

These, as found in Leviticus, are the hinge upon which the King's case for an annulment hangs. Here, for the first time, "wily Winchester" shows his facility for forging links between Henry's self-interest and the preservation of an essentially orthodox theology.[85]

Proceeding now to the question of the Supremacy, Gardiner argues that if the King is the head of the realm, he is the head of *all* in that realm, clergy no less than laity. But Gardiner goes on to describe Henry frankly as "summum in terris caput Ecclesiae Anglicanae",[86] which is altogether wanting in the earlier ambivalence of Fox and Sampson, and for that matter, Gardiner himself.[87] But what does Gardiner mean here? How does he conceive of a royal supremacy over the Church? The key to his intentions are found in his now famous proposition which does not describe the supremacy, but the Church:

> ... the churche of Englande is nothing elles but the congregation of men and women of the clergie and of the laytie united in Christes profession...[88]

It is easy to lay too much emphasis on this definition, taken in isolation, and Fr. Hughes, for instance, has lamented the nominalistic bias in the formula.[89] But recalling that in *Se sedes illa* Gardiner had denied that any schism had taken plan, we may find cause to revise this judgment. I would suggest that the "Church of England" as the Bishop here describes it, is conceived as a legal entity, and that we would be mistaken to think that his definition is intended to characterize, much less exhaust, his notion of the universal Church. Nevertheless, it is true, particularly in light of his later profound defense of specific doctrines of Catholicism, that his ecclesiology was, and would remain, remarkably inadequate.

A similar ambiguity hangs over Gardiner's treatment of the Supremacy. Nowhere does he suggest—as Cranmer soon would do[90]— that the King initiate reforms in doctrine, though he does offer, as an example of a prince who exercised an ancient supremacy "Justinian that made lawes concerning the glorious Trinitie and the catholike faithe."[91] But this too is open to being misconstrued. For one thing, Gardiner's Protestant translator has given "made" for the original "aedidit" which might be better rendered as "put forth". And this corresponds to the actual historical situation. Justinian, after all, was the most orthodox of emperors: his "lawes", for the most part, were coercive enactments, in the Marsiglian sense, of previous canons of the Church Councils. For those bent on doctrinal innovation, Justinian was hardly a promising prototype.

But whatever reservations surround Gardiner's treatment of the Supremacy and the Church, his attitude to the Roman primacy is beyond doubt. Here his arguments follow the trail blazed by Marsiglio, and his two predecessors, Fox and Sampson. More generously than the last, he will grant that the early Roman see enoyed a certain limited prestige by virtue of the sanctity of its pastors and the political pre-eminence of the city. But he firmly insists that Roman authority never rested upon God's law.[92] He reiterates the now commonplace assertions: unlike later popes, Christ himself sought no earthly kingdom.[93] Peter's supremacy consisted solely in being the first called of the apostles; in any case, it never was of any worldly sort.[94] And contrasting the present full blown papal claims with the original commission given the apostles, Gardiner outdistances his competitors in verve and irony, an irony, which, in one instance, unwittingly redounds upon himself, when this most lordly of English prelates since Wolsey maintains that servants of the Word ought not to meddle in too many offices![95]

Gardiner concludes by returning to the subject of obedience to the prince which, is enjoined upon all Christians. It is a mere repetition of the previous tracts.

Though the most comprehensive of the treatises vaunting the Supremacy and repudiating the jurisdiction of Rome, *De Vera Obedientia* was not the last of their number. Until the spring of 1539, the government printed, or allowed to be published, a number of apologias for the new settlement. Most were penned by known favorers of the old religion. If Cromwell's attempts to corral bishop Stokesley offer any guide, a good portion of these offerings were taken on an impromptu basis from sermons delivered at Paul's Cross, or else before the court during Holy Week. Such was the case with the writings of Simon Mathew, John Longland and Cuthbert Tunstall. The style of these works suggests that they passed from pulpit to printer with very little editing. All caught the government's eye by their rejection of the primacy or their praise of the new order. Since they add nothing to either subject that had not been discussed before, we shall delay treatment of them until the fifth chapter where they will command our attention by their awareness of the burgeoning Protestant menace.

With rare exceptions, Catholic writings in support of the Supremacy have failed to win the sympathy of later historians. General opinion has followed the lead of John Foxe, and continues to look upon them as the inconsiderable spawn of time-serving and base servility. The Marian retractions of their authors (those, in fact, who survived) has grafted to them the rancid smack of bad faith, an impression amplified by an undeniable repetitiveness and unoriginality which so often characterizes hack work. It is suggested throughout this volume that closer study of these writings in their ambience may soften this verdict; for the present, let us note merely that propaganda in general, and sermons in particular, are wedded to redundancy if they hope to be efficacious. Furthermore, from the point of view of the authors, originality was the last thing they aimed at: by definition, they wished to remain as traditional as possible.

Having summarized these tracts, we must classify their similarities. First of all, whether directly inspired by the *Defensor Pacis* or not, each is cast in the Marsiglian mold. By this, we mean not only the obvious rejection of the primacy and its supplanting by a univocal, temporal jurisdiction, but also the retention of substantially orthodox theology. No less Marsiglian is the tendency of these tracts to remain muted on the question of how the institutional Church is to adjudicate upon and proclaim true doctrine. Plainly the various national churches cannot do so; on the other hand, it was equally clear that on Marsiglian principles, no General Council might be called, or its decrees enforced, without a *consensus princpum*. And while such a proposition might be entertained in the early fourteenth century, it was scarcely realistic in the third decade of the sixteenth. Here, indeed, was no mere theoretical weakness as the Henrician Catholics were to discover to their cost.

Nevertheless, there can be little doubt that, at the outset of their venture, Henrician Catholics remained blind to the potentialities for theological discord inherent in the doctrine of the Royal Supremacy. Nor is this surprising. Catholic apologists neither desired nor anticipated theological innovation: the faith, for them, was a fixed thing, and Henry, in this scheme, was to be a bulwark of received orthodoxy. When Richard Sampson speaks of the King's duty to chastise his clergy—in Marsiglian terms, to exercise coercive jurisdiction over them—it is the correction of their morals, not their theology, he has in mind.[96] Nor, as we have seen, was Stephen Gardiner of a different opinion, the celebrated reference to Justinian notwithstanding.[97] Though the bishop of Winchester too, speaks of Henry's duty to reform his clergy, the matters he specifies are disciplinary or temporal.[98] Simon Mathew, as we shall see, also took the faith as a settled thing, one and universal, while at a still later date, the sermons of Longland and Tunstall evade the subject of a theological Supremacy altogether. We may conclude that, contrary to what is often suggested, the Henrician Catholic leadership took a "low" line on the Supremacy.

Secondly, all these polemics lay strong emphasis on obedience. For Cuthbert Tunstall, disobedience is nothing less than the primordial sin of Adam, and those who will not subject themselves to their governors have the "archangel Lucifer ... (for) their father".[99] Tunstall's vision of obedience transcends the pragmatic and legal justification for the settlement: obedience is the freely willed submission of all creatures to the hierarchical order of God; its rupture is the great 'aboriginal calamity' which has ushered in its wake pain, travail, destruction and death.

To be sure, this insistence on obedience has less exalted origins. However the government sought to gloss the matter, the new laws were felt by many, even of the simpler sort, to constitute a breach with a venerable tradition.[100] Their rich potentiality for discord and treason were amply confirmed by the risings of 1536. On a wider scope, we are all familiar with the prevalent insecurity of Tudor England, and Reformation Europe in general. It was obvious enough to construe obedience as the sole alternative to a ruinous anarchy. Only we must add that the insistence on obedience was by no means a merely Henrician Catholic phenomenon: we need go no further than Tyndale, Cranmer, Barnes and Morison to discover Reformers equally vehement in their insistence on undeviating obedience.[101] Indeed, if the first Henrician Catholics made much of the virtue of obedience, this may well have been as a substitute for coming to grips with the explosive concept of the Supremacy. Simply, it was easier to justify obedience to a Royal injunction (which was surely enjoined in scripture) than to offer a convincing rationale for the amorphous novelty of the Royal Supremacy.

A third similarity which links these Catholic tracts is the proposition that the settlement had effected nothing novel. We must be careful here. Protestant thought, too, might claim to be 'traditional' and often spoke of a return to the evangelical purity of the early Church. What distinguishes the Henrician Catholic is the insistence that no schism had taken place, and that the English Church remained a province of the visible Catholic Church. Gardiner explicitly confirms this point when he grants that while in pressing need of reform, the Roman Church is a true Church. The same point is made in so many words by Simon Mathew, Tunstall, Stokesley and Thomas Starkey.[102] No such sentiment can be ascribed to the Reformers who were already following in the wake of continental precedent, and describing the see of Rome as the throne of the Antichrist.[103] The Henrician Catholic took the primacy for an accidental deformity grafted upon the body of an essentially healthy Church. Unlike the Reformers, he did not disdain the vast accretion of doctrine, tradition, ceremonies and visual auxiliaries to piety as things to be both identified and jettisoned with the pope.

A fourth and final consideration is the manner in which the primacy was rejected. In each of these writings, the repudiation of Roman authority is as vigorous, direct and unequivocal, as the acceptance of the Supremacy is ambivalent or muted. Gardiner's injunction that "those born and bred in England shall have nothing to do with Rome" is perhaps well enough known.[104] Less so is Tunstall's invective against the pontiffs who

> ...make theym selfes felowes to god, contrarye to his word ... who doo exalte their seates aboue the sterres of god, and doo ascende aboue the clowdes, and wyl be lyke to almyghty god.[105]

A like vehemence may be noted in each author we have mentioned in this chapter. In light of later suspicions of their authors' sincerity, it is worth noting that no part of these writings carries more conviction than the diatribes against Rome.

It is true that from the inception of the break with Rome, the Reformers took to castigating their opponents as papists, yet this was no real issue until the advent of the Edwardian Reformation. In the immediate years to come, the storm center would focus around traditions and ceremonies: whether these should be kept, or cast out; whether they were divinely ordained or merely tolerable; or again, merely indifferent or positively harmful. In general, Catholics favored the first line, Reformers, the second. Yet far from presenting a fast front, Catholics were themselves disturbed and uncertain about these questions. It would come down to drawing a distinction between essential doctrine and *adiaphora*—what was perhaps useful, but in itself, indifferent. To grasp the Henrician Catholic position on these matters, we must discuss the third factor which went into its making: what for convenience, we shall call Erasmianism.

4

Erasmus and Adiaphorism

Recent studies have laid such heavy emphasis on the Erasmian contribution to the English Reformation,[1] that our most eminent Tudor historian has complained of the penchant for turning up Erasmus under every Henrician reform.[2] It is no intention of ours to review this prevalent influence which culminated in a Protestant government's determination to place the *Paraphrases* in every parish church in England.[3] Nor do we intend to slight Erasmus' role in the formation of English Protestantism, particularly his emphasis on the "simple Gospel" and his corrosive critique of both scholastic theology and the paraphernalia of late medieval worship.

But quite pertinent to this book (and much less universally recognized) is Erasmus' authority with the men who were to provide the post-Supremacy Catholic leadership. His influence embraced nearly every eminent stalwart of the old faith—Tunstall, Stokesley, Sampson, Gardiner, Longland, Aldrich, Starkey, and even Edward Lee, with whom a decade before he had engaged in bitter controversy. Some, like Gardiner and Tunstall, knew the great man on an intimate basis, others were correspondents of that voluminous letter writer. Strikingly, it was among Catholics, and not the Reformers, that Erasmus enjoyed personal sway.[4]

Before describing the particulars of this influence, it is necessary to characterize briefly the theology of the elusive humanist. On a variety of issues over which the two camps were to fracture such as the eucharist, the primacy, religious orders, ceremonies and Councils, Erasmus' position was not always clear, nor was he unduly burdened by consistency.

Erasmus is a headland where converge two separate streams—a simplistic Northern pietism, and the Italian critical method. Certain of his themes, such as the marked separation of essential from peripheral doctrine, we have met before in Marsiglio and Gerson.[5]

From the practical piety of the *devotio moderna* he poured off the last dregs of an asceticism to which he was little inclined, and with it, the mystical strain which is its frequent concomitant. The filtered residue was a moralism uniquely his own which stressed commonplace good works, and which laid him open to Luther's charge of Pelagianism.

Perhaps a less recognized consequence of this moralism was a certain flattening of the spiritual life. One may conjecture whether this levelling was a factor in the undistinguished spiritual performance of a number of the Henrician Catholic leaders, itself noted by two later historians of different religious persuasions.[6] It must be confessed that Erasmus' devotional works, in spite of their wide circulation, were scarcely manuals of heroic sanctity.

More positively, Erasmus was the undisputed master of the "New Learning",[7] the application of a philological and critical method to the emendation of scripture and the Fathers. Here the great Dutchman confessedly realised the legacy of Valla, yet it would be difficult to exaggerate the magnitude of his example, or the enthusiasm with which his prodigious labors were received. The impact of the "new Learning" on the sixteenth century is comparable to that of the discovery of Aristotle in the twelfth century, or the impact of Newton upon the eighteenth.

Though it rankled Erasmus to be taken for a progenitor of Luther's,[8] his peculiar fusion of pietism and criticism bred contempt for the highest attainments of the middle ages: seen from the prospect of the *philosophia Christi*, the broad currents of scholastic theology were but meandering, sullied rivulets which served to cloud the purity of the originate spring. The new illumination of antique Christian sources by philology was bound to prove disturbing to the early sixteenth century since nearly all Christians concurred in the opinion that the early Church, proximate to its founder, was more pure and virtuous than the present, and was, as well, possessed of the entirety of revelation. As we have suggested, "development of dogma" remained an unexplored concept, hidden in the womb of time. Revelation was consequently construed as static, truth being, in the classic formula: "quod ubique quod semper quod ab omnibus creditum est."

In the eyes of his contemporaries, it was Erasmus' particular glory to have refurbished the time-smudged image of the early Church. As Erasmus himself put it congratulating Colet,

> You . . . do your utmost to restore that ancient and genuine theology, now overgrown and entangled with thorny subtleties, to its pristine splendor and dignity. . .[9]

The glamour of this project was not a little enhanced by Erasmus' satiric gifts, which drew attention to the flagrant discrepancies between the ancient and Renaissance Church.

There is an obvious correlation between Erasmus' veneration of antique Christianity and what might be called his doctrinal minimalism. Throughout his life Erasmus held consistently to a reductive view of dogma. In 1519, with the Reformation barely under way, he professed that schism might be healed if

> . . . instead of wishing to fix and define every little detail, we were to let suffice what is clearly contained in Scriptures, and is indispensable to salvation. . .[10]

And in the evening of his life he repeated the same theme to no less a correspondent than Pope Paul III:

> The definition of dogmas should be reserved to a council. However I do not think it necessary for a council to pronounce on any and every opinion but only on those crucial points on which the Christian teaching hinges . . . Just as a variety of ceremonies does not disrupt the harmony of the Church, so too there are points of view on which it is possible to disagree and still preserve Christian peace intact.[11]

In the above passage, the like of which could be multiplied in his writings, Erasmus gives clear voice to adiaphorism, a point of view often ascribed to Melanchthon and Starkey,[12] both of whom were deeply indebted to Erasmus. The last, in his turn, owed his adiaphorism to his study of the Fathers, particularly Augustine, and to Gerson.

The Erasmian catalogue of "things indifferent" was an extensive one, embracing pilgrimages, excessive feast days, monastic vows, rules of fasting and abstinence, veneration of saints, auricular confession, celibacy, and above all, a too precise definition of doctrine which he associated with the despised scholastic subtleties.[13]

Yet for all his emphasis on essential matters (and a corresponding tendency to reduce the secondary to triviality) Erasmus remained a moderate, preserving an equilibrium unique in that age. While his inclination toward a more "spiritual" Christianity is evident, he understood no less the love and need for material imagery on the part of the mass of the people. At the same time, he recoiled from a religious materialism that was dangerously akin to idolatry—the mistaking of the outward form for the substance. A case in point was his attitude toward the eucharist. Clearly he inclined toward some doctrine of a "spiritual" presence, and he ridiculed those who "wherever they see a priest exposing the Host . . . rush up and gaze fixedly upon it". But in his last years, he felt constrained to "acquiesce in what the Church has handed down, namely, that the living body and blood of the Lord are here present".[14]

So protean a figure could scarcely command unqualified acceptance from any party, and the Henrician Catholics were no exception. Richard Sampson, though a fervent admirer, disallowed Erasmus' exegesis of a passage of Jerome which seemed to favor the primacy,[15] while Stephen Gardiner, who as a young man had been privileged to serve at the scholar's table, later reproved both his early opinions of the eucharist and his less than respectful comments on the duties of magistrates.[16] So far as Henrician Catholics were concerned, these criticisms sum up neatly what remained unacceptable: Erasmus' persistent attachment to Rome as a symbol of unity, his eucharistic ambiguity, and his coolness toward erastianism.

But this said, Erasmian attitudes account for much that is otherwise inexplicable in conforming Catholicism. In nothing is Erasmus' sway so apparent as in the attitude taken by the Catholic leadership to the suppression of the monasteries, places of pilgrimage, and veneration of relics and images. Whatever popular resentment surged forth on this score, Catholic leadership gave little voice to it. Intimidation will not serve as an explanation here, for the same leadership was vociferous when an essential dogma such as the Real Presence or the necessity of works was challenged.

But we are not reduced simply to an argument from silence; a number of surprising instances serve to confirm the penetrating influence of Erasmus with Henrician Catholics. Stephen Gardiner, for one, raised not a murmur in defense of the monks, but he was left more than a few words attesting to his contempt for the friars. He can scarcely mention his critics, Robert Barnes and John Bale, without sniping at their former profession. Barnes if that "trim minion friar" in whom railing may be excused since it is the bane of his calling,[17] while Bale is characterized as an "inepttientis fraterculi latratus" and his cohorts, "nebulones".[18] Moreover, the Bishop of Winchester saw a sinister connection between the old friars and the new Reformers, one that quite carried over their transfer of religious loyalties. Defending the doctrine of good works against its slanderers, he remarks that the former friars plying the "merchaundise" of pardons from Rome, are now too frequently the "new bretherne" who having cheapened good works, are prepared to dispense with them altogether, and he prays

> ...the kynges maiestie as he hath banyshed freres by the Frenche name, wolde also banyshe these that call them selfe brethern in Englysche...[19]

Gardiner not only followed Erasmus in his dislike of the regulars, he frowned upon "supersitition" as well. In a letter to Somerset, otherwise vigorously defending Catholicism, he voiced his regret that certain objectionable practices had not been expunged when the opportunity had offered itself in 1542.[20]

Gardiner's opinion of certain popular devotions was apparently shared by Robert Aldrich (bishop of Carlisle after 1537). As a young man, vhe had accompanied Erasmus on a pilgrimage to Walsingham, celebrated in one of the more pungent *Colloquies*. Here, according to Erasmus, Aldrich has made sport of a monk who was displaying a phial of the Blessed Virgin's milk for the edification of the credulous.[21] In spite of his identification with the "New Learning", the seventeen questions of 1540 show Aldrich to be among the most consistently orthodox of the respondants.[22] Seven years later, he would emerge as a regular opponent of the Edwardian Reforms, in spite of which, he managed to retain his diocese, dying as an incumbent in the following reign.[23]

Cuthbert Tunstall was yet another friend and correspondent of Erasmus. Indeed his wide learning, suave latinity and relative tolerance[24] mark him as the most distinguished Erasmian on the bench of bishops. In the years between 1535-40, and again, in the teeth of the Edwardian reforms, Tunstall was the most respected of the Catholic controversialists, and one, moreover, who followed Erasmus' advice, rather than practice, in eschewing personal abuse of his opponents. His attachment to the essentials of Catholic doctrine led him into respectful controversy with Henry, and then to deprivation and imprisonment by Northumberland in 1551. Tunstall's polemics invariably centered around the key issues of the mass, holy orders, confession and freewill. But though courteously outspoken on these matters, he raised no word in defense of monasticism, ceremonies or pilgrimages.

Far more unlikely Erasmians were John Stokesley and John Longland, respectively Henrician bishops of London and Lincoln. Stokesley was nothing less than the leader of the Catholic faction in the crucial years 1534-39, Gardiner being first in disgrace, and then ambassador in France until 1538, while Tunstall was largely occupied by his duties in the North. Until his death in September, 1539, Stokesley proved the least resilient but the most resourceful of the conservative bishops,[25] an aggressive persecutor, and a stubborn opponent of concessions to Protestant theology.[26] Yet according to the chronicler Edward Hall, it was no Reforming bishop or modcrate, but Stokesley who called for the dissolution of the greater monasteries, and this at a time when the government had yet to show its hand. In 1536, the bishop of London reminded Parliament that Henry had taken the lesser monasteries by

> . . . the consent of the great and fatts abbottes . . . in hope that their
> great monasteries continued still. But even at that time one sayd . . .
> that these were as thornes, but the great abbottes were putrified olde
> oaks and they must nedes followe & so will do other in Christendom
> qt Doctor Stokesley bishop of London or many yeres be passed.[27]

It should be noted that Stokesley, along with Kite of Carlisle (d. 1537) was the bishop most justly suspected to favoring a return to Roman jurisdiction.[28] In the early Protestant narratives of the Reformation, Stokesley appears as the most hidebound of reactionaries, yet as carly as 1519, Erasmus describes him as one of the luminaries of Henry's court.[29]

Every bit as improbable an Erasmian was John Longland whom we have already marked as a persecuting bishop. To Cromwell's continual annoyance, Longland seems to have misconstrued the Supremacy as a *carte blanche* for the extension of episcopal authority, particularly over the regulars. (This aspect of the Bishop of Lincoln's career has received attention in the work of Professor Bowker.)[30] Earlier, as a protege of Wolsey's, Longland had been an agent in the requisitioning of some smaller monasteries to the making of Cardinal's College. He was both a correspondent and patron of Erasmus, who felt he knew the Bishop's mind well enough to complain to him of the mendicant orders which diverted the flow of charity better dispersed to the poor.[31] Owing to Protestant polemics, we have a tendency to regard Stokesley and Longland as the most obscurantist of the Henrician prelates, and so far as the progress of the Reformation goes, this is a true enough surmise. Yet both to a degree were Erasmians, and adhered to the great humanist's contempt for monkery and its attendant paraphernalia.

It is important to see that the decision to cut away the vast undergrowth of monastic piety and its attendant devotions was by no means confined to English Catholics. Even as Henry and Cromwell were going about the business of suppressing the lesser monasteries, a groundswell among continental Catholics to curtail monasticism and a variety of forms of medieval piety abhorrent to the New Learning, reached its crest in a curious document known as the *Consilium de emandanda Ecclesia*. This program for a far-reaching reform of the Church was presented to Pope Paul III in March 1537. Among its signators were Contarini, Sadoleto, Pole and Giberti, prominent Erasmians all. Sections 11 through 13 deal with monastic abuses, and the cosignatories urge the Pope to "prohibendo ne novos possint admittere" a solution, which if adopted, would have eliminated monastic houses on the continent as effectively, if not so swiftly, as those of England.[32] So far as the document contemplated the continued survival of religious houses, these would be active, educational institutions—precisely the transformation Thomas Starkey was simultaneously urging upon Henry VIII. The entire *Consilium* encapsulates the Erasmian program, and among the many abuses scored by the document are inflated claims of papal powers, rampant simony in the Curia, centralization, pluralism, absenteeism, benefice hunting, premature vocations, and the sort of scholastic debate whose triviality induces irreverence.[33]

The attack on scholasticism brings to mind still another Erasmian influence on Henrician Catholics. The English defenders of the old order but seldom resort to medieval theologians in their conflict with the Reformers. They chose instead to meet their adversaries on the Erasmian field of Scriptures and the Fathers. To be sure, another factor accounts for much of this decision. The Reformers had issued the challenge, and in great part, there was no choice but to meet them on their own grounds. Yet on the continent, the foremost exponents of Catholicism, Cajetan, Eck and Cochlaeus, had no hesitation in resorting to the scholastic doctors.

It was quite otherwise in England. Though we are assured that scholasticism still prevailed at the universities, there was but one scholastic theologian of repute—William Peryn, and he belatedly—who came forward to meet the challenge of the Reformers.[34] It was rather Cranmer who twitted Gardiner on the latter's ignorance of Scotus,[35] though it must be added that neither the Archbishop nor Tunstall, who between them enjoyed the greatest reputation for learning among the prelates, seem to have had a very profound grasp of medieval theology. One must conclude that in England, the Catholic apologists, no less than their opponents, had in their early years turned away from scholasticism to the New Learning. The rationale of their apologetic would be historical and humanistic.

But if the Catholic advocates, almost to a man, were Erasmian, can the settlement itself be so described? Some historians have not hesitated to do so, and can advance persuasive arguments for their position. By 1546 the Church of England had abolished monasteries and pilgrimages. Superstitious veneration of relics and images had been suppressed, the shrines despoiled, and a number of pious frauds exhibited to the public. On the positive side of the ledger, the people had been given the Scripture in English, and a good start made toward a vernacular liturgy. Adiaphorism (of a sort) had appeared in the official formulae,[36] and had (to some degree) survived the seeming catastrophe of the Six Articles.

All this was no mean accomplishment, yet it may be wondered if the government ever realized an Erasmian program, or for that matter, ever attempted to. A sort of litmus paper of Erasmianism is the curious career of Thomas Starkey. Or should we speak of two careers? that a relatively obscure man in his own time?[37] and that of a ghostly apotheosis in the twentieth century? For Professor Zeeveld, Starkey is nothing less than the progenitor of the Anglican *via media*,[38] a proposition endorsed in varying degrees by professors Dickens, Slavin and

Elton.[39] This opinion we will have cause to challenge. What cannot be doubted is that Starkey was the purest example of an Erasmian humanist in England: not even Tunstall so nearly approached the great Dutchman in the breadth of his concerns. Like Erasmus, and almost alone among the Henrician Catholics, Starkey's vision transcended purely theological matters to embrace the Erasmian ideal of the *respublica christiana*; his concerns were as much civil as ecclesiastical.* It is indeed his social criticism that commends him to our attention today, and no doubt accounts for the inflation of his historical importance.

He first appears as an Oxford humanist who attached himself to Reginald Pole, accompanying him during his scholarly sojourns in the south of France and Padua. In late 1534 he returned from Italy to play a part in the impending changes, and managed to attract the attention of Cromwell. In his guileless way, he assures us that he was avid to "lyue in a polytyke lyfe."[40] For this he proved singularly ill-suited both by temperament and circumstance. Though Cromwell was sufficiently impressed to have him appointed a royal chaplain in February 1535, it is apparent that the King never viewed him as more than mere bait to snare Pole. With the latter's explicit defection from the royal cause in May 1536, Starkey was all but ruined. After a number of pathetic intercessions, he managed to reingratiate himself with Cromwell who seems to have toyed with the idea of turning Starkey's talents against the Northern rebels. A little later, we catch a glimpse of him sitting on a commission to investigate a nest of sorcerers. In August 1538, he was dead, leaving us to conjecture how he might have weathered the fall of the Pole family in the "Exeter conspiracy" of that year.[41] By any standard, this was an abortive and pitiful career.

The surviving letters, treatises, and one published tract yield a consistent view of a character continually wavering between timidity and indiscretion. Like Erasmus, he was not of the stuff martyrs are made, yet no post-schismatic, "official" writer so regularly surprises us by the boldness and freedom of his opinions.

His most profound work, the justly famed *Dialogue*, drafted in 1533, remained unpublished until 1871. It is both too well known and too tangential to warrant discussion here. We may note in passing that the *Dialogue* grants an honorary primacy to the pope, and that its radical social critique culminates in the suggestion that Henry VIII establish the machinery for an elective monarchy to determine his future successors! Professor Mayer has shown that the work was

* See p. 166.

largely completed before its author was well apprised of the domestic siutation.[42]

That the *Dialogue* failed to find its way into print should not occasion much surprise, though the fact might serve to trim the tendency to vaunt Thomas Cromwell as a patron of learning.[43] Starkey's next foray in the government's service, the *Exhortation*, nearly met with a like fate. Cromwell returned the first draft to its author, funnelling the King's complaint that Starkey's ideas were insufficiently scriptural. Properly amended, it was published, probably by April 1536.[44]

Unlike the *Dialogue*, the *Exhortation* is largely constrained to theological matters. A goodly portion of the tract is given over to arguments against the Roman primacy;[45] with most of these we are already familiar: scripture offers no ground for Roman authority, nor any evidence for its existence in the apostolic or ancient Church. The primacy arose as an historical expedient; it is no longer such. Set up to confirm unity and concord, the papacy has lately furthered division and strife. Under the reckless ambition of the popes, superstitition has flourished. Starkey's arguments are more finely shaded and less vehement than his predecessors, so giving a greater impression of impartiality and weight. But however we appreciate this today, it did not commend him to his contemporaries.[46]

The *Exhortation* has been much admired as the fount of adiaphorism, and indeed, Starkey hangs his discourse on the distinction between necessary and "indifferent" things. But even in England, Starkey was well anticipated, and by such unlikely and disparate figures as Tyndale, Latimer, Frith, Simon Mathew and Edward Lee.[47] Behind all of these (and their continental comperes like Bucer, Melanchthon, Pflug and Contarini) stood Erasmus. And behind Erasmus, Gerson.

More specifically, the adiaphorism of the Ten Articles and the *Bishops' Book* has been ascribed to Starkey.[48] Pending the discovery of direct evidence, I find this most unlikely. It is far more probable that the adiaphorism of the official formulae was due to the difficulties encountered in the negotiations with the German Lutherans. These made it incumbent on a divided clergy to paper over discrepancies with ambiguity, and with the polite fiction that disagreement existed over inessential matters.[49] If the influence of single persons may be guessed at, these are likely Cromwell and Edward Fox. It was during these months that Cromwell, according to Prof. Elton, pressed the "mean" even more strongly upon Starkey,[50] while Fox, just returned from Germany, was plainly anxious to pilot an agreement through convocation. The adiaphorism of the official formulae is far more plausibly the work of a polished diplomat for whom even doctrine was negotiable.

Still other considerations exist to counter the notion of Starkey as the founder of the *via media*. For one thing, there is no evidence that the *Exhortation* was highly thought of by any of the men who were destined to be the founders of Edwardian or Elizabethan Anglicanism.[51] More notably, the *Exhortation* does not figure in the later writings of the first "high" Anglicans, such as Hooker, Andrewes or Taylor. There is, I hope to show, good reason for this. Starkey is not recognizably an Anglican in any pre-Puseyite sense. As far as his position admits of definition, Starkey was an Erasmian and a Henrician Catholic.

Even under the pressure of Cromwell and the King, the *Exhortation* defends General Councils, pilgrimages, veneration of the saints and their images, purgatory, fasting and holy days.[52] True, Starkey holds that all of these have been abused under the popes' rule, but he confirms Erasmus' view that ordinary folk

> ...without some exterior and outward sygnes and ceremonies ... could neuer be lad to true religion, nor of god to conceyue the divinitie.

From which we may deduce the author held some form of these to be essential to the economy of salvation. Moreover, Starkey challenges the Reformers' imputation that such practices as pilgrimages and devotion to images were "maynteined only by them whiche take profyte and lucre thereby": on the contrary, they were instituted by

> despisers of all worldly gayne, profyte, and pleasure, [who] ... loked only to the preferrement and encrease of virtue and of true religion.[53]

Still later in the treatise, pilgrimages are certified by the analogue of Magdalen's anointing of Jesus' feet. To the apostle's objection, Jesus pointed to Mary's

> inward and aboundant deuotion, though the outwarde deede appere to the worlde a superstitiouse operation.[54]

On the subject of General Councils, the doctrine propounded by the *Exhortation* is, at first sight, difficult and even contradictory. The Church, it is true, survived for centuries without them, and their decrees in adiaphora need not be received or maintained by common local authority.[55] Specifically, Starkey, like Marsiglio, holds that binding laws (i.e., those upheld by coercive jurisdiction) are the province of the civil government alone.[56] But it is a "corrupt" judgment

> to flee the order of a generalle counsel, and of al interpretation of scripture there comonly receiued. For to this succedeth . . . the ruine of scripture it self, the authoritie whereof . . . hangeth much uppon generall counsell.

To be sure, the truth of God's word does not depend upon man's judgment, yet they

> whiche we haue and take to be the true gospelles . . . we knowe not surely so to do, but onely by feyth and confidence that we gyue to the definition of generall counsell and consent of the same.

In his unpublished correspondence, Starkey was still more conciliarist, both before and after writing the *Exhortation.*[57] Finally, in attempting to compose the bitter dispute between faith and works, Starkey's own solution is markedly Catholic:

> A more pestilent opinion & more pernicious to Christes doctrine was neuer I trowe amonge menne then this, to saye that faythe alone, without charitable workes, is sufficient to mans saluation.[58]

The above considerations are set forth to suggest that the *Exhortation* had little influence on the subsequent development of Anglicanism. The real fathers of the Church of England—historical Anglicanism as it existed between the sixteenth and nineteenth centuries—Cranmer, Ridley, Jewel, Parker and the rest, would make a very different list of adiaphora than Starkey.[59] Indeed, it is plain that Starkey's program was more nearly realized in places like Scandinavia and Nurnburg, where Lutheranism came gently to terms with a residue of medieval Catholicism.

Another famous thesis of the *Exhortation* was in fact already anticipated in the writings of Sampson, Simon Mathew and Gardiner. This is the insistence that ancient Catholic communities had existed and continued to exist, orthodoxy intact, without recognizing Roman jurisdiction.[60] The argument, not unique to Starkey, but common to all Henrician Catholics, appeared in the *Bishops' Book* and again, in the *King's Book*, and is clearly related to the Catholic assertion that the new settlement did not constitute a schism.

The *Exhortation* was not long in print when the bombshell of Pole's denunciation of the recent settlement arrived in the King's hands. Since Pole's manuscript was yet unpublished a last flicker of hope remained for his conversion, and Starkey, with Tunstall and Stokesley, were set to reason against it. Their reasonings did not prevail with the exile, and when, in December 1536, he accepted the red hat, Starkey's eclipse was complete, and he had himself to repudiate the imputation of "popyschness".[61]

It was sometime between Pole's defection in May and the apparent pregnancy of Queen Jane that Starkey wrote to the King.[62] The letter may be roughly dated by its author's counsel to Henry to recognize the succession of the Princess Mary pending.

> . . . such frute as hyt schal pleyse god to send to your hyghnes to our comfort by this last matrimony schal put al thynges out of dowte and ambyguyte. . .[63]

This letter is surely the most remarkable communication dispatched to the king during a long reign, and not all its flattery could disguise the fact that it was crammed with unsolicited, unwelcome, and unheeded advice. It also reveals inadvertently how far Starkey remained from the counsels of Henry and his first minister. In spirit and matter, the letter returns us to the Starkey of the *Dialogue*.

Starkey begins by taking account of (and detaching himself from) Pole's recent judgment. He expresses his shock at the exile's "corrupt sentence", but imprudently attributes his dismay to his previous good opinion of Pole's character. He laments that the King and the realm are now "bereft of such a wyt to the wych I euer trustyd he wold have grown to haue byn a grete ornament".[64] The probable cause of Pole's secession was his "grete affection" which

> . . . playnely he showeth, that the dethe of them wych suffryd in the cause hathe so stonge hys hart & oppressyg hym wyth sorrow, that he seemyth to forget vtterly his dewty to hys cuntry & to your grace . . . [65]

Turning, for the time, to more general considerations of present policy, Starkey treats the king to a lecture on ways to augment his "polytyke wysdome". He is certain Henry

> wold neuer promote nor stablysch any acte in thys your Reame & cuntry but such only as schuld tend to your gracys honowre and goddes glory . . . [and] to the the quyetnes of thys present age but also of al our posteryte . . .

In keeping with this, Starkey expresses his joy that the King has plucked away the one cause of a contrary suspicion: . . .

> for thys I thynke may truly be sayd, that so long as that woman lyued, whom hyt plesyd your hyghness . . . mouyd by opynyon of vertue to sett in such hygh dygnyte, few actys coud procede by the conyecture of wyse men wych myght be durabul with our posteryte . . .

and the late Queen, Anne, somewhat ungallantly, is compared to a sore which only apparently healed may erupt forth again to the grave harm of the body politic.

Touching the succession, Henry is urged to recognize the claim of the Princess Mary who by "the consent of al men . . . [is] the floure of al ladys & the very glas & image of al vertue & nobylyte". [66] (It is possible this appeal was issued while Mary was still obstinately refusing to recognize either the first divorce or the Royal Supremacy.)[67] Though Starkey expresses a hope for further royal heirs, the present recognition of Mary's claim would certify both domestic and foreign tranquility. One wonders if Starkey knew that Chapuys was presenting identical arguments to the King, and that Henry had very firmly set his face against this advice?

Returning again to the subject of the martyrs, Starkey comments that it was unfortunate that the Supremacy had to assert itself in the execution of these men. Admittedly supersititious and stubborn, they were nonetheless persons of great virtue and repute.[68] Though ostensibly keeping to his difficult mean, Starkey is far less generous toward the new "precharys" who he hopes

> ...schalbe brought to a certayne stey & not haue lyberty to ex- pownde the darke placys of scrypture aftur theyr owne fantasys, slypping raschely bothe from the sentence of the auncyent interpre- tars of Chrysts doctryne & from the consent & custume of the church, vsed from the begynnying vnto thys day...[69]

Their temerity has ruptured charity among Christians, and they preach to their congregations as to infidels ignorant of all Christian doctrine. Worse, under the pretence of attacking "popery", they have chased away all "virtue and holynes". As for the attack on purgatory, this has had no happier issue than a general scepticism about the afterlife altogether. (Both the manner and matter of these observations are reminiscent of Erasmus' pragmatic defense of the old way.)[70] This appeal to halt the Reformation in its tracks is reinforced by the odd opinion that had the Catholic martyrs thought that changes would be confined to repudiation of the pope, they would have given their assent to the Supremacy.[71]

Next, Starkey deals with the suppression of the lesser monasteries, an act which he thoroughly approves. However, Starkey is certain that Henry

> ...wyl most lyberally dyspose thys tresure ... to the ayd, succor and comfort of your most louyng & obedyent pore subyectys...[72]

In this way, monastic wealth, formerly applied to the "nouryschyng of an idul rowte" may now be turned to the benefit of "profytabul cytyzens lyuying in some honest exercyse in thys your commynalyte". The sequestered goods should be applied to the establishment of learning and the art of war. (By the last, Starkey intends the economic re- enforcement of an arms-bearing, yeoman class.)

Starkey confesses that the suppressions have occasioned "no small controuersye" among the King's subjects

> ...specyally seying that by the consent of al your lernyed clergye hyt ys agred that such a place ther ys wherein soulys departyd remaynyng

may be releuyd by the prayer & almys dede of ther posteryte. . . [73]

But more scrupulous than the government, he assures Henry that the sequestrations can be justified *if* the wealth is applied to the good works intended by the original benefactors. Otherwise these would be

> . . . defruadyd of the benefyt of prayer & almys dede ther appoynted to be done for releyffe by theyr last wyl & testament. . . [74]

Yet the consent of this army of the dead may be "presupposyd" to a higher good. If these same benefactors were now living and were aware

> . . . how lyttel lernyng & relygon ys tought in the same, ye & how lytyl chrystyan hospytalyte ys vsed therin, they wolde . . . cry out with one voyce, saying . . . to the pryncys of the world, "alter these foundatyonys wych we of long tyme before dyd instytvte & turn them to some better vse & commondyte". . . [75]

True, some men would hold that the situation requires "a just reformatyon" and not a "ruynose suppressyon". To these it may be retorted that

> . . . though god delyte much in charitable mindes therby declaryd, yet to conuerte ouer possissyon to that end & purpos & to appoynt ouer many personys to such offyce . . . be not wythout grete detryment & hurt to the chrystyan commynwele, gud ordur & true pollycy. . . [76]

This leads Starkey to considerations of English demography. Having resided in Northern Italy, he found his native land by comparison stagnant, unflourishing, and underpopulated. The last consideration makes it

> . . . hyghly expedyent . . . to mynysch thys numbur of prestys & relygyous personys . . . and to . . alter thys law of bound chastyte, though hyt hathe byn neuer so longe recevythe. . .

But there is a "thynge wych many wyse men feare & gretely dystrust", namely that these monasteries

> ...schalbe leysed & set vnto grete lordys & gentlemen of much possessyons & to them wych heue no grete nede at al...

which if done, will much "dymynsch the profyt of your acte". Rather, the land ought to be leased

> ...to yunger bretherne lyuyng in seruyce vnprofytabully & to them wych be of lower state & degree...[77]

which would serve to increase the number of gainfully employed persons, diminish pauperism, and so augment the wealth of the realm.

Like Gardiner some ten years later, he feared the ruin and decay of the monastic buildings, and like the Bishop, his apprehensions seem largely aesthetic. The king is cautioned that the "cuntrey myght appeare so to be defacyed as hyt had byn lately ouerrun wyth enemys in tyme of ware".[78] As for the present inmates, they might be dispersed to the greater abbeys, where they can better observe the rule, and deport themselves in a more edifying manner.[79] Notably, Starkey's solution is more "Catholic" than that of either Pole or Stokesley.

Yet it must be confessed that like many Erasmians of his generation, Starkey has little feeling for the contemplative life. He remarks that the souls of the departed would draw greater profit from their bequests if these were turned to "the commyn comfort of theyr posteryte" rather than a few living "in the monastycal lyfe & solytary". His notion of a monastery (like Pole's) is that of a virtuous retreat house where weary worldlings may withdraw into a stronghold of pious studies and edifying conversation.[80]

The remaining section of this letter is devoted to Church unity. Much of it is a repetition of the *Exhortation*. Once more he notes that the Roman primacy rose as an expedient, and only as such, was confirmed by Church Councils. But what is expedient is no part of divine law, and may be set aside. He hopes that other princes will follow Henry and repudiate the pope, but for just this reason, it is necessary for Henry to set a good example. To do this, the king must maintain an "indyfferent mean" between the "old and blynd superstycyon & thys lyght & arrogant opynyon lately entrying here amonge us".[81]

That, by the last, Starkey does not only mean radical sectarianism is clear from the subsequent lines which refer to "vndyscrete preachyng". Henry is counselled to sanction only "syldon and rarer prechyng made with gretar lernyng & dyscretyon". True enough, in ancient times Christianity was broadcast by preaching but now it "hath byn stabyled so many yerys and both by educatyon & tradytyon so well confyrmed, ther ys thereof I thynke no huge necessitie". Only men of "approued vertue & grete puryte of lyfe" should be licensed at all.[82]

To those familiar with the reign, the above words indicate that Starkey's sympathies lay with the Catholic faction. And the letters concluding lines admit of no doubt: the primacy, Henry is assured, will be put to oblivion if no changes are made in the doctrine and rites of the Church. A General Council should be called by the consent of all the princes, independently of the Pope, to confirm the King's doings, and to apply them to other principalities. As to the composition of such a Council, it is to be remembered that

> ...byschoppes & prestys be the chefe membrys in the chrystyan common welys, havyng powar of god to rleyse men from al syn...

This is nothing but a repetition of the same point that Tunstall and Stokesley had made to Pole, and the very bone of contention between Tunstall and the King.[83]

I have dwelt upon this letter at same length for it throws several aspects of Henrician Catholicism into high relief. It is no less instructive about the "settlement" itself and Starkey's role in it. One must reiterate the point that Starkey is put out of focus when seen as the first true Anglican and father of the *via media*. If this was so, it was a remarkable oversight on the part of his contemporaries and successors to ignore the fact. His reforming proclivities and insistence on the mean may be ascribed to Erasmian and Aristotelian influences, while his rejection of the Roman primacy is rooted in Marsiglio. In neither case was his position unique. In surrendering the primacy, Sampson, Lee, Tunstall and Stokesley had taken the position that Roman jurisdiction was adiaphora, that is, no part of the divine law.

Let us add that one ought to be wary of attaching the terms "liberal" or "tolerant" to either Starkey's thesis in particular[84] or to sixteenth century Anglicanism in general. A persistent theme of all Tudor religious settlements was "uniformity". And granted that the century saw no less than four distinct settlements, the government was markedly successful in achieving it. French, Bohemian and Polish Protestants were able to maintain temples of worship under their Catholic regimes, something Catholics and non-conformists were unable to obtain in England. Nor was tolerance Starkey's aim. Having established his own specific area of adiaphora, he allowed the details of doctrine and worship to be determined by the common counsel of King and Parliament: any swervings from these determinations are rightfully punishable by the sovereign. We might ask, too, if a certain insularity is not evident in perceiving sixteenth-century Anglicanism as a particular focus of adiaphorism. In their denial of the Real Presence, their iconoclasm and repudiation of the time-hallowed forms of worship the makers of Edwardian and Elizabethan Anglicanism went far beyond the most radical of the continental Lutherans, a fact of which they were keenly aware.[85]

As to adiaphorism itself, the principle would appear to be too broad to admit to useful specification. Roman Catholics, Calvinists, Lutherans and Anglicans alike all admitted a distinction between necessary and expedient canons. The difficulty lay in that each sect had its own ledger of adiaphora. Both before and after Reformation, Romanists were prepared to make wide accommodations, including clerical marriage and eucharistic reception in both kinds, to the Utraquists and Oriental Churches. Calvin himself proved an adiaphorist on the matter of bishops and vestments.[86] The real nub is those doctrines each faith considered non-negotiable.

Finally, we might take Starkey's career as an index of how far the Henrician Reformation fell short of the goals of Erasmian humanism. Even as he fell from favor, both parties drifted toward separate moorings, each equidistant from an Erasmian mean. The Ten Articles, said to represent adiaphorism, reflected only a bitter truce which both parties strove to overthrow at the first opportunity.

Starkey's letter to Henry, with its pro-Catholic bias, anticipates our next theme: the burgeoning Catholic awareness of the Protestant menace within. Increasingly, the Catholic apologists of the Supremacy swung their turrets around toward the Reformers.

5

Attack on the Reformers:
First Phase 1533-40

The foregoing four chapters have attempted to delineate those elements which constituted and gave form to an autocephalous Catholic program in the first years of the new settlement. Conciliarism, Marsiglianism and Erasmian humanism were continental phenomena, licit gestations from the womb of Catholic tradition. With this distinguished pedigree, it was possible to present Henrician Catholicism as a theology which transcended the insular conditions and royal whims that presided over its actual establishment. Consequently the first polemicists addressed themselves to the point that no novelties had been introduced at all.

It was not long, however, before the introduction of conspicuous Reformers into key offices of the Church made it increasingly difficult to maintain the earlier pretence. Catholic apologetics, cautiously at first, then to the exclusion of all else, came to reflect the challenge of a nascent Protestantism.

The student is soon made aware that Catholic polemical activity falls into two distinct phases separated by a five year caesura. The first phase extends from 1533 to the aftermath of Cromwell's fall in 1540. For the next five years there is little that is noteworthy save the official *King's Book* of 1543. Then following a few surface rumblings, there is the astonishing spurt of activity which bursts forth in the King's last year, and lasts until the triumph of the Reformers closed the domestic press to their antagonists in 1548.[1] Thereafter no Catholic works will be published in England until the reign of Mary.

In the earlier phase, the Henrician Catholic polemic exhibited a two-edged sword, the sharper edge turned toward Rome and the task of disallowing the primacy. In this guise, we have dealt already with most of these writings. We must now turn to examine them from the aspect of their hostility to Protestantism.

A typical in these early years was the *Sermon* of Simon Mathew, preached on 27 June 1535 and published by Berthelet a month afterward. Mathew, a prominent theologian and canon of S. Paul's, was very possibly the spokesman for the anxieties of his bishop, John Stokesley.[2] Certainly the oration with its explicit repudiation of the primacy and its justification of the recent executions commended itself to the government by virtue of the known conservatism of its ponent.[3] More remarkable were its author's open animadversions on the recent Protestant encroachments on the settlement which simultaneously excited the complaints of Stokesley to Cromwell.

Mathew begins well enough with the prescribed insistence on obedience to divinely ordained superiors, and a prayer for the preservation of the King, Queen Anne, and "my lady Elizabeth princesse and lawfull heire" but his supplication for the Church of England is also joined to an explicit bidding of the "catholike church of Christendom", and to the repeated assertion that we take that Church for "one misticall body, hauying dyuers membres deputed to dyuerse offices."[4] Christ is the "one principall heed"[5] of this mystical body, and we are reassured that

> ...diuersitie of regions and countreys maketh not ... diuersities of churches but the unitie of fayth maketh all regions one churche... "[6]

Rather neatly, this argument that we are one by faith and participation in Christ's mystical body is turned against the papacy: Did not the Apostles act independently of one another, yet they shared as the same faith as Peter? A year before Starkey, Mathew is "ryghte sure that many thousandes are saved whiche newer hards of Peter, nor yet of the bishop of Rome"[7] That we must obey the pope as vicar of Christ is "depnable techynge ... which have caused men to leave the commandementes of god undone forthe humeyne traditions".[8] Rather abruptly, however, this line of thought is broken off, and we hear echoes from the London pulpits as the author rebukes those who under the pretext of defending the "kynges matters ... rage ... and rayle" calling "the byshopps of Rome the harlotte of Babylon, or the beasts of Rome".[9] (We may recall that within half a year, the Archbishop will be numbered among them.)

But earlier in this sermon, Mathew confronts another Protestant encroachment on tradition—the attack on purgatory. In the list of things he invites his congregation to pray for he would include the dead

> ...though the laste sonday the preacher coude not fynde in his conscience to pray for the soules departed, saying, that he thought his prayer shuld nothynge auayle them...

Mathew will bid them otherwise, and he hopes his auditors will recall how he has

> ...proued by auctrities of hierome, Augustine Ambrose and Chrysostome, and also by Scriptures, as saynt Augustine understandeth them, that we sholde do".[10]

In his awareness of the mystical body, the unity of faith, the value of tradition, and his upholding of purgatory, Mathew goes considerably further than any comparable Catholic polemicist at this early date. The *Sermon* is permeated with the consciousness of an incipient Protestant challenge, and is contrived as much to meet this as to satisfy the demands of government propaganda.

Quite different is the tone of two Good Friday sermons of John Longland, bishop of Lincoln, delivered respectively in 1536 and 1538.[11] Both sermons are examples of Catholic devotional preaching, a form already languishing but not yet extinct in these years.[12] Though each strikes a blow at the new doctrines, Longland's strictures are more in the nature of afterthoughts: in these sermons at least, he is not primarily concerned with heresy.

Like so many luminaries of this reign, Longland had begun his career as a protege of Wolsey, who had been instrumental in placing him as the King's confessor, and one story has it that Longland acted in this capacity as the Cardinal's agent by insinuating scruples about the first marriage in the King's mind.[13] Whether true or not, Longland's connivance was maintained by Chapuys and others.[14] The same rumor accounts for the curious fact that Longland was the only Catholic bishop whom the Yorkshire "rebels" called upon the King to punish.[15]

At the same time, Longland's orthodoxy admits of no doubt. Not only did he grudge doctrinal innovations[16] and hinder the new preaching at every turn,[17] he also shared with Stokesley the dubious distinction of being the most vigorous persecutor on the bench.[18] Throughout the ascendancy of Cromwell he was continually at loggerheads with the minister, and where not impeded by him, he assiduously hunted heretics throughout his huge diocese. According to Foxe, he prosecuted two heretics to their doom in 1541.[19] It is probably Longland's tenacity which accounts in part for the relative orthodoxy of the older university where he was chancellor from 1532 until his death in 1547.[20] Further evidence of his Catholicism might be inferred from his two most distinguished protegés: George Day, future bishop of Chichester, who signally refused to promote Edwardian reforms in 1550; and Richard Pate, Longland's nephew, who gave his uncle a nerve wracking month when, in 1541, while ambassador to the Emperor, he went over to the Papal standard.[21]

If, however, we knew none of the above, the two sermons we are about to consider testify amply to the Bishop's theological convictions. In no comparable literature is the pre-Reformation piety of England so evident.

The sermon of 1536 was a Lenten exercise delivered before the "kynge his maiestie at Granwiche", and notably omits mention of either the Supremacy, or the renunciation of the primacy. Instead, the auditors are offered a somewhat discursive meditation on the passion of Christ, and the human depravity for which that passion made atonement. The sermon stands in marked contrast to the standard fare issued since the government had undertaken the programming of London pulpits in service of the new regimen.[22]

We are catapulted at once into the warm bath of late medieval piety: Christ of "his grette abundant charyte" has been crucified for our sins. The Father has given "his deere darlynge, his son" to atone for our manifold wickedness.[23] The fathomless love of Christ in especially manifest in that he died for his enemies, and Saint Bernard is invoked to assure us that both Jesus *and Mary* are perpetual intercessors for us with the father. Rather startling is the evocation of Mary's "breste and pappes" offering succor to a sinful mankind.[24] We are warned, however, that God's mercy often expresses itself in the taking away of things we love lest from "to moche pleasure we ronne into eternall dampnacio"[25]-an interesting observation in light of the Royal proclivity to treat adversity as a sign of Divine displeasure.

A fairly lengthy interlude considers the eucharist in the familiar orthodox way: it is Christ corporeally present under the species of bread. Longland then turns to dwell on those vices which preclude our salvation. First among these is sensuality, and this sermon is a reminder (should one be required at this date) that during the dawn of the Reformation, it was not the Protestants who had a corner on 'Puritanism.' All the fleshly delights are flayed, and, somewhat sinister in light of the charges soon to be laid against Queen Anne, daring too, in light of the common rumor of Henry's earlier relation with her sister, incest is specially singled out for castigation.[26]

Heaven, the Bishop assures us, "is not wonnen wyth eatings and drynkynge, with delyinge and playinge, with sportynge and baytynge",[27] but with penance and acquiescence in adversity. Above all, we must learn to forsake ourselves, and this theme of self-mortification reaches its apogee with the image of Christ at Gethsemane who suffered

> ...that horyble conflicte between sensualitye and reason ...and cried fader, put away this chalis of deathe. Sensualitye wolde live. Reason wolde die.[28]

Longland then interjects the sole controversial reference in the entire sermon. Though Christ has died for us, we must beware the arrogance born of excessive confidence:

> Lit no man therefore, bee too suerre of himselfe to saye Christ hath suffrede for me. Chirste hathe shedde his bloode and washed me, Christe hathe payed my rawnsome ... howeuer I lyue, I whall be sauede ... Christe hath satisfyed for me....

Such faith (which is the characteristic mark of the new teaching) is a dangerous "presumpcion" and leads to a "fleshly and carnall lybertye". Salvation is not won by mere trust, but by the imitation of Christ in both works and suffering.[29]Having discharged this single shot at the doctrine of *sole fide*, Longland concludes, asking his auditors to kneel and recite "v. pater noster, v. Aues, and oon Credo, in honour of this bloode".[30]

In some respects Longland's 1538 sermon is more conformable to government expectations, which no doubt explains the "cum Privilegio" which adorns the title page.[31] There is the obligatory attack on Roman pretensions, spun around Longland's own preoccupation with episcopal authority. Christ is our "hyghest bushop ... the bushop of bushoppes" and the Bishop of Rome ought to be "abashed" and "ashamed" by his blasphemous appropriation of titles proper to Our Lord himself.[32] The Pope is enjoined to be

> ...content with thyne owne dioces, with thyne owne chardge, as other bushops are with tyeyrs, for futher then thyne own dioces, thy iurisdiction doo not stretch.[33]

Perhaps in conformity to the Ten Articles and the *Bishops' Book*, both ordained since his previous sermon, Longland contends that "all virtues are *dona dei*", but he hastens to attach to this a perfectly Catholic sense: "no more can I haue Charyte, faythe, hoope nor any other virtue but of the gyfte of god".[34] The order of words relegates "faythe" to its traditional role in Catholic theology.

As in his previous sermon, Longland scourges worldliness in exhaustive detail, and the body is decried as "the greatest enemye that man hath".[35] Particularly menacing are the innumerable temptations against chastity (a subject which to all appearances held him in thrall): women are to be handled brusquely, for the soul is ever in peril "as longe as thou delytest wantonly to tangle and talk with them". Abruptly, however Luther is recalled (and rebuked) when we are told that "concupisentia" is no sin; only yielding to it is.[36] The sermon then culminates in a moving passage on the Augustinian theme of the two cities and two loves—love of God, and natural self-love.[37]

Puzzling then, is the abrupt change of tone as the Bishop takes up the subject of simony. In the context this seems a non-sequitur until we recall that no bishop was more jealous of his jurisdiction, or contested so obstinately the Vicar-general's attempt to impose his own candidates in the diocese. A clue here is furnished by the circumstances of the sermon. Since Henry was present at the occasion, it is likely that Longland was appealing over Cromwell's head directly to Royal authority. And it may be fairly assumed that heresy, no less than simony, was at the root of Longland's indignation.

No less bold is Longland's reference to the scriptures. We may be certain that he was not the least of those bishops who had small relish for the Englishing of the Bible, but now, in 1538, Cromwell's injunctions gave orders for the placing of the English New Testament in every parish church.[38] Apropos of this, the Bishop sniffs:

> We haue all the scrypture in Englyshe, and we haue knowledge of god and [of the] lawes, and yet doo we not lyue thereafter. . . .[39]

Well might an indignant Reformer retort that the vine had had scant time to fructify! Still, the implication of this remark, that the Reformers are hearers of the Word rather than doers, we have heard before, and will hear again—it is a classic allegation of Catholic polemicists.

The remainder of the 1538 sermon is indubitably Catholic. Put simply, Longland is as orthodox as can be without stumbling over the new formulas and injunctions. In truth, he is not always that prudent. The government having made clear its aversion to the term "purgatory", the Bishop is careful to avoid it. But he plainly accepts prayers for the dead, and all which that implies. As if to emphasize this, he makes specific reference to "limbo", that equally tendentious concept of medieval theology.[40] And some of his auditors at least, must have been no less dismayed by his reference to the stigmata.[41] Finally, it was skating on very thin ice indeed in this year which saw government inspired attacks on the superstitious veneration of the saints, to conclude his oration with an invocation to saints Margaret and Catherine,[42]

Longland's second sermon is important as a barometer of Catholic sentiment in the year in which the Reformation made its greatest strides. Though its author is careful to observe at least the letter of the laws, the entire sermon vibrates with the tension of unspoken obstinacy. Clearly the Catholic leadership was alarmed by the consistent chipping away of the old verities, and Longland's sermon is a harbinger of the impending crisis, and a signal that Catholics were finding further concessions insupportable.

We have remarked before that these sermons are notable in being among the last examples of pre-Reformation devotional literature. They are heavy with the musky fragrance of the medieval twilight. At his best, Longland is able to inflict the passion of Christ upon his auditors with a pulsating immediacy. We are told that at one time, Longland was Henry's favorite preacher, and even now the patient reader of these sermons, after discounting an undeniable repetitiveness and grotesquerie, may still perceive in them a certain rough art. This is most true when the Bishop makes no concessions to the propaganda demands of the day. Particularly admirable are those passages where the themes of God's love and self love, mortification and pleasure, are woven together with great dexterity.

If Longland's sermons evoke echoes of a departing age, Tunstall's more famous sermon of 1539 seems to anticipate an Elizabethan future. For all his reputation for learning, the bishop of Durham was anything but a prolific author. Prof. Elton is surely correct in surmising that the gorgeous flattery of Henry VIII which adorns this discourse was a factor in its speedy reproduction by the government printer.[43] Still another was its timeliness. In the spring of 1539, the political horizon was darkened by a potential coalition of Charles V and Francis I. There loomed the dreaded prospect of a papal crusade against a schismatic King. Anticipating that Henry's hour of reckoning might be near, the Pope once again dispatched Reginald Pole northward. Under these circumstances, the government welcomed the support of the realm's most prestigious Catholic prelate.

In several respects Tunstall did not disappoint the King. His Palm Sunday sermon of 1539 is the last fling of that Catholic literature in support of the new settlement which originated in the apologias of Fox and Sampson. As such, Tunstall's discourse was hardly original,* but it covered all the bases, and with many a felicitous turn of phrase.

The sermon is a meditation on humility and obedience spun out from the epistle for that sunday (Philippians, 2, 5). Jesus himself is the very model of both virtues: in his Incarnation he submits himself to the ordeal of the flesh in perfect obedience to the Father. Contrarywise

> ...how farre they be from Christ, and howe contrarye to his doctrine, that doo gyue them selves to disobedience.... [44]

Those who disdain to submit themselves to their governors have the archrebel Lucifer for their father.[45] Disobedience, ingratitude, and want of humility all bear the stamp of the sovereign sin of pride, and have as their model Satan who fell "From heuen like lyghtnyng ... not kepynge the order of his creation".[46] The arch-demon's vaunting pride is emulated by "the bysheppes of Rome ... who doo exalte their seate aboue the sterres of god"[47], and Roman pretensions flout the scripture itself which requires us to be "subiecte to euery human creature

* See p. 171

forgoddes sake".[48] There follows a lengthy resumé of previous arguments against the primacy. We have marked all of them before, but the bishop of Durham presents them with great clarity, thus belatedly confirming Dr. Layton's opinion that no man in the realm was more suited to set out this matter.[49]

Tunstall then turns his attentions to the particulars of Pole's mission and potential foreign invasion. There is a lively effusion of national feeling which culminates in the superb tribute to Henry as a hearty lion.[50] We may assume the King was no less gratified by the attack on Pole, Tunstall's erstwhile friend. The Cardinal is scourged as a traitor to his country: his treachery is such that "any heathen man wolde abhore to doo" while his ingratitude for the many benefits conferred upon him by Henry will make him "to be reputed more wilde and cruell than any tigre,"[51] (Ingratitude was the unfailing motif of any official attacks on Pole:[52] it not only made for convincing propaganda but reflected the heartfelt opinion of the King towards those who failed to conform themselves to his will.)

In the above particulars, Tunstall's sermon certainly conforms to the inflexible standards of Henrician propaganda, but it contains much else besides, including the sharpest attack to date on the Reformers' doctrine of justification, and a riposte to the King on a matter over which they had already locked horns (and would again)—the status of holy orders. On this point hinged the autonomy of the clerical estate.

Tunstall's attack on the Reformers is in good part a repetition of points made earlier by Starkey and Longland; yet by comparison he is more deliberate and concise. No more than Longland did he view the recent policy of "the open Bible" with equanimity. And he makes it plain that he does not equate the recent appetite for vernacular scripture with any increase in virtue. The Gospel he notes

> . . . is gyven us to know God thereby, and to be a rule to lyue by, but we muche do talke of it . . . (and) vse it as if it were a boke of problems to dispute vppon, and care not to amede our lyuynge. . . .[53]

Turning to matter of *sola fide*, the Bishop is still more explicit, and singles out for castigation the proposition that "faythe alone iustifieth us, and not our workes."[54] To this he retorts that good works are required by scripture, and warns his auditors that Christ will destroy the fruitless vine.[55] True, he grants that good works are contingent upon the grace of God, but so then is faith. Here Tunstall is doing little more than taking the familiar Catholic position, and one notes how far it is from the Pelagianism with which they were regularly taxed by the Reformers.

Tunstall's sermon, however, does more than merely reiterate the usual Catholic complaints against solefidianism and the vaunted benefits of a vernacular Bible. His distinctive contribution was to perceive, expose and challenge the implicit threat to the sacerdotal order which lurked within the Supremacy. We know from the inception of the Reformation this particular issue had given him cause for uneasiness, and as early as 1531 Henry had written him personally to set aside his reservations.[57] In 1536, the Bishop's signature was prominent on a document, already discussed, which however hesitantly, delivered the *potestis ordinis* from the grasp of the prince.

The matter was by no means academic. If the government was to control the Church, it must divide the bishops and weaken convocation. By 1536, as we have seen, it had so far succeeded that convocation was hardly able to compose any issue without an appeal to Royal authority. But the issue did not end there.It was a continual temptation to the government to espouse the Lutheran principle of the priesthood of all believers, thus eliminating a sacramentally distinct clergy altogether. This surely is the meaning of the government sponsored probe into the portent of those embarrassing scriptural texts, Acts 20 and John 20, which must somehow be navigated if the Church was to be reduced to a limb of the Caesaro-papist prince. And it was the Reformers, and they alone, who could offer the government reliable support in this cause.

Did Tunstall divine Henry's inclinations in this matter? It would be interesting to know: if so, he showed considerable fortitude in advancing his own convictions in a public sermon graced by the Royal presence. If not, he was soon to be enlightened in a private exchange of letters with the King.

The essence of Tunstall's position appears in the relationship he perceives between the autonomy of holy orders and the power to shrive. It is in the scriptural texts supporting the letter that we grasp most clearly a specific apostolic commission: "whose synnes so euer ye shall forgyue, be forgyuen, and whose synnes ye shall reteyne be reteyned" (John 20, 23) and "what thynges so euer ye shall bynde upon erthe shal be bounde in heauen (Matt 18).[58] Tunstall's argument will soon be carried forward in his dispute with the King over whether auricular confession is necessary or (as the King and the Six Articles would have it) merely expedient.[59] In this sermon, as he would later, the Bishop insists that confession is incumbent upon those who would receive the eucharist whereto we may "not go in our fylthy and spotted cote."[60]

In this sermon, too, Tunstall unequivocally asserts the apostolic commission of a teaching church. Here the text Luke 10, 16, is introduced: "He that herith you, herith me ... and he that despyeth you, despyseth me."[61] This is consistent with Tunstall's earlier public assertions of the authority of the eight general councils. In this sermon, Tunstall is very careful to distinguish between ecclesiastical and magisterial authority, for while the apostles were heirs to no worldly kingdom,[62] they have a discrete and divinely ordained authority in their own right.[63]

As Henrician propaganda, Tunstall's sermon must be judged a rather belated testimonial. And the same verdict must be passed on a portion of his anti-Reformist polemics. Yet the sermon is anything but stale. Its excellence derives from the author's clarity of mind and (saving the untypical bombast against Pole) a unique temper among Tudor polemicists. Whether he is undermining the Papal claims, or implicit Royal pretensions to a sacerdotal monarchy, or confronting the Reformers with scriptural texts certain to embarrass them, Tunstall, alone of his contemporaries of whatever persuasion, manages to give off more light than heat. It is this quality that won him the admiration of certain Protestant contemporaries such as Cranmer and John Foxe.

The Palm Sunday sermon was delivered on the eve of yet another call to compose once and for all those religious differences which now rent the country. In April 1539, a new Parliament met, and a committee was constituted, consisting of the Vicar-General and eight prelates, to arrive at a satisfactory formula. The eight bishops were the two primates, Goodrich, Latimer, Capon, Clerk, Aldrich and Tunstall. Once more, deadlock was a foregone conclusion. It is quite possible that the committee was no more than a niccty since it could not have met more than three or four occasions before the matter was whisked from its hands, and the notorious "Six Articles" was introduced to the House of Lords by a layman—the Duke of Norfolk.[64]

The Articles themselves were decidedly Catholic, especially when compared to the previous formulae produced by convocation and ecclesiastical "committees". We cannot escape the conclusion that Norfolk, a thoroughgoing conservative, but no theologian, was a stalking horse for the Catholic leadership. In a letter written the following autumn, the Saxon theologian and negotiator, Burckhardt, ascribed the authorship of the Articles to Stokesley and Gardiner[65]—both conspicuously absent from the bypassed committee. Foxe intimates that the personal presence of the King during certain of the sessions had much to do with the Articles' speedy passage: all we can be certain of is that Henry favored the celibacy clause as surely as he diluted that on auricular confession.[66]

In light of what had gone before, and indeed, what was soon to follow, why did the King and Cromwell allow, and as it appears, connive at their passage? With their insistence upon transubstantiation, private masses and clerical celibacy, the Articles could only handicap the six-year campaign to whittle away at the authority of the old order. Particularly the clause on private masses would seem to eliminate all theological justification for extinguishing the monasteries—a process now entering its final stages.

Two related answers suggest themselves. The alacrity with which the articles were subscribed to, and the ferocious penalties which accompanied them (the efficacy of which were soon curbed by the government) attest to a lingering Catholic fervor among the laity, and no doubt as well, the desire among many to have done with six years of religious contention. It would seem that thus far, the Reformation had yet to take deep root among the nation's representatives. In fact, the Six Articles may be read as the Indian Summer of English Catholicism: never again would the national mood show itself so homogeneously orthodox. The temper of the next decade was more ambivalent, as Protestantism made deeper inroads into the established classes, and within the court itself.

Closely allied to the temporary prevalence of orthodoxy was the constellation of foreign affairs in the spring of 1539, and the potential threat of a Franco-Imperialist alliance. Henry, who was at least as skilled a diplomat as any of his ministers, saw that the coalescence of these two giants under the banner of a Papal crusade posed a menace for which an alliance with the German Protestant princes offered slender compensation. At such times, it behooved him to parade as a mere schismatic, at least until he could detach one or another of the great sovereigns from the Papacy. In short, Henry felt he could not move "leftward" until France or the Empire moved with him.

This opinion is supported by Martin Bucer who told his correspondent, Philip of Hesse, that Henry had been persuaded to acquiesce in the Articles by Gardiner, who argued that further Reformation would lead to a revolt of the English lords, and that Francis I could never then be brought around to follow Henry's lead and to renounce the Pope.[67]

It remains to be asked whether the Six Articles, as is so often asserted, represent a triumph of Henry's personal theology? We have already suggested the answer. Before the year was out, the King once more was flirting with the German evangelicals, and yet another embassy was sent to London to hammer out the theological details. To be sure, it came to nothing as did the intimately related marriage to Anne of Cleves. But in April or May of the following year, the "Seventeen Questions" reopened in the most provocative manner the matters suppositiously settled by the Six Articles. The King's comments on a set of these answers indicate not only that the questions were introduced with his approval; his marginal jottings reveal him to be far from the consensus of his catholic prelates.[68]

Indeed, the furor set off by the Articles (June 1539) had begun to subside before the season changed. In July, Henry pardoned several hundred persons indicted in the first surge of enthusiasm. By October, Burckhardt could assure the anxious Melanchthon that far from all being lost, the Reformers stood in greater favor than ever.[69]

The Saxon envoy's sentiments must have been confirmed by the appointment that month of Edmund Bonner to the see of London. The dreaded Stokesley had died in September, and the new bishop was still very much Cromwell's man (and Gardiner's enemy), and a compliant agent in the printing of the "Great Bible" in this year.[70] In October too, bishop Longland, presuming too much on the new statute, complained to Cromwell of a Reformer at Balliol College[71] only to have the tables turned on him. Instead, the Bishop was ordered to absolve the vicar of Horncastle, a notorious heretic in his diocese.[72] The same month, Owen Oglethorpe, future Marian bishop of Carlisle, wrote to the all powerful minister begging for patronage and assuring him that he was no longer an "addicte" to man's doctrine and schoolmen's fantasies.[73] Cranmer too, was so far from being intimidated by recent events that he asked to have the prominent Reformer Edward Crome made dean of Canterbury.[74]

That the earlier Catholic triumph in a matter of months had begun to turn into a rout is made clear in a curious interrogation conducted in December. A certain Chaitour, a servant of Tunstall's was apprehended in what seems to have been an attempt to abort an intrigue to replace Cromwell. The drift of the interrogation was plainly to implicate Chaitour's master. The servant had gone about indiscreetly telling others that Tunstall might have first place in the kingdom, but had refused it with the words "lubricus est primus locus apud reges". Apparently Browne and Kingston, two lay, conservative members of the Council were propelling the reluctant Bishop forward.

One of Chaitours's conversations took place with a man named Cray, and while Cray could not directly implicate Tunstall either, he confirmed that Chaitour had told him that the Bishop had refused the bait because of the inconstancy of the King. The two men then discussed the Six Articles and their aftermath. Noting that Bishop Sampson had been expelled from the Council, Chaitour opined it was due to religious contention.

"Jesus," said Cray, "I thought that schism and diversity of opinion had been pacified by the last Parliament."

"Marry," replied Chaitour, "even so had we, but now we see experience to the contrary".

As further examples of the shift of favor, the two men noted the expulsion of Gardiner from the Council for protesting the appointment of Barnes as envoy to the German princes, and the Primate's sending a popular Catholic preacher to the hinterlands. The rumor also ran that Cromwell had arrange the Cleves marriage with "one of his own sort", and that the new bride would not arrive in England until the last abbey had been pulled down.[75]

Though Tunstall could not be proven to be a party to this intrigue, the information elicited must have been galling to Henry, and no doubt damaged the Bishop's repute with him. Very likely this was Cromwell's intention, or at least the one he had to make do with.

The expulsion of Gardiner and Sampson from the Council, and the attempt to net Tunstall indicate that, for whatever reasons, Cromwell had abandoned his former strategy of working with the Catholics. It was henceforth a fight to the death. As matters would prove, his attempt to carry all was premature. What Cromwell had lost sight of, Tunstall had perceived obliquely as the King's "inconstancy"—Henry's determination to keep a free hand by maintaining an equilibrium between the opposed factions.

In truth the plot to take Tunstall revealed a more dangerous threat to the Reformation than the Six Articles: Cromwell was no longer in sure control of the Council. Nor could the collapse of the Cleves marriage have helped to retrieve his position. True in April 1540 he was created Earl of Essex, but the honor appears to have been his undoing. Blind or reckless, he now seems to have been persuaded to gamble on an all-out purge. In the last week of May he precipitated the fatal crisis by arresting Sampson a few hours after the latter had been translated to the new see of Westminster.[76] It was a brutally ironic rehearsal of his own unexpected apprehension two weeks later at the Council table.

Cromwell's execution in July was followed hard by the burning of three prominent Reformers, Barnes, Garrett and Jerome. Like Cromwell, the three were apparently attainted for Sacramentarianism—the denial of the Real Presence. Dr. Scarisbrick states that all three were innocent of the charge.[77] Certainly Barnes was a Lutheran, and far from denying the presence, his assertion of it is confirmed by the contemporaneous Catholic account we are about to consider.[78]

We must deal with Barnes in more detail later. Suffice to note for the present that at the stake, Barnes made a touching protestation of both his faith and innocence.[79] Shortly afterward, it was published, and its wide circulation provoked a reply from Dr. John Standish, a fellow of Whittington College.

Standish's painstaking reply to Barnes' protestation is an unusually competent work. In contrast to the government's charges, its author is anything but vague as to the specific heresies for which Barnes was executed. He readily grants that Barnes was orthodox on the question of the eucharist, and goes on to upbraid him for repelling accusations of anabaptism "as thought there were no heresye but that alone".[80]

Like Gardiner after him, Standish dwells on the theme of Barnes ingenuousness: Barnes confutes accusations never hurled at him, while refusing to confront those of which he was guilty. He denies, for instance, holding the notorious opinion that Our Lady was no better than a saffron bag, but Standish testifies that he personally heard Barnes in a sermon declare that she was no better than any other woman.[81] Barnes real errors, writes Standish, were to preach:

> ...agaynst all the ordynaunce of Christes Churche agaynste the

> orseruyng of dayes, both of fastynge & prayeng . . . denyeng godly
> ordynaunce to bynde to deadly sine, and that ecclesia no possit
> restringere ea quo libera sunt par euanglium.[82]

Now far from being a libel, this is wholly in accord with what we
know of Barnes' preaching. Indeed, Standish explicitly condemns
Barnes for repudiating the magisterium of the visible Church. The
ex-friar's plea that he preached only what "scripture ledde me vnto" is
attacked on a twofold basis.

First, Standish contends that Barnes, like all heretics, falls back on
scripture only to twist it to his own fancy. The scripture, for instance,
clearly ordains that we make restitution to God for sin through alms
and works.[83] Secondly, scripture itself rests on the authority of the
Church and not vice-versa. The Gospels of Nicodemus and Bartho-
lomew were rejected though the reputed authors knew Christ, while
Mark and Luke, who did not, were taken into the canon by the
authority of the Church guided by the Holy Spirit.[84] (This point will
become a keystone of later Catholic apologetics.)

Because Barnes denies the authority of the Church, he is led to
absurdities as when he questions the value of praying to the saints
since it is not enjoined in scripture. How should it be? Most scripture
was written while the saints were still living! If Barnes were a Catholic,
Standish states flatly, he would accept the testimony of the Church in
this matter.[85]

Standish then takes his deceased opponent to task for misrepre-
senting Catholic doctrine: Catholics do not pray to the saints *apart*
from the merits of Christ: the formula of these prayers always concludes "per christu dominum nostrum".[86] No less wrong-headed is
Barnes' insistence that "there is nother satisfaccion vnto the father but
this deth and passyon onely". Standish retorts that Catholics believe
that Christ atoned for "originall synne and actuall also", but the economy of salvation requires us to do penance after we fall into actual sin
"not that we can suffycyently satysfye for one deadly synne" but because God wills us to do so.[87]

The bone of contention here—satisfaction for sin—lies at the core
of the Reformation debate, and Standish's polemic deserves notice as
a thorough and unequivocal attack on Lutheranism, the first in fact,
since the silencing of Fisher and More. Moreover, unlike the government's attainder, Standish's indictment is unmistakably specific.

Barnes, we are told, preached:

> ...a carnall lybertye with a damnable uistifycacion of onely fayth ... and that god is the author of suynne, and that workes do not profyte, and that Christes death is suffycyent so that penaunce is voyde and superfluous, and that contrarye to the order of our sauiours praier we must be forgyuen of god before we can forgyue. ...

And these are the errors that Barnes himself retracted at Paul's Cross.[88]

It is particularly to Barnes' solifidianism that Standish addresses himself. And it is noteworthy that certain of his points, viz. that Lutherans reverse the order of the Lord's Prayer, will be repeated again in the later polemics of Gardiner.[89] On the question of good works, Standish attempts to dispute the Lutheran point of view from scripture itself: if our good dedes were not meritorious God wolde not haue promessyd us a penny for our day hyre".[90] And striking at the very heart of the new doctrines, Standish contends that S. Paul in Romans 8 does not imply that good works can not justify, but merely that "the olde lawe" could not.[91]

A curious personal note adorns the conclusion of this tract. Barnes' downfall (as we shall note) had been triggered by a public attack upon Gardiner at Paul's Cross. There followed a chain of apologies, retractions, interviews and recantations. At the stake, Barnes forgave all his persecutors, but Gardiner especially by name, "yf he haue sought or wroughte this my death other by worde or deed".[92] Standish pours scorn upon this "feyned charyte" and extols the Bishop as "thys honorable and reuerend father in god whiche hathe euer bene a great mayntayner of Christes relegyon agaynste heretics".[93]

Standish's tract is of considerable interest to the student of Henrician Catholicism. Though ostensibly an "occasional" piece, it is, in fact, the first thoroughgoing refutation of the new German heresies to appear in England since the abrogation of Papal jurisdiction. While pointing forward to the later polemics of Gardiner, Smith and Peryn, it attains the lonely eminence of a well-raised sign post in a wilderness. In contrast to the sermon literature of the 1530's which contented itself with glancing blows, Standish's book is marked by an "unwearied industry" and "drudging" noted by a later biographer.[94] His comprehensive defense of Catholicism is unique at this time, and extends well beyond the limits of the Six Articles to embrace the notion of a mystical body, visible and inerrant. Against Barnes and his cohorts, he is bold enough to repeat the ancient formula "extra ecclesiam nulla salus"[95] and his defense of the old religion extends to the minutiae of Catholic devotional life.[96]

We may take leave of Standish's tract noting its bland assumption that Henry's Church is the Catholic Church in England. Though he stigmatizes Barnes as one of those who

> ...under the colour of the usurped power of the bysshope of Rome rayle agaynste the godly order and laudable uses in the Churche of Christe....[97]

he makes no attempt to defend the English Church from the charge of schism from the Papist quarter, nor yet any defense of the Supremacy as such. Not for the last time, we note the cloud of ambiguity which cloaks the problem of the magisterium.[98] In this case the author's complacency is surely explained by the date of his tract. With Cromwell gone, and Henry enamored of Catherine Howard (herself a flower of the Howard-Gardiner connection), the Catholics appeared to have achieved a brief pinnacle of hegemony.

But Henry soon returned to the policy of equipoise. In truth, the apparent Catholic triumph was no more than a mirage. The new decade was to see a swift increase in popular Protestantism—the winter of reaction had barely frozen the surface: beneath the seedbed the new doctrines were gestating for a more exhuberant spring.

6

Attack on the Reformers:
Second Phase 1540-47

To an eye as discerning as Stephen Gardiner's, signs of an evangelical resuscitation were not wanting. In 1542, the Bishop, backed by a Catholic majority in convocation, had failed to obtain the recall of the *Great Bible*. Catholics had hoped to prune the more controversial passages, replacing English terms with less provocative Latin ones. Between them, the King and Cranmer took the matter out of convocation's hands, and placed it in the lap of the universities—where nothing was done.[1] In the following year, Henry married Catherine Parr, a lady whose inclination to the new doctrines soon became evident. And no less significant, a groundswell to undo Cranmer came to grief leaving the Archbishop more strongly entrenched than ever, and free to pursue his discreet revolution with little further impediment.[2]

Yet amidst the slow erosion of their position, Catholics must have been heartened when, in 1543, the so-called *King's Book* appeared. Drawn up by a committee in convocation, approved therein, and certified by Henry himself with a preface, the new book marked something of a retreat from the demi-Lutheranism of the *Ten Articles* and the *Bishop's Book*. Though testimony on the point is conflicting, the *King's Book* was apparently the work of bishops Day, Heath, and Thirlby, and three theologians: Redman, Robinson and Cox. Curiously, it would appear that neither Cranmer nor Gardiner played any great role in its making.[3]

On most points, the *King's Book*, was more orthodox than its predecessor,[4] yet of its chief architects only Day and Redman hitherto had enjoyed a reputation for irreproachable orthodoxy. Heath and Thirlby were previously Cromwell's men, and both at this time were close associates of the Archbishop. The first particularly seems to have travelled some theological distance since the days when the German evangelicals had found him more sympathetic than his colleague Edward Fox. A comparison of the answers of these men to the seventeen part questionaire of 1540, finds all of them, save Redman, to the left of Catholic "hardliners" like Edward Lee, Tunstall and Aldrich.[5] Noticeable then, is a drift toward Catholicism among previously uncertain members of the bench. Among this number we must, by 1543, include Bonner of London, Skip of Hereford, and Salcot of Salisbury.[6]

But these apparent Catholic gains were more than offset by heavy losses: the deaths of Kite (1537), Stokesley (1539), Clerk (1541), and Edward Lee (1544) removed adamant upholders of the old ways, while the translation of Sampson to Coventry and Lichfield (and so to the presidency of the Council of Wales), and Tunstall's increasing involvement in the North, removed both from an active religious role in the 1540's.[7] Gone too was the prevailing influence of John Longland though he survived as bishop of Lincoln until 1547. Whether subdued by his arrest in 1541, or simply entering dotage, he disappears as an important integer in this decade.[8] No less significant are the men who won promotions during these years of the so-called "Catholic reaction": nearly all were to prove broken reeds in the storms to come.[9]

By 1544, the first stirrings of a reinvigorated Reform movement were evident. At court, around the person of the new Queen, and in the household of Prince Edward, a demi-Protestant spirit prevailed. Sporadic attacks on the Reformers were turned back at the doors of this inner sanctum. In the Council too, Seymour and Lisle, both inclined to the new religion, began to increase at the expense of Wriothesley and Gardiner. The latter, still indispensable to Henry, was increasingly away on diplomatic missions arising from Henry's reassertion of England as a continental power.

In the same year, quite likely prodded by the embarrassing attacks on Cranmer, the Queen, and certain gentlefolk at court, Parliament mitigated the severe penalities attached to the Six Articles. And plans were now afoot to English portions of the liturgy, and to remove a variety of lingering "superstitions": with regard to the latter, Henry was willing to exhibit himself as a prime mover. In the following year (1545), Parliament, no doubt moved more by the rising costs of war than by any specifically religious motives, voted Henry the chantries and collegiate endowments.[10] This was the assembly to which the King made his extraordinary peroration exhorting *both* factions of the national Church to charity and mutual forbearance.

As usual, the Royal summons to concord was answered by a fresh outburst of acrimony. The Chantries Act might seem to imply the nullity of masses "satisfactory" (a doctrine expressly asserted by both the Six Articles and the *King's Book*), and on Passion Sunday, 1546, Dr. Edward Crome, following the dictates of logic rather than good sense, launched a public attack on the sacrifice of the mass.*

Crome, a favorite of Cranmer's preached that the new act told against the existence of purgatory, and the benefit of masses *pro mortem*. However sound his reasoning, it was unwise to anticipate Henry's theology. Under hard interrogation, he revealed a nest of Reformers, and his confession led to the last purge of the reign. Crome himself survived the worst consequences of his indiscretion by making a public recantation.[11]

Yet so labyrinthine had the old King's intentions become that it is possible to speculate whether Crome, with the cognizance of the King, was floating a trial balloon for reforms which never matured. We do know that in 1546 Henry, in collusion with Cranmer, was preparing to launch other innovations which were blocked only by Gardiner's warning that further reformation would imperil the projected alliance with the Emperor. All of which did not prevent the King from tempting Francis into making common cause against the Council of Trent. If we are to believe Cranmer (or Morice), Henry proposed nothing less than the joint abolition of mass in both countries.[12]

There are difficulties with Morice's tale, but it cannot be easily dismissed. That it has been entertained by serious historians confirms the miasma which surrounds the King's intentions during these final years.[13] It may be that Cranmer wished to believe that Henry was prepared to abandon the mass in 1546, as this was the year that he, yielding to his chaplain Ridley's persuasions, gave up his belief in a "real" or physical presence. Without going into the niceties of the Archbishop's eucharistic theology, we may note that by his own confession, this was the year that he passed into the ranks of the sacramentaries. Certainly he would be so classed by the old King and most of his fellow bishops. In light of the future, it was a momentous development.[14]

* See p. 176

The above comments, far from being exhaustive, are intended to provide the minimal necessary background for the final phase of conforming Catholic polemics. With the sole exception of Standish's tract, and some collected sermons of Roger Edgeworth,[15] Catholics appear to have consoled themselves for the five years between 1539-44 that theirs was the "official" position, and that the Six Articles and the *King's Book* between them, provided the old faith with an adequate platform.

Smarting under the harness of restraint, the Protestants did not allow themselves to grow so complacent. On the contrary, from its origins, the English Reformation had its radical wing whom prudence and a stern rejection of accommodation had driven overseas. Horrified by the Six Articles and the preeminence of conservatives in the Council, they began a barrage of pamphleteering against the Catholic leadership. Moreover, after 1540, most of these exiles had passed quite beyond Lutheranism and were to be found in the camp of the sacramentaries. To be sure, the prodding of these radicals had been a persistent feature of the Reformation from its outset, but now their energy welled forth in a spate of tracts whose tone is passionate, popular and rancourous.[16]

Typical of their number is *The Epistle Exhortatorye ... agaynst the pompouse popyshe Bysshoppes*. Its pseudonymous author was none other than John Bale, and the work is a zestful and plebeian broadside. In anticipation of future Marxist polemics, Bale indulges in zoological abuse of the Catholic prelates whom he compares, "in one wildly mixed metaphor," to "cruel wolves ... cloysteringe togyther in corners lyke a swarme of adders in a dunge hill."[17]

"Wynchestre" is singled out as the ringleader of the vile crew, "a wylye watterer of the Popes olde garden" who has not hesitated to prowl in the King's own household in pursuit of "true fauerers of the Lordes verities", and who was checked only by "God ... [and] by the hygh wisdome of our sayd Kyng". Gleeful mention is made of the execution of Germane Gardiner, the Bishop's secretary,[18] and Gardiner himself is accused of being a papist informer.[19]

In a paroxym of alliteration, Bale rails at the "blasphemouse beggeryes of the bloodye Bishoppes of Rome", and Bonner, now on his way to notoriety, is apostrophied as the "blodye byshop of Londe".[20] The leading Catholics are enumerated as

> ... lewde Londe, lurkynge Lyncolne, dreamynge Durham, Yorke

without wytte, chatteringe, smylynge Salisburye . . . and that double faced trayter Wilson . . .[21]*

Aside from this torrent of abuse, the author attempts to defend such key Protestant concepts as *sola fide*, but with a wont of discrimination that spurns serious engagement.[22]

Only a little less popular, every bit as bilious, and far more learned were the works of Bale's fellow exiles, George Joye and William Turner. These were to be Gardiner's first adversaries in the coming controversies. It would appear that government efforts to prevent the importation of the exiles' books was sporadic and ineffective.

The first printed evidence of Catholic unease with the status quo surface in 1544 with two published sermons of William Chedsey and Cuthbert Scot respectively, and with a lost work of Gardiner's against William Turner.

Chedsey, then a fellow of Corpus Christi College, Oxford, and a chaplain to Bonner, was later to distinguish himself as a Catholic champion at the university during the reign of Edward, and this discourse is a relatively tame affair, largely a plea to brake the decay of the universities. One is at first puzzled as to why Paul's Cross should have been chosen as the site of this sermon, but Chedsey tips his handwhen he laments the paucity of contemporary benefactors: good learning, he assures us, is a sure foundation of the faith. The author then goes on to attack preachers of novelties,[23] an early confirmation that Catholic reverses had revived the courage of their opponents.

Cuthbert Scot was a fellow of Christ's College, Cambridge, and in the spring of the following year, he would denounce a heretical play to the university's chancellor, Stephen Gardiner. This led to a lively exchange of letters between the Bishop and the vice-chancellor, Matthew Parker, who attempted simultaneously to shield the culprits and to cover the Bishop's informant with opprobrium. Gardiner was not deceived.[24] No doubt he recalled his beleagured colleague in later years: in Mary's reign, Scot was made bishop of Chester.

Scot's sermon was altogether a more substantial work. Its topic is the priesthood and those who would bring it into contempt. Priesthood, writes Scot, is derived from Our Lord himself who is "high priest" of the Christian religion. A priest has the venerable office of repeating the sacrifice of Christ in offering up "his blessed body & blood in y sacrament of thaulter".

* See p. 176.

From the first, Scot confesses the low esteem into which the clergy has fallen so that "it is now nothing elles but a laughynge stocke for the people'. And he is quick to grant that the clergy themselves are much to blame for this state of affairs: they must foreswear stubbornness, anger, drunkenness, brawling, and covetousness. On the other hand, should the entire estate be condemned because of the viciousness of a few? Do we condemn the apostles though Judas was of their number? Moreover, Scot writes

> I do greatly meruayl that seynge in these dayes men be so well [versed] ... in scripture, that they can not spye amonges all other thinges howe they shold use them selues towardes prestes.

Paul has taught us (I Thes. 5) to be obedient to those who have "ouersyght of you".[25]

While some priests are unworthy, even more foolish are those who "omitte theyr own deuties, and be so curyous in fyndynge faultes with other men". Paul has reminded us that those who would judge would do well to condemn themselves first.

Turning to the lay critics of the clergy, Scot points our that "euery true christen man is a preest (I Peter 2)". You must not think, he hastens to add, forfending any Lutheran reading of the text, "a preest so that he sholde ministre y sacramentes, or interprete & teach goddes worde", but each is so in the sense that he offers up his appetites and body in imitation of the sacrifices of Christ.[26] Particularly those given to scorn of the clergy seem unable to harness their own vices and cupidity.

The subject of hypocrisy leads Scot to a brief digression on Papal authority. The pope who began by describing himself as "seruum serourum" has metamorphosized into "dominus dominorum". But, God be thanked, "his combe is somewhat cutte" and "we for oure parte be delyuered from his tyranny.' Alas, notwithstanding this deliverance there are many which "be poysened with this same venim ... pride of herte". Chief among these are those who "haue in theyr handes the new testament and talk much of goddes word" but neglect Paul's ordinance to gentle obedience.[27]

Noting a new fractiousness in the realm, Scot compares the discontented to a gaggle of wayward children who disobey their parents while insisting they have reached the age of discretion. Worst of the lot are those brazen enough to search the dark places of scripture in defiance of the ancient doctors and the laws of the Church. If you inquire of these bold persons how they have the temerity to behave so, they reply,

> I am one whose eyes it hath pleased god to to haue opened that I shold see his truthe; the churche hath erred, the doctours haue ben disceaued, as I know i myselfe can not be, for I am ... one of the predestinate and elect .... [28]

The remainer of Scot's sermon strikes at the hypocrisy of specific vested interest groups and merits the attention of the social historian. Particularly arresting is his attack on the London clothing merchants, notoriously a hotbed of heresy.[29] The merchants are charged with something remarkably evocative of "hard sell" techniques and sharp practices. These persons, Scot assures us, are not of God and have a lying spirit.[30]

The Preacher's concluding words let fly at the crimes and privileges of the rich, and he marks their ablility to elude the punishments meted out to the poor. Joined to the rich are the multitudes who abuse high office. Well might they beware for "multe sunt Regem aures et oculi". And if a mortal king may be deceived, the King of Heaven cannot.[31]

It should be apparent from this brief resumé that Scot's discourse does not attempt anything like a comprehensive refutation of the new doctrines. Rather, he confines himself to a number of sharp shafts, and *ad hominem* arguments. Though its author was, as we have suggested, a scholar of considerable repute, the sermon itself is pastoral in intent, and reminiscent of the homely, moralizing meditations of Longland.

It was not until the last year of Henry's reign that the comprehensive defense of the old religion swung into high gear. So far as written polemics go, the undertaking was that of three men: Stephen Gardiner, William Peryn and Richard Smith; their energy and learning offered partial compensation for the multitude and vigor of their adversaries. Since both Peryn and Smith went dangerously beyond Gardiner, and (at least by implication) called into question the very premises of the new establishment, we shall defer discussion of their works to the following chapter. And this decision is confirmed by the unique prestige of Gardiner, and the singular force of his writings.

That the bishop of Winchester should now emerge as the chief apologist of English Catholicism should give one pause. The minister who, with Wriothesley, dominated the last phase of the reign, and who was continually burdened with the work of the Council, diplomacy, and the provisioning of Henry's expeditionary force to France, was a sore-pressed, much overworked man. It must be confessed that as a domestic statesman, he does not rise to the stature of a Wolsey or a Cromwell. But then neither of his predecessors graced their life's labours with a formidable corpus of theological works of no mean literary or intellectual merit, written in good part during the years of his pre-eminence. G.R. Elton has rightly drawn our attention to the multifarious energies of Thomas Cromwell; no less amazing, if more dissipated, are the labours of Stephen Gardiner.

To be sure, Gardiner's intellectual competence was already manifest as early as 1535. But the two works defending the new settlement were written in enforced retirement, and moreover were the works of a skilled advocate rather than a theologian *per se*. The Gardiner who emerges in this following decade is an altogether different article. This is not to deny that he was, and would remain always, something of an amateur, or that there is some truth to his opponents' claim that his theology smacked of the law court.[32] One marks the advocate's elan, and the exuberance with which he set to exposing the confusions of his antagonists, their inability to reach a consensus, and their inherent contradictions. (But in these aspects, he also offers a striking anticipation of Bossuet.)

In estimating the man and his work, it should not be forgotten that the rage of his enemies is in great part a measure of the fear he inspired in them. He was at one and the same time their chief political and polemical adversary. The fact is astonishing: the range of the man is singular.

This same range is noticeable in his works, and in his capacity to achieve a variety of tones: it excuses, if it does not explain, the quality of *de haut en bas* in these polemics. It was no small accomplishment to strike the correct note in countering both the lofty Ridley and the scabarous Bale.

It is difficult to form a just appraisal of the man. Recent historians, perhaps savouring the exotic diction of the Tudor age, refer to him still as "wily Winchester".[33] Surely he was no saint, and the evidence for his ambition, pomp and choleric temper seem incontrovertible. Bluff, open and intensely convivial (qualities he shared with his great patron,

Wolsey), he may well have appeared overwhelming and something of a bully to more timid and hesitant personalities. On the other hand, one may question the appropriateness of the epithet "wily" to a man who, at the various climactic points of his career, seems to have been somewhat wanting in tact. Indeed, from beginning to end, his career is studded with an astonishing number of costly miscalculations. They are not those of a prudent man.

Even the passage of time has not dulled his ebullient sense of the ridiculous. He found it irresistible—or politic—to share a joke even with potential enemies.[34] Through the last half of his life he had to continually repel charges of maliciousness from Latimer, Barnes, Bale, Joye and others. We are certain that some of these accusations are false. He could indeed be kind, and his lack of vindictiveness is shown in his later treatment of Peter Martyr and Thomas Smith, with both of whose views he had scant sympathy. There is also a story that he attempted to save Cranmer.[35]

Between 1545 and 1554, he published some eight works and penned at least three more. It is only with the earliest of these that we have to deal in some detail. Gardiner's first polemic of the new decade was the *Contemptum humanis legis*, written in 1541, but unpublished until 1930. It was the first of four writings fired off at Martin Bucer, his erstwhile supporter. The two had met at the Diet of Ratisbon, and there fell out over the question of clerical celibacy.[36]

The *Contemptum* is not a work of much moment, though it offers a good example of its author's Latin style at its most sparkling. Curiously though Gardiner reveals himself here as an implacable anti-Lutheran, he does approximate Luther's position in his insistence on the submission we owe even to an evil prince.[37]

The Bishop's next work, a lost tract against William Turner, was published late in 1543 or early the following year. Reconstructed by J. Muller from Turner's riposte.[38] It shows a marked advance in the author's theological maturity.

Gardiner first comes to grips with the common jibe of the Reformers that because a practice has been retained by the Roman Church it is *ispo facto* wicked. But the very devil confessed Jesus to be the son of God: is the proposition any the less true for that?[39] Having parried this, Gardiner then thrusts to the heart of the Reformers' liturgical style:

> ...thes men speak much of prechyng, but note well thys, the wold
> we shuld se nothynge in remembrance of Christ, and therefore can
> they not abyde image ... they would haue all in talkyng ... so as all
> the gates of our sences and wayes to mannis understandynge shuld
> be shit up, savying the eare alone. . . .

True worship, Gardiner retorts, is intentional, and it is human that the
senses should incarnate and express intention. This does not imply
that sensuous objects are "ydols". Christ himself used clay to heal a
man's blindness. If Turner had been standing by Christ

> ...when the woman was heled of hyr diseas by tourcyng of hys
> garment Turner would demand why he had made his garment an
> other god. . . .

Turner's confusion, and that of the other Reformers, is marked by a
failure to discriminate between worship and idolatry. And Gardiner
clearly implies that this muddle rests on an impoverished understanding
of the "Word made flesh". The material signs used by the Church are
images of the divine economy:

> ...and all that is good to man is wrought by God in Christ, for
> Christ, and by Christ where he in all creatures may do soche minis-
> teriall service as it shall please God. . . .[40]

This splendid Catholic reading of the Incarnation is easily the high-
point of this tract, but the work under consideration is packed with
argument. On the matter of the reception of the eucharist in one kind,
Gardiner is terse: "we deny that the supper hath any halfe at all". The
laity "reverently absteyn" from the cup, but having received the whole
Christ in the host, forfeit nothing. It is the faith of utraquists like
Turner which is tainted: if they believed in the Real Presence, they
would not be such sticklers for the chalice.

The keeping of Lent, which Turner has stigmatized as "popysch",
"hath been, as Origen testifieth, in the Greke Chirche even from the
beginning". And Gardiner scornfully notes "the man speaketh wisely
of the Grekes fallyng from the pope, that never was with him."[41] Here
the bishop of Winchester appeals to a Catholic tradition wider and
more antique than papalism, rejecting again Turner's identification of
Catholicism with popery.

For the rest, Gardiner defends a host of Catholic practices common to the day, fasting, abstinence, holy water, holy bread, creeping to the cross, and the like. The surviving fragment concludes with the author setting to rights a previous dispute with Bucer that had got mangled with the retelling.

Gardiner's next English work was written in late 1545 while in Bruges on a mission to Charles V.[42] Published the following year, the tract is an answer to a book of George Joye, an exile and one time associate of Tyndale's. Joye had undertaken a refutation of the articles Gardiner had enjoined upon Barnes before the latter's rearrest and execution in 1540. But Joye's polemic went beyond theological differences: he bluntly charged the Bishop with malice, with setting out to destroy Barnes.

Gardiner's reply, then, is especially interesting since it contains not only a defense of the original articles, but a personal apologia in the form of a review of his relationship with the executed heretic.

The tale of Barnes' tangled association with Gardiner is too lengthy to be unravelled in this book, though it would well reward a thorough investigation. Both were Cambridge men, Barnes perhaps a decade younger. At the time of their first meeting Gardiner must have been on the verge of entering the great world under Wolsey's aegis. In this tract, he recalls a "trim minion friar Augustine of merry scoffing wit", a phrase which would seem to betray both fondness and contempt. (But a secular priest and an Erasmian, Gardiner had no good opinion of friars.)

Yet in the beginning, Gardiner does appear to have genuinely liked Barnes, enough indeed to have counselled him when he was hauled before Wolsey for preaching an indiscreet sermon at the church of S. Edward's, Cambridge, during the Christmas of 1525. Subsequently Barnes was compelled to do public penance, and sentenced to imprisonment within a London house of his own order. Later the friar would complain of the harshness of this verdict, but by 1527 he was free enough to entertain some Lollards in his rooms, and to sell them a copy of Tyndale's New Testament. When this fresh evidence of heresy was uncovered, he fled to Germany and entered Luther's orbit.[43]

He was an unlikely martyr. Indeed, as Gardiner sketches him, there was more than a little of Falstaff about Barnes. Of his first brush with the law, we are told that it might have been overlooked since no one paid much note of "railing" in a friar. But Barnes had so far forgotten himself as to protest the principle of Christians taking oaths. Ten years later, this would have been enough to earn him a speedy demise in any state, Catholic or Reformed. But the 1520's were a more tolerant decade, and even bishop Fisher found little to cavil against save that Barnes had the temerity to address himself to the Cambridge "butcher" rather reserving his thoughts to the inner circles of academia.[44]

Under Luther's tutelage, Barnes divested himself of demi-anabaptist notions, and when, in 1534, he returned to England, it was in the more respectable guise of a Lutheran, and a protegé of Cromwell's. For the next five years he was to flit back and forth between England and the continent, a prominent emissary in the on-and-off again negotiations with the German evangelicals.

Sadly, he found it easier to dismantle his theological radicalism than to harness his mercurial temperament. He remained something of a gadfly and crowd pleaser whom a pulpit tempted to unpremeditated excesses. It was in 1538 that he preached the sermon containing an unflattering reference to the Virgin which burned itself into John Standish's memory.

The developing antipathy to Gardiner must have been exacerbated when the Bishop complained of his appointment as a commissioner to the Lutheran states, and was himself dropped temporarily from the Council in consequence. But the demeaning of Gardiner led Barnes into a dangerous and unwarranted exhilaration. Then, in the spring of 1540, he found himself abruptly replaced by the Bishop in the roster of preachers at Paul's Cross. In his response to Joye, Gardiner insists that these arrangements were made unbeknownst to him by his chancellor, and that he had hastily to compose a sermon for the occasion.[45] However this may be, Gardiner rose to the challenge superbly with a rousing attack on the principle of *sola fide*. In the "newe teaching" all is turned backward, even the paternoster

> ...where we sayd, forgyue us our debtes, as we forgyue our debters, now it is, as thou forgiuest our debtes, so I will forgyue my debters ... so God must forgyue first....[46]

Rather twisting the knife, Gardiner then went on to note that the old friars now being gone with their bought pardons, they are now replaced by the "newe bretherne" who assert that heaven requires no works at all. And these "new bretherne" are all too frequently ex-friars!

Certainly this was provocative stuff, and it is understandable that Barnes fumed, but his subsequent counter-move argues to a want of judgment. A fortnight later, the ex-friar mounted the same pulpit, and throwing that Sunday's text aside, preached to the same which Gardiner had, a thing, the Bishop notes, which "had not bene seen in that place before". And not content with refuting his adversary's very words, he made the fatal error of abusing Gardiner by name.

Barnes was then summoned into the Royal presence and ordered to confer with Gardiner over the points at issue. On the second day, a suddenly abject Barnes threw himself at the Bishop's feet and.. spoke so many wordes to my glory and in prayse of my lerning, as I was ashamed to heare them, and dare not for vaineglory reherse them now.[47]

Somewhat impulsively, Gardiner invited Barnes to come reside with him, and offered to favor the penitent with a rich living. (This is confirmed by Gardiner's opponents who later charged the Bishop with attempting to bribe Barnes.)In the warmth of reconciliation, Barnes promised to become the Bishop's "scolar", but having been instructed for two days

> ...he waxed wery of that humilitye & came the thyrde day & signified to me, that yf I wolde take him as one that came to conferre, he wolde come styll, but els he wold no more come....

and so Gardiner concludes, "was I rid of my waywarde scolar".[48]

But Barnes was shortly in trouble again "to the conceyuinge whereof I was no pryuie" and made by Henry to recant publicly. Gardiner, present at this ceremony, was suddenly mortified to have Barnes cry out to him for forgiveness. Stunned, he remained immobile until Barnes called out to him a second time whereupon Gardiner hesitantly complied. The slowness of his response, with its implied lack of charity, humiliated the Bishop before the throng. (Gardiner's account, by the way, vividly evokes Barnes' sense of theatre.) But now, even as Gardiner's ears burned, the unpredictable Barnes concluded his formal recantation, and immediately began to preach the contrary of it! Moreover a friend was foolish enough to write a letter making sport of his duplicity, which fell into the hands of his enemies in the Council.[49] This time Barnes had overplayed his hand, and he and two cohorts were sent to the Tower. To the final attainder Gardiner admits he was privy, but "amonge the rest".[50]

After this intriguing overture, Gardiner plunges into theological embroilment. The substance of the tract against Joye is the Catholic economy of salvation compared to that of the Reformers. Like Standish before him, Gardiner regards the Protestant account of the old religion as no better than a travesty. No more than the Reformers do Catholics assert that we are saved by merits: only Christ is our mediator. "The contention", writes Gardiner precisely

> ...is not of the preciousnes, validitie and effect of Christes passion, but of the use of it. And where your doctrine should onely implye that it is sufficient to thynke and talke of christes passion, we say it is also necessarie to some* to taste ... and also to drynke of it, as Christ sayde....

We must "participate" in Christ's life.[51]

When Barnes had asserted that Christ asks nothing of men, he, Gardiner, replied that all men must then be presumed to be saved by Christ's redemptive act. No, said Barnes: they must believe. So there is, Gardiner retorts, *one condition.*[52] (Here indeed, are echoes of the law court.)

Gardiner next proceeds to criticize the Reformers' proclivity for patchquilt interpretation of scripture. The Word is not to to be taken piecemeal, and reveals its meaning only in proper context:

> Two stones that be knocked together put fourthe a sparke of fyre which appeareth not in any one of the stones alone.[53]

This point leads Gardiner to the heart of his argument: the contingency of solefidian theology on those Pauline passages which imply predestination. After commenting on these, Gardiner passes on to S. Augustine who is

> ...playne in the condempnation of necessite, for it doth clearly extinct all virtue and vice, and lykewyse heauen and hell when it is thoroughly thought on.[54]

Of predestination itself, the author remarks that the problem has been confused by the human tendency to predicate time within God. We can be worse muddled here by a crude scriptural literalism. When we are told, for example, that Abraham begat Isaac, this is not to be understood in the same sense as the Creed when it asserts that Christ is the only begotten son of the Father. Likewise

> ... when the Scripture telleth us: God hath chosen, God hath predestinate, god hath forseen al ... here these verbs, hath chosen, hath predestinate, hath forseen, do declare these actes in God to be most perfet, but not any suche tyme to passe as man dreameth of. For these actes in god be without time.[55]

As S. Gregory Nazianzen has said, we cannot comprehend the work of God either in "tyme or place" for the ability to do so would imply that we understand as God does, and therefore, we would be as God. But "Gods secrete workes exceed our capacite & may not therefore be measured by our laguage".[56] As an instance of this, we know that the perfection of God transcends time, therefore predestination, whatever it means, cannot imply a past in God.

(Gardiner's discussion of temporality is grounded in S. Augustine. He views time as a necessary but subjective category of human thought, and a limitation of contingent beings.)

The Reformers "because they can not tell howe to joyne ... gods choise and mans together ... mangle and deny mans choice".[57] Excessive speculation on this question, he hints, may well lead to blasphemy and atheism. In a prophetic passage, he writes that "nowe men be suffred to loke on gods secrecies, they wyll begyn to tell him howe he myght haue done better", e.g., if God foresaw man's fall, might he not have taken more effective preventive action?[58] Having delivered himself amply on this matter, the bishop of Winchester, anticipating a later papal judgment, enjoins silence upon all parties in the dispute.

Gardiner appears to have been satisfied with his *Declaration*. Though Joye saw fit to reply to the tract within the same year, the Bishop made no response, though we know that with more formidable opponents like Bucer and Cranmer, he returned to the charge again and again.[59]

In this case, at any rate, the Bishop was on to bigger game. This time it was "old Nick" himself, or rather his "sophistrie" as manifest in a multitude of his minions. It is perhaps a measure of Gardiner's growth as a theologian that he now wished to deal with the Reformation on a larger canvas than that offered by the nit-picking concerns of embittered exiles. There was always something of the 'grand' in Gardiner's manner.[60]

Like the polemic against Joye, a *Detection of the Devils Sophistry* was published in 1546—the annus mirabilis of Henrician Catholic tracts. This time Gardiner's subject was a defense of the Catholic doctrine of the eucharist. His concern for this doctrine is mirrored in that of his fellow polemicists, William Peryn and Richard Smith, who addressed themselves to the same problem. That the real presence should be the focus of these works indicates that Zwinglianism had ousted Luther's doctrines as the primary menace to Catholic security.

Though in all probability none of these writers anticipated that disaster was only months away, it is apparent that the Catholic leadership anticipated some new crisis. The opening pages of Peryn's *Thre godlye and notalbe sermons* make it clear that the author's bishop, Edmund Bonner, had pressed him to publish these sermons to counter the "horrible heresye of Berengary and Wikclyfe sacramentaries abhomynable ... raysed agayne ... by meanes of euell and pestiferous bookes"[61], while the hurried and prolific industry of Richard Smith similarly testifies to a sense of urgency. At the same time, John Feckenham sounded the alarm from Paul's Cross in a sermon daring enough to earn him a rebuke from the Council.[62]

Certainly apprehension is keynoted in the opening pages of Gardiner's tract:

> Consider gentle reader how ful of iniquite thys time is, in whiche the hyghe mysterie of our religion is openly assaulted. Byleue not euery spirite, and mystruste thyne owne iudgment, aboue the reache of thy capacitie....

And once again, the Bishop asks his reader to "conforme knowlege to agre with obedience."[63] But if this injunction recalls *de vera obedientia*, the remainder of the book does not. The old theology was no longer to be affirmed by a mere summons to obey divinely ordained authority, and the *Detection* is a densely argued and detailed assault on the new eucharistic doctrines.

Gardiner perceives the present errors as rooted in "carnal" reasonings, and he likens the Reformers to the ancient epicureans who thought "the sonne was but two foote brode, because theyr eye iudged it to be no bygger." Always swift to spot the inconsistencies in his opponents' arguments, he points to the fact that the Reformers accept even greater and more paradoxical mysteries than that of the real presence. For

> ...lyke as in the other mysteries of the Trinitie, the creation of the
> world, and the Incarnation ... and also the resurrection of the fleshe
> ...carnal reason is excluded by certentie of faith, so shulde it be in
> all other mysteries....[64]

He then rehearses the familiar parade of radical charges against the real presence: that it is an "ydol", that it may be eaten by a mouse, that it becomes mouldy, and so on. To the allegation that this "papisticall god" is corruptible bread, he retorts that the same might be alleged of the flesh that the Son himself took—this last a shrewd thrust which has become a hallmark of Gardiner's polemics. On a loftier plane too, the contention may be seen as evidence of the Bishop's deepening understanding of the Catholic theology of the Incarnation.[65]

These remarks are followed by a more conventional exposition of the real presence which culminates with the warning that the doubts sown by the sacramentarians will ultimately undermine all piety leaving "no stedfaste faith ... but wauering opinion."[66] And John 6 is brought to bear against those who contend that Christ always speaks in metaphors and parables.

Next Gardiner introduces a long excursus in which the 9th century Greek father, John Damascene, is introduced in support of a corporeal presence. Large chunks of John's *de Fide Orthodoxa* are served up in Greek, Latin and English, and the original is culled from Oecalampidius' edition so the Reformers will have no pretext to carp against a popish twisting of the text.[67] These lengthy and pedantic digressions will become an increasing feature of Reformation polemics; even in the following reign, the volumes of controversy are noticeably more swollen, and the authors' arguments correspondingly more difficult to follow amidst the brambles of patristic quotation and commentary.

Having reinforced his contention with the authority of a venerable Greek father, Gardiner reiterates his assertion that "we shold not measure goddes doinges by our natural inbecilitie": all the specifically Christian dogmas transcend our natural reason and appear paradoxical to it. To the now familiar Protestant objection that Christ cannot be in the host and heaven simultaneously, he replies that Christ appeared to Paul *after* His ascension.[68]

The Fathers are now paraded triumphantly to show their consensus on this venerable doctrine, while the disarray of the Reformers is gleefully exhibited. Luther and Melanchthon accept a corporeal presence, while it is denied by Zwingli and Oecalampidius, and "amonge us by Frith, Joye, Bale & Turner."[69] The point made earlier against Turner, is repeated again, that utraquism, though itself indifferent, argues to a deficit in faith since one receives the "hole Christ" in the single species.[70] The tract concludes with the author's assurance that Christ is "present really in the sacrament of the aulter, without leauing his seate in heauen."[71]

By 1546 then, it is clear that Gardiner had emerged as an effective polemical champion of the old religion. Though his grasp of theology was growing increasingly profound, he retained a lightness of touch and a literary grace certainly denied to Standish, Smith and Peryn, all of whose works at this time are marked by a solemn aridity. Gardiner's weakness is betrayed by his increasingly uncertain ecclesiology. One must presume that he could not have been blind to the fact that his recent disputations had carried him out far beyond the wading pools of the Supremacy. In his polemics with foreigners (like Bucer) or exiles (Turner and Joye) there could be no appeal to the deference due to the secular authority. Bucer's magistrates, for instance, were the frankly Protestant city fathers of Strasbourg. To be sure, there is no question but that Gardiner thinks of his opponents as heretics pure and simple. But heretics by the determination of what authority? The Pope? The Councils? Gardiner dares not appeal to the first, and will not to the other. We are left instead with a rather lame appeal to the practice of the "Greke church" to justify the orthodoxy of his eucharistic opinions, and that "faythe is set a worke by charite."[72]

But even as Gardiner penned these works, Catholic prospects were becoming occluded. The bishop's pro-imperialist policies were no longer those of his King, and once again he fell into disfavor, this time for refusing an exchange of lands. As the year drew to a close, Norfolk, the last pillar of the lay Catholic aristocracy in the Council, was clapped into the Tower, enmeshed in the downfall of his erratic son. Wriothesley changed sides, and Seymour and Lisle were now clearly in the ascendant. In January 1547, the old King was dead. The most notable omission in his will was the name of Gardiner who was given no seat on the Counil of the Regency. Before the spring was out, the Bishop was energetically protesting the new reforms that crested in July with a proclamation ordering the churches to take in a translation of Erasmus' *Paraphrases* and a *Book of Homilies*. The latter contained several penned by Cranmer in the cause of solefidianism, and which ran clean contrary to the spirit of the still official *King's Book*. This was but the first gust in what was to become a vertible typhoon of reform. As usual, Gardiner's objections were all too pertinent, and in September, he was incarcerated in the Fleet, so depriving the Catholics of their sole effective leader in the coming Parliament. The Reformers were on the inside track, and home free.

7

Conclusion: Mid-Tudor Aftermath

Our purpose has been to treat the dilemma of Henrician Catholicism: precisely, the ideological dilemma. Governed by this principle, we have focused on but a portion of the larger question—how to explain the failure of Henrician Anglo-Catholicism?

To begin with, it simply will not do to dismiss the Catholic party as the devil's spawn, or as papists without the courage of their convictions, or again, as prudent men swamped in a rising tide of idealist fanaticism, or yet as men whose spirituality and fortitude were inferior to that of their antagonists. Such theories have found exponents from Foxe to contemporary historians and tracing their lineaments would be another book in itself. What I hope to have accomplished is the presentation of the problem in another dimension.

Certainly there is a problem. When Henry broke with Rome in 1533, the overwhelming majority of Englishmen were Catholic, though few had very strong attachments to Rome. In the view of the episcopate and most of the educated clergy, the future must have held prospects of a schism of uncertain duration. No doubt this was uncomfortable, but the situation, as we have seen, was not unprecedented. And whatever uneasiness was felt in some quarters, compensation offered itself in the anticipation of salubrious reforms. Yet with the exception of Cranmer, not a single bishop anticipated any doctrinal change of moment; and none, save Cranmer, felt any pull toward the new continental heresies.

Two years later this had quite changed. The primate had gained five colleagues on the bench, and during the convocation of 1536, the upper house "showed itself as a house divided". (The lower house, still conservative and in a surly temper, issued a compendium of sixty-eight "mala dogmata"[1] ignored by their superiors and the government alike.)

It is clear then that from its inception, the Royal Supremacy operated to divide the Church, and so emasculate it that it proved incapable of offering corporate resistance—not only to the King, as has been commonly noted—but to the new doctrines. Such is the import of those bipartite ecclesiatical commissions whose carefully structured indecisiveness invariably placed all decisions in the government's hands. It is just possible that this strategy originated with Thomas Cromwell, but unlike many of the minister's policies, this one did not die with him. As early as 1536, Henry had been prepared to assert (truly or not) that he "conceived" the none too orthodox Ten Articles; after Cromwell's fall he continued as before: taking Biblical revision out of Convocation's hands in 1542, contributing a new preface that went well beyond mere authorization to the *King's Book* (1543) and, in 1545, making a speech before Parliament in which he frankly laid claim to the role of doctrinal adjudicator.

In his stern letter of 1531 to bishop Tunstall, the King had disavowed in anticipation any such role: the supremacy, he explained, meant no more than a claim to temporal jurisdiction over all Englishmen.[2] Five years later, the Royal theologian had made a complete *volte-face*. In his corrections of the *Bishop's Book*, the King did not scruple to amend the work of his clergy—as indeed the preface of that work invited him to do.[3] With regard to the sacrament of holy orders, the very fulcrum of autonomous ecclesiastical jurisdiction, we find Henry in agreement with Cranmer's view of 1540. Beside a passing note that Acts 20 grants a "jurisdiction appertaining unto priests and bishops", the King wrote: here *cure* is spoken of, not jurisdiction or power" (italics mine).[4] And again, after a passage asserting the "power and authority ... given ... by Christ and his apostles unto certain persons only, namely bishops and priests", the King remarked significantly, "note, there were no kings christian under whom they did dwell."[5] It is impossible to mistake the drift of these addenda.

What then was the King's theological orientation after the rupture with Rome? His disdain for a corporate Church, and a pronounced tendency toward *sola scriptura* make it difficult to describe him even loosely as a Catholic. Equally, his consistent rejection of solefidianism separates him from the Protestant camp. Was he then an Erasmian? To the extent that he inclined to semi-Pelagianism, and exhibited an increasing hostility to 'supersitition', there can be no quarrel with this description. On the other hand, we have noted that the genuine Erasmians of the day, like Tunstall and Starkey, appear no less discomfited by this regime. Unlike the Erasmians, the King showed scant respect for the *consensus patrum*, and still less for the judgment of the visible Church. And, most important, Erasmus himself was no erastian: in his opinion, the kings and princes of Europe stood no less in need of reform than the Church. This view did not commend itself to Henry. As his famous address of 1545 confirms, the King was untroubled by self-doubts, and saw himself as transcending both factions within the national Church.

Catholics then, were a mere party within the settlement, and their attempts to capture the English Church were never wholly successful, for the Supreme Head stood above and not with them. Stephen Gardiner's proud charge that the King used the Reformers without ever being of their number was no less true of his own faction.

In truth, from the outset, Henry seems to have been determined to keep the factions in equilibrium. When it served his interest, the Reformation was allowed to make modest strides. But if the Reformers were to be utilized effectively as a counterweight, it was incumbent upon the government to give them a real base within the settlement. By 1535, this had been accomplished.

No less menacing was the pruning of Catholic devotional life, a process which advanced during the entire reign. The extinction of the monasteries and friaries, the abolition of pilgrimages and a slew of saints' days, and the curtailment of fasting and the veneration of images, all these led to the atrophy of a specifically Catholic spirituality. By 1547, Catholic apologists were left defending the nucleus of the old faith, but multitudes had been cut adrift with the extinguishing of the old piety.

But the supremacy disadvantaged the Catholics on more than the practical plane. Theoretically, the old faith was put in an impossible position, for Henry's supremacy went far beyond either the dreams or practice of Byzantine caesaropapism. Theologically venturesome though some of the ancient emperors were, they had to deal with the Church as a corporate body. It was the particular genius of Henry and Cromwell to create a schism within the body itself, so rendering the Church impotent while reserving the ultimate magisterium to government inititative. In practice, this meant the Church abdicated its doctrinal authority to the state. To be sure, this strategy was unthinkable without the Reformation challenge to the sacrament of orders. Luther's doctrine of the priesthood of all believers and corollary of the "godly prince" was a blatant invitation to the usurpations of secular authority. And we have noted that, on this point, Henry's views were those of the Reformers.

Abstractly, it could be argued that Royal Supremacy contained implicitly the germ of doctrinal innovation and, in the fractured political structure of Christendom, a permanent potentiality for schism. Yet since the termination of the iconoclastic movement in the ninth century, the Orthodox states of the east had maintained Catholicity intact without a major schism, and that under infidel as well as Christian rulers. The Catholic apologists, particularly Starkey, Tunstall and Gardiner grasped this point—though precious few of the details—in their appeal to the Greeks and the early ecumenical councils.

A qualified acknowledgment of this theory found its way into the official formulae in the insistence that the faithful must "abhoore and deteste all heresies and schismes" though this orthodox sentiment is somewhat blunted with the codicil: "whereby the true interpretation and sence of scriptures ... maye be peruerted." This same *Bishops' Book* will even grant the " ...churche of Rome with all thother partycular churches in the worlde, compacted and unyted togeyther ... make but one catholyque churche or bodye ... " but hastily adds that this "misticall bodye" is a "mere spirituall unitie."[6]

But what if spiritual unity should be disrupted by quarrels over what was the "true interpretation and sence of scriptures"? In the early sixteenth century this was no academic question. What voice might then be trusted to speak authoritatively? The plain Catholic answer was, if not the pope, then an ecumenical General Council.

But the Henrician Church was no means ready to return so unequivocal an answer. True, the official formulae retained the appeal to a Council, but so hedged with provisos, and so contingent upon national acceptance, as to make the concept meaningless. Once more we note that the Reformers, following the lead of Luther, threw great dubiety on General Councils. The same scepticism was allowed to insinuate itself into the formulae of English religion. But to question that the visible Church could define doctrine, or for that matter had any need to, was to surrender to the Reformers' twin principles of the sufficiency of scripture and the invisible Church. It was at this juncture that Henry's Church yielded itself most completely to the Reformation.

The Catholic response to this surrender was twofold, and in both cases, inadequate. Some, like Tunstall, continued to argue for the infallibility of the eight General Councils, and to insist on the visible, corporate unity of the Church. The difficulty with this solution was that its proponents were expressing but a private opinion which found only the scantiest support in the official formulae. Indeed, these insisted that no canons of any Council were compelling unless received by the whole consensus of Christian princes. This was to say no more or less than the ultimate arbiter of doctrine was not a Council, but the consent of the "godly prince."

Consequently, the most forcible argument of the Catholics, that of a visible Church whose doctrinal authority was guaranteed by a General Council inspired by the Holy Spirit, found no authoritative reception in the new settlement. Discouraged, most Catholics fell back on other lines of defense.

One of the most wayward of these was the interesting suggestion of Richard Smith that Catholic unity is maintained in the true body and blood of Christ in the eucharist—we are all one in receiving Him.[7] Conversely, those who reject transubstantiation are no members of Christ's Church.[8] But this view, however prescient of the eucharistic theology of today, found few supporters among Smith's contemporaries. And Smith himself more often resorted to what was to become the second line of Catholic defenses.

This was the tactic of defending the old faith from tradition and the Bible. As far as the latter went, this stratagem had the advantage of meeting the Reformers on a ground which both parties recognized as valid, and one to which the government could take no umbrage. Since English Reformers seldom went to lengths of Luther who was prepared to cast doubts on the authority of an Epistle of James or Revelations, argument could be confined to interpretation of the received text.

It was otherwise with 'tradition' where the situation was frought with difficulties. For one thing, the radical Reformers recognized no such thing at all, and these extremists were by no means a negligible force in Anglican life, even at this early date. Among Catholics too, there was no exact agreement as to what constituted tradition, though all insisted that scripture must be interpreted in light of it. Most, no doubt, accepted implicitly what Richard Smith proclaimed baldly when he insisted that

> ...many thynges necessary both to be belieuedand also obserued of us christen people, are not expressly writte ... but are left to vs by the holy apostles, and other thauncient fathers, and godly mennes tradition.[9]

Some Catholics took tradition as extending well into the Middle Ages. Such were bishop Longland who quoted S. Bernard as a "father" in his sermon of 1536, or bishop Aldrich of Carlisle who invoked the authority of Thomas Walden, a relatively obscure late scholastic and confuter of Lollardy.[10] Most daring in this regard was the same Richard Smith who deferred to the authority of the "fathers" at the Council of Constance.[11]

More cautious exponents of tradition restricted it in fact if not in theory to the fathers of the first five or six centuries. Such limits were prescribed by the Erasmian program of *ad fontes*, and the outer limits of Protestant credulity: in the west, Isidore, in the east, John Damascene, marked the *non plus ultra* of patristics.

Here, the moderate wing of the Reformers, led by Cranmer, were prepared to accept the rules and contest the ground. Midway into the reign of Edward VI, Catholic-Anglican apologetics had assumed its familiar form, as the short, hard-hitting sermon or tract gave way to swollen volumes of patristic quotation and commentary that will characterize the next four centuries of polemics. As the ages wore on, Smith, Gardiner, Turner and Cranmer gave way to Jewel, Harding, Hooker, Bellarmine, Taylor, Newman, Salmon, Gore and Butler. The subject of the great debate was, which Church was the true heir to the Church of the Fathers?

From the Henrician Catholic point of view, the difficulty lay in beng driven onto ground where no easy or decisive victory was to be expected. Moreover, the field of battle was a specifically Protestant preserve since the last court of appeal was historical, not the authority of the living Church. Both parties now set about with extraordinary energy to the task of assembling a valid reconstruction of the ancient Church.

But for the Catholic, this quest for the rule of faith amidst the brambles of historical scholarship was an implicit confession of defeat. Perhaps this was unavoidable, since any debate must discover some common ground to which both participants subscribe, and the Reformers would consent to no principle save antiquity. Catholic polemics, divested of an appeal to the rule of the contemporary Church, fell back on an essentially historical defense of two key doctrines— good works and the mass.

• • •

If one must single out the primordial error of the conforming Catholics, it was not the repudiation of the Roman primacy, but the acceptance of the Supremacy. In the latter, they bought something more than a schism.

To be sure, there were a number of extenuating circumstances for their failure to make a stand. In the five years between Henry's letter of reassurance to Tunstall and the Convocation of 1536, Supremacy had come to mean quite another thing. The transition had been so neatly managed that there had been no single moment when the Catholic leadership might have gathered itself to cry halt. A variety of factors must be weighed here. We cannot ignore the timorousness induced by a careful and selective policy of isolation and terror. One notes that beginning with Tunstall, the leadership was selectively and in turn, threatened and intimidated. Tunstall in 1534 amd 1539, Edward Lee in 1535 and 1537, Stokesley in 1536 and 1538, Longland and Clerk 1541. Gardiner, closer to the King, was singed periodically throughout the reign.

On the other hand, even at the worst of times, in say 1535 and 1538, the Catholic leaders might console themselves with the hope of yet another turn of the wheel of policy. Nor, as long as Henry lived, were such expectations entirely forlorn. The lurches to the right which accompanied the fall of Anne Boleyn and Cromwell, the Six Articles and the *King's Book* (the list is not exhaustive), all seemed to augur a decisive Catholic triumph. Above all, the King himself continued to attend mass, and to keep a part at least of the old ceremonial.

Yet again, the Catholic leaders were deeply divided. Some like bishop Kite and (possibly) Stokesley were covert papists at heart, separated from Rome by a blend of fear and opportunism. But even those conformists for whom the papacy at best was a peripheral thing—no matter to die for, in the proximate words of Edward Lee— were themselves in disarray.

In practical matters, this want of coherence became manifest at the inception of the new reign. In June 1547, Gardiner, in a letter to Somerset which undertook to defend the old faith, charged his colleague Tunstall with giving advice "to envey . . . innovation", and then went on to disassociate himself from the person and works of Richard Smith.[12] The leader of English Catholicism here repudiates in a single letter his two remaining peers! In the case of Smith whose very qualified apostasy had been proclaimed at Paul's Cross three weeks previously, the bishop was very likely animated by disgust.[13] But the misapprehension of Tunstall's position argues to an incredible lack of communication and joint policy among the Catholic chiefs. The bishop of Durham remained firmly Catholic in sentiment, testified for Gardiner at his later trial, and voted against both the first Act of Uniformity and the new ordinal. It was after his imprisonment and deprivation that he wrote his defense of the old theology of the eucharist and a brilliant attack on the predestinarians.[14]

Between Gardiner and Bonner, the second of the Catholic bishops to fall under the Council's displeasure, there had once been very bad blood.[15] Apparently the two had composed their differences after Cromwell's fall, but there is nothing to suggest a collusion of interests after that time.

In any event, the detention of Gardiner and Bonner was followed by defections in Catholic ranks. Early in 1548, Cranmer had addressed another of his leading questionnaries to certain prominent clergy, this time concerning the nature of the eucharist. Among the respondents were seventeen bishops and two (Reformed) theologians. Bonner, Heath, Skip, Repps, Day and Warton responded *en bloc*, and in an essentially orthodox manner—the only evidence we have of Catholics acting in concert. Separate but equally Catholic replies were submitted by Tunstall, Capon (Salisbury), Bush (Bristol), and Aldrich (Carlisle). Among the Reformers are Cranmer, Barlow (St. David's), Holbeach (Lincoln), Ridley (Rochester), and the two theologians, Cox and Taylor. Holgate (York), Goodrich (Ely) and Sampson (Coventry & Lichfield) are uncertain about the benefits of the mass, but clearly defend some notion of the Real Presence.[16] Breaking this down, ten out of nineteen (or seventeen if we discount the select theologians) are Catholic, while three others are more easily aligned with the old school on this crucial dogma.

Before the full year had turned, the first Prayer Book had been introduced into Parliament—a work whose eucharistic doctrine could only with the greatest strain be interpreted in a Catholic sense.[17] And voting with the Reformers for its passage were Holgate, Goodrich,

Sampson, Capon, Bush and Warton (the last by proxy). Three moderates and three Catholics had gone over to the Reformation.

In 1552, the Second Act of Uniformity with its radically Protestant Prayer Book was submitted to a vote. By this time Gardiner, Bonner, Heath, Day and Tunstall were deprived, while Skip and Repps were dead. Only Aldrich and Thirlby remained to vote no.[18]

What meets the eye in even the most cursory glance is that Catholic leadership failed to organize resistance to these innovations, or even to hold ranks. Setting aside the patent Reformers, one notes that men appointed in the previous reign who had subscribed to the Six Articles and the *King's Book*, went along with or passively acquiesced in the changes without protest. Such were bishops Holgate, Warton, Sampson, Holbeach, Capon, King, Skip, Chamber, Kitchin, Bush, Bird and Bulkeley. No less than nine of these appointments had been made in the years of Henry's suppositious Catholic reaction—between 1540 and 1547.[19] It is yet another touchstone whereby we may estimate the sovereign's orthodoxy.

To be sure, in the future committments of men there is always an element of uncertainty; decisions were made which not even Henry can be presumed to have anticipated. As late as 1540, Sampson had shown himself to be a convinced, if not very courageous, Catholic. Yet his answers to the 1548 questionnaire indicate that he had undergone a considerable doctrinal evolution.[20] Conversely, who could have foreseen that Bonner, Cromwell's man and diplomatist, contributor of a radical preface to *de vera obedientia*, and midwife of the Great Bible, would emerge as a leading Catholic foe of the Edwardian innovations?

Yet the exceptions, interesting as they are, but confirm the rule. Catholic confusion stands in a stark contrast to the purposefulness and cohesion of the Reformers. Despite grave uncertainties in essential doctrine, the latter maintained a real unity from the origins of their party to the vestarian controversy of 1551.

As we might expect, Catholic divisiveness prevailed on the theoretical level as well. Catholic apologists may be divided into those who took the Supremacy seriously, and those for whom it was a thing indifferent, or a positive impediment. (But all Catholics, it must be emphasized, took a "low" line on the Supremacy in that they held the sacerdotal order to be a thing divinely ordained, and separate from the prince's appointment.)

Chief of the first group was Stephen Gardiner whose *de vera obedientia* was the most important attempt to accommodate the Supremacy to the scheme of Catholic theology. The glaring weakness of Gardiner's work was its ecclesiology. Unity of doctrine could presumably be maintained only by the action of the Spirit on the individual soverign. So, all evidence to the contrary, Gardiner was commited to a defense of Henry's orthodoxy.

And this was the position that Gardiner conscientiously upheld until 1550. In the extraordinary series of letters he wrote in 1547, defending the old settlement from impending innovations, the bishop undertook to repel Cranmer's suggestion that Henry was "seduced" or "compassed" into subscribing to the formula of the *King's Book*.[21] Quite the contrary, he retorts, Cranmer himself was compelled to yield the point of "only faith" to the King for

> ...our soverigne lord was neither seduced nor deceyved. For he dyscussed yt thorowly and travailed in yt with you vnto whome fynally your Grace cessyd ...[22].

Henry, insists Gardiner, was too learned and wise to be hoodwinked in such matters; moreover, if Henry was deceived, might not the present government be deceived as well?[23] The upshot of Cranmer's argument will be to bring the Royal Supremacy into the same disrepute as Roman authority.[24]

All this was well said; lethal in fact—but no less for Gardiner's position than Cranmer's. As time would reveal, neither man was prepared to surrender what each regarded as true religion to the operation of the Supremacy. In truth, the implicit proposition governing Gardiner's theology might be given as: 'the Holy Ghost, operating through the Supremacy, would conserve Catholic orthodoxy intact.' This was pure Marsiglianism, and it bound orthodoxy straitly to historical fact: the Prince and the Council will continue to be Catholic. It is hardly necessary to add that this expectation was thoroughly crushed by the rule of the Edwardian regents.

It is difficult to account for so inadequate an line or argument in the arsenal of an increasingly subtle and sophisticated theologian, but that Gardiner remained convinced of the Supremacy, that he did not stick at its ruthless application, cannot be doubted. In a letter of 14 June 1547, the bishop singled out for special castigation "Dr. Smyth of Oxford who affirmed fondly in words that wee [convocation] might make laws [unless] The King's majesty hath authorized and approved it."[25]

"Dr. Smyth" is none other than Richard Smith, Gardiner's disa-vowed comrade in arms. If Gardiner was the foremost leader of the Catholic supremacists, Smith as truly summarizes the school which sought to minimize the erastian factor. In this category one must place Tunstall, Longland and (with reservations) Starkey.

Even less than Gardiner can Smith be convicted of 'popish' leanings. His early advancement had been owed to the King who appointed him the first Regius Professor of Divinity at Oxford in 1536. For ten years we hear little of him. Then, in 1546, he burst into print with two books in defense of the old mass, and one work upholding "unwritten verities." This was the first spurt in a veritable torrent of polemical activity which lasted until his death at Douai in 1563.

The man himself would seem to have fallen short of the stature of his work. Somewhat deficient in fortitude, his career was shadowed by allegations of equivocation, apostasy, and sexual scandal.[26] In his first book, he prayed that he might not forsake his convictions through "anye kynde of payne, or the feare of it."[27] His opinions were temera-rious enough to warrant this anxiety, and though the old King did not live long enough to call him to account, Somerset's Council did so in the spring in 1547. His errors were deemed important enough to warrant a public retraction at Paul's Cross, and when this was found inadequate, he was ordered to make public satisfaction at Oxford. Though both these works were printed[28] in the hope of embarrassing the Catholics, they were too full of equivocation to be found entirely satisfactory, and their author was replaced as Regius Professor by Peter Martyr, whose views on the eucharist Smith then promptly assailed.[29]

Smith's first two works (and possibly the third on unwritten vertities) belong to the history of Henry VIII. Excruciatingly prolix, neither charm of style nor occasional vivacity of phrase intrudes upon their cumulation of argument. If the Council found them odious, this was because of the boldness and huge learning of their author.

The *Assertion and Defence of the sacramente of the aulter* is a 260 folio attack on those who assert that the eucharist is a "bare figure."[30] Defending the doctrine of transubstantiation, the author will resort to the Bible, the ancient fathers, and the "infalible canons and rules."[31] The book is a catena of sources followed by the author's commentaries.

Some idea of Smith's thoroughness may be garnered from the fact that no less than seventeen errors concerning the eucharist are isolated, discussed and reproved, from those of Berengar to Smith's contemporary, Frith.[32]

Hot on the heels of the *Assertion*, Smith now published *A Defence of the Sacrifice of the Masse*, a still more provocative and brazen work (but no less dull) which revealed more clearly than any other Catholic polemic the potential strain between the old faith and the Royal Supremacy. Smith tells us that the book was:

> . . . made in hast win the space of a moneth, whan I myght steale an houre from my other business or studye. . . [33]

—a prodigious feat since it consists of 189 folios of closely packed argument.

Though some of the material overlaps, the two books are concerned with separate aspects of the sacrament. While the *Assertion* attempts to validate the doctrine of transubstantiation, the *Defence of the Sacrifice*, as its title suggests, contends that the celebration of mass is a "sacrifice propitiatory for both the quick and the dead,"[34] —a proposition denied alike by Lutherans and sacramentaries who contended that Christ's sacrifice on the cross was unique and wholly sufficient, and that the mass in no sense participated in this sacrifice, but was a memorial of it. Not surprisingly, it is Luther who is particularly singled out for refutation in this second work.

In 1546-47, Smith's doctrine of the eucharist was still in accord with officially prescribed belief of the Six Articles and the *King's Book*, though it may be wondered if a government which had just granted the King the chantries might not be embarrassed by so hearty a champion of "masses satisfactory." (By early 1547, the new Council was preparing to justify the impending seizures with Protestant underpinnings.) What was truly perilous in Smith's new book was the thoroughness with which he was prepared to argue for both the autonomy and infallibility of the Church, and the corresponding insufficiency of scripture.

Taking up the now familiar argument that the Church herself is the sole guarantee of scripture, Smith notes that the great heresiarchs from Marcion to Luther have been prepared to dispense with whole books of the Bible,[35] while conversely, they read scripture all too selectively.

An example of the latter is Luther's "peruerse" reading of S. Paul, who surely insisted that sacrifice is the prerogative of priests, not all Christians, as Luther would have it.[36] And he makes the telling argument (telling, because the Reformers abhorred the prospect of anabaptism no less than the Catholics) that those who would insist on infant baptism must appeal to extra-scriptural authority as there is not a word of it in the New Testament.[37]

The mass, Smith insists, is a sacrifice propitiatory because the Church tells us it is. Would not the Holy Ghost have protected Christ's spouse, the Church, from so gross an error these thousand of years?[38] Christ promised to be with His Church to the end (Matt. 28) and to

> ... send the holy gooste, the spirit of trouth to teache the churche all truthe necessary for christen people to knowe, and ... shall always and euer abyde with it, the whyche he hath undoutedly performed before Luthers byrth, and especyally to the general councels representynge the whol churche and congregation of christen people, so that they beynge lawfully gathered together ... dyd not erre in the faythe of Christ nor yet coulde erre therin ... [39]

Here at last, and far too late, was an unequivocal Catholic riposte to the challenge of the Supremacy. Catholic, be it noted, but not papist, for the author sharply insists that the Church receives its doctrine from the apostles, not Rome.[40]

Perhaps but a month, or at best, two months later, Smith published the third in this trinity of books, *A brief treatyse settynge forth diuers truthes necessary both to be belieued of chrysten people & kept also whiche are not expressed in the scripture but left y church by the aposotles traditio.* Here the author expanded his defense of the old religion to cover the time worn ancient rites and practices. His intention is to confute that "ungodly opinion which affirmeth that euery necessary truth is wrytten in the Bible."[41] Rather oddly, the work opens with a puzzling digression, a furious attack on clerical laxity and simony. Benefices are now given as

> ... common merchaudise, with oute all regarde & respecte had vnto the learnynge & honesty of the preest, to whom they are sold .... [42]

A reader unfamiliar with the Catholic polemics of the time may at first find this surprisingly Protestant in tone. In fact, we note the same themes in Longland, Starkey, Cuthbert Scot, and Gardiner's chaplain, James Brooke. What is singular in Smith's diatribe is the extension of the term simony to cover lay impropriations of Church benefices.

For the rest, the *brief treatyse* is an anything but terse catalogue of Catholic practices defended by an appeal to the early fathers. The root of Smith's position is given as John 16, Christ's promises to his apostles that the Spirit would teach them many things he had not.[43] Again, the book offers an awesome, if not entirely discriminating scholarship.

The *brief treatyse* proved too much for the new men in control of the Council. It was then that Smith was called up to London to face an interview with Cranmer, and to be called upon to retract. After his loss of the Regius professorship and the debate with his successor and Cox, Smith was cast into prison. He was freed sometime at the end of 1549, and made his way to Louvain.

It was probably the following year that he published at Rouen a refutation of Cranmer's book which denied the corporeal presence in the eucharist.[44] Free of the trammels of censorship, Smith's style, for the first time, assumes a sort of corrosive humor.

For our purposes, the *Confutation* is of interest because of what it reveals of previous Henrician polemics. Presumably as a guest of Louvain, Smith had to declare himself a Roman Catholic. Yet a close reading of his work shows its author to be a lukewarm papist indeed. The sole evidence for Romanism in the *Confutation* is its author's defense of the Lateran Council—summoned by Innocent III—as an authoritative ecumenical council. But the pope, throughout the work, is referred to as the bishop of Rome.[45] And when Smith comes to expound Christ's promise to pray for Peter, he construes the passage in the classically non-papist manner. The prayer means that Christ

> ... will praye for Peter, *that his faythe*, that is to say, *the faythe of the catholique churche* ... wyll not decay ... (italics mine)[46].

In light of such a passage, one wonders if many historians have not too hastily followed the early Protestant practice of imputing covert popery to many of these conformists.[47]

What does emerge from the *Confutation* is that Smith was a full-blown conciliarist. It is the authority of the Councils, not Rome, which is continually insisted upon—above all, the authority of the "foure generl concels."[48] Error, we are assured, can never "whollie" prevail in the Church due to Christ's promise,[49] The kernel of Smith's argument is

> . . . that it perteyneth onlyc vnto the churche of christe to expounde the scripture & to discusse al doutes of our fayth . . . and that also the general concils ought not to be despised, but much regarded, obediently receaued and foloued. . . .

But they cannot be followed if a nation or people is constrained to obey the decisions of a local authority of Christendom. Since Christ promised to be with the Church, doctrine belongs to her and "not unto one person, nor to any one countrey or region."[50] The errors of S. Cyprian and eighty assembled African bishops had to be corrected by a General Council.[51]

With the *Confutation*, the Henrician Catholic position had come round full circle to the position of 1533—an appeal to a General Council with no pretense that England had the authority to define doctrine independently of the universal Church. As Smith makes clear, doctrine belongs to no one person, country or region. The Supremacy is rejected. The dilemma of Henrician Catholicism is that the old faith is incompatible with doctrinal autarchy.

• • •

In March 1553, King Edward VI died; two weeks later, his sister Mary sat on the throne of England. Her religious inclinations were well enough known, and Catholics dared to resume the ancient religious practices, though formal reunion with Rome was still two years away. With reluctance, the new Queen assumed her father and brother's title of Supreme Head. No sooner had she gained her capital than she plucked Gardiner from the tower to make him her chancellor.

In November 1553, Gardiner's former chaplain, James Brooke, now master of Balliol, preached at Paul's Cross to the text of the resurrection of the daughter of Jairus. But his real subject is the resuscitation of "our Mother the holye Catholique Churche." Interestingly, Brooke does not mention the pope at all, either under his old or more recently ordained titles. For the rest, the sermon reiterates the points already made by Smith: "The churche can neuer be diuorced from Christe . . .

nor yeat at any time be ledde out of the way of the trueth."[52] Tertullian is brought forth to argue the infallibility of the Church, and the Church may authorize custom "in such thynges wherein the scripture doeth determine no certentie."[53]

A very forceful and sophisticated argument is presented for the Church's authority over scripture:

> The Churche hath ... geuen to her by GOD, authoritie to discerne the true scripture from the forged, the autentical from the Apocryphal ... otherwise why should we allow & receiue S. Markes gospel which neuer saw Christ nor hard Christ, and disalowe and reiect Nicodems Gospel now extant...?

Conversely, Mark and Hebrews are accepted "notwithstandinge many haue doubted of thautours of them."[54]

Meanwhile, in spite of Mary's (temporary) resumption of the title Supreme Head, Brooke insists that

> ...obedience ought to be had (touching thinterpretation of Scripture) to the rules in the churche, namely *suche as* hath their successio fro the apostles... (italics mine).[55]

These are bishops, and departure from their jurisdiction is heresy. There are "iii notes: Antiquitie, uniuersitie, and consent, whereby ... catholike veritie is discerned"[56] —the Lerins canon being invoked again as the certificate of orthodoxy. It is the final irony of Henrician Catholicism tht it attained its apotheosis under the shadow of its surrender to Rome.

Bibliography
Primary Sources

Manuscript Sources

British Museum, Cottinian MSS, Cleo. E, IV, V, VI. Lambeth Palace Library, MSS, 1107, 1108

Printed Primary Sources

Aless [Alane, Alesius], Alexander, *On the auctorite . . . agaynst the bisshop of London* (Leipsig, 1538?).

Bale, John [pseud. Henrye Stalbrydge], *The Epistle exhortatorye of an Englyshe Christiane . . . against the pompouse popyshe Bysshoppes* (Basle, 1544?).

[Bancroft, Richard?], *Tracts ascribed to Richard Bancroft*, ed. A. Peel (Cambridge, 1953).

Brokes, James, *A Sermon very notable, fruictefu and Godlie made at Paules Cross* (Rouen, 1554).

Burnet, Gilbert, *The History of the Reformation in the Church of England*, 7 vols., ed. N. Pocock, Vols. IV, V, VI, original source material (Oxfort, 1845).

Calender of Letters, Documents and papers relating to the Negotiations between England and Spain . . ., ed. Goyangos, Mattingly, et al (London, 1862-1954).

Chedsey, William, in *Two Sermons*, folios Ai-Fiii, Bound with a sermon of Cuthbert Scot (J. Herford, London, 1545).

Cranmer, Thomas, *A Defense of the true and catholike doctrine of the sacrament of the body and bloud of our saviour Christ* (London, 1550).

_____ , *The Remains of Thomas Cranmer, D.D., Archbishop of Canterbury*,ed. H. Jenkyns (Oxford, 1833).

_____ , *The Works of Thomas Cranmer, Archbishop of Canterbury, Martyr*, 1556, 2 vols., ed. J.E. Cos (Parker Society, Cambridge, 1844-46).

Edgeworth, Roger, Sermons conflated in 1557. (Caly, Rouen, 1557).

English Historical Documents, ed., C.H. Williams (Oxford, 1967).

Erasmus, Desiderius, *The Colloquies of Erasmus*, ed. and trans., C.R. Thompson (Chicago, 1965).

_____ , The Essential Erasmus, ed. and trans. J.P. Dolan (New York, 1964).

_____ , *Erasmi Epistolae*, 12 vols., ed P. Allen (Oxford, 1906-58).

_____ , *Proverbs of Adagies*, trans., R. Taverner (London, 1539).

_____ , *Selected Letters of Desiderius Erasmus*, ed. H. Hillerbrand, trans. M. Haworth (New York, 1970).

Fox, Edward, *Opus eximium de vera differentia* (Berthelet, London, 1534), translated by Henry, Lord Stafford as *The True Differences of Foxe* (Copeland, London, 1548).

Foxe, John, *Actes and Monuments* The Book of Martyrs, 8 vols., ed. G. Townsend (New York, 1965).

Gardiner, Stephen, *A Detection of the Devils Sophistrie wherewith he robbeth the unlearned people of the true byleef, in the most blessed sacrament of the aulter* (J. Herford, London 1546).

_____ , *Declaration of Such True Articles as George Ioye hath gone about to confute as false*(J. Herford, London, 1546).

_____ , *An explicatio and assertion of the true Catholique fayth, touchyng the moost blessed sacrament of the aulter* (Caly? Rouen? 1551).

_____ , *Letters of Stephen Gardiner*, ed. J. A. Muller (Cambridge, 1933). Includes a reconstruction of Gardiner's lost tract against William Turner.

_____ , *Obedience in Church and State*, ed. with introduction by P. Janelle (Cambridge, 1930). Includes the original latin tracts,

Si sedes illa, De vera obedientia and *Contemptum humanae legis*, the first two with contemporaneous translations.

Hall, Edward, *The union of the two noble and illustre famelies Yorke and Lancaster* [known as Hall's Chronicle] ed. H. Ellis (London, 1809).

Harding, Thomas, *A Detection of Sundrie Foule errours* ... (Louvain, 1568).

Harpsfield, Nicholas, *Harpsfield's Life of More*, ed. E.V. Hitchcock, introduction, R. W. Chambers (E.E.T.S., Oxford, 1932).

[Henry VIII?]*An Epistle of Henry VIII to the Emperor, Christian princes and all true Christen men* (Berthelet, London, 1538).

Hooker, Richard, *On the Laws of Ecclesiastical Polity*, 2 vols., ed. C. Morris (London, 1907).

The Institution of a Christen Man [known as *The Bishops' Book*]. Preface by Edward Fox (Berthelet, London, 1537).

Jewel, John, *An apologie or aunswer in defence of the Church of England*, trans. Ann, Lady Bacon (London, 1562).

Joye, George under Pseudonym Sawtry, James, *The defense of the Marriage of Priestes Agenst Gardiner and Repps* (Auryk? 1541).

Kidd, B. editor. *Documents of the Continental Reformation* (Oxford, 1911).

Letters and Papers, Foreign and Domestic, of the Reign of Henry VIII, 1509-1547. Editors, Brewer, Gairdner et al (London, 1862-1932).

Letters to Cromwell and Others on the Suppression of the Monasteries, ed. G.H. Cook (London, 1965).

The Lisle Letters 6 vols ... [ed. Muriel St. Clare Byrne] (Chicago, 1981).

Longland, John, *A Sermond Spoken before the Kynge his maiestie at Grenwiche, uppon good Fryday* (London? 1536).

_____ , *A Sermonde made before the Kynge his maiestye at grenewiche upon good Frydaye* (Petit, London, 1538).

Marsilius of Padua, *The Defensor Pacis*, ed. and trans. by A. Gewirth (New York, 1956). This is the second volume of Professor Gewirth's *Marsilius of Padua, The Defender of the Peace.*

Matthew, Simon, *A Sermon made in the cathedrall churche of Saynt Paul at London* (Berthelet, London, 1535).

Melanchthon, Phillip, *The Epistle unto Kynge Henry the Eight* (Wesel? 1547).

_____ , *The Loci Lommunes of Philip Melanchthon*, ed., C. L. Hill, (Boston, 1944).

_____ , *A Very Godly Defense*. Trans. by Lewes Beuchame (Leipsig? 1541).

Merriman, R. B., *Life and Letters of Thomas Cromwell*, 2 vols. (Oxford, 1902). The second part of volume I, and volume II are the minister's correspondence.

More, Thomas, *The Correspondence of Thomas More*, ed. E. F. Rogers (Princeton, 1947).

More, Thomas, *The Yale Edition of the Complete Works of St. Thomas More* (New Haven, 1963 -).

Morison, Richard, *An exhortation to styr all Engliyshe men to the defense of theyr countrye* (Berthelet, London, 1539).

_____ , *An Inuective Ayenste the great and detectable vice, treason* (Berthelet, London, 1539).

Narratives of the Days of the Reformation, ed. J. G. Nichols (Camden Society, London, 1859).

A Necessary Doctrine and Erudition for any Christen man [*the King's Book*] (London, 1543).

Original Letters Illistrative of English History, ed. H. Ellis, 3rd. series (London, 1846).

Original Letters relative to the English Reformation, ed. H. Robinson (Cambridge, 1846).

Parker, Matthew, *Correspondence of Matthew Parker*, D. D., Editors J. Bruce & T. T. Perowne (Cambridge, 1853).

Proceedings in the Parliaments of Elizabeth I, ed. T. E. Hartley, (Leicester, Wilmington, DE., 1981).

A Protestation made for the most highly and redoubted kynge of Englande & his hole counsell and clergie (Berthelet, London, 1537).

Records of the Reformation, The divorce: 1527-1533, ed. N. Pocock, 2 vols. (Oxford, 1870).

Roper, William, *Life of More*, ed. E. V. Hitchcook (E.E.T.S., Oxford, 1935).

Scot, Cuthbert, in *Two Sermons*, folios. Fiv-Jviii. Bound with a sermon of William Chedsey (J. Herford, London, 1545).

Smith, Richard, *The Assertion & Defense of the Sacrament of the Aulter* (J. Herford, London, 1546).

_____ , *A bouclier of the Catholike fayth of Christes Church* (London, 1554).

_____ , *A brief treatyse settynge forth divers truthes necessary ... whiche are not expressed in the scripture but left to y church by the apostles traditio*(T. Petit, London, 1547).

_____ , *A Confutation of a certen booke ... sette fourth ... in the name of Thomas Archebysshoppe of Canterburye* (? Rouen, 1550).

_____ , *A defence of the Sacrifice of the masse* (Wm. Myddylton, London, 1547).

_____ , *A Godly and faythfull Retraction made and published at Paules crosse* (London, 1547).

_____ , *A Playne Declaration made at Oxford* (R. Wolfe, London, 1547).

_____ , *The Seconde parte of the books called a Bucklar of the Catholyke fayeth* (Caley, Rouen, 1555).

Standish, John, *A Disciourse wherein is debated whether the scripture should be in English for al men to reade that wyle, (Caly, Rouen, 1554).*

Starkey, Thomas, *Starkey's Life and Letters, England in the Reign of Henry VIII*, ed. S. Herrtage (E.E.T.S., Oxford, 1878).

_____ , *An Exhortation to the people instructing them to unity and obedience* (Berthelet, London, 1536?).

State Papers of the reign of Henry VIII, II vols. (London, 1830-52).

Stokesley, John and Tunstall, Cuthbert, *A Letter ... sent unto Reginalde Pole, Cardinall* (R. Woulie, London, 1560).

Strype, John *Ecclesiastical Memorials*, 3 vols. (Oxford, 1822).

_____ , *The Life and Acts of Matthew Parker,3 vols.* (Oxford, 1821).

_____ , *Memorials of Thomas Cranmer,2 vols.* (Oxford, 1840). Both this and the above contain much printed source material.

A Supplycacion to our ... soueraigne lorde Kynge Henry the eyght anon. (uncertain, 1544).

A Treatise Concernynge generall councilles, the Byshoppes of Rome and the Clergy [anon]. (Berthelet, London, 1538).

Tudor Royal Proclamations, vol. 1, 1485-1553, editors P. L. Hughes and J. F. Larkin (New Haven, 1964).

Tunstall, Cuthbert, *Contra Impios Blasphematores Dei Praedestinationis opus Cuthbert Tunstalli Dvnelmensis episcopia* (Antwerp, 1555).

_____ , *A Sermon ... made upon Palme Sondaye last past* (Berthelet, London, 1539).

_____ , *De veritate corporis & sanguinis Domini in Eucharistia* (Paris, 1554).

Turner, William, [pseud, James Sawtry], *The Defence of the Mariage of Priestes* (Auryk? 1541).

Tyndale, William, *The practyses of Prelates* (Marburg? 1530).

Wilkins, David ed., *Concilia Magnae Britanniae et Hiberniae*, 3 vols. (London, 1737).

Wriothesley, Charles, *Chronicle of England*, 2 vols. (Camden Soc., London, 1885).

Secondary Sources

Bainton, Roland, *Erasmus of Christendom* (New York, 1969).

Bernard, G.W., "The Pardon of the Clergy Reconsidered" *Journal of Ecclesiastical History* (April, 1986).

Bradshaw, Brendan, "The Controversial Sir Thomas More," *Journal of Ecclesiastical History* (October, 1985).

Bowker, Margaret, *The Henrician Reformation: The Diocese of Lincoln under John Longland 1521-1547* (Cambridge, 1981).

Block, Joseph, "Thomas Cromwell's Patronage of Preaching" *Sixteenth Century Journal* (April, 1977).

Burn-Murdock, H., *The Development of the Papacy* (Faber, London, n.d.).

Cambridge History of the Bible: The West from the Reformation to the Present Day, ed. S. L. Greenslade (Cambridge, 1963).

Clark, Francis, S. J., *Eucharistic Sacrifice and the Reformation* (Oxford, 1967).

Clebsch, WIlliam, *England's Earliest Protestants* (New Haven, 1964).

Congar, Yves, *Tradition and Traditions* (New York, 1967).

Constant, G., *The Reformation in England: The English Schism and Henry VIII* (London, 1934).

Dickens, A. G., *The English Reformation* (London, 1964).

_____ , *Thomas Cromwell and the English Reformation* (London, 1959).

_____ , *Lollards and Protestants in the Diocese of York, 1509-1558* (Oxford, 1959).

Dix, Dom Gregory, *The Shape of the Liturgy* (Westminster, 1945).

Dowling, Maria, "Anne Boleyn and Reform", *Journal of Ecclesiastical History* (Jan 1984).

Elton, G. R., *Policy and Police* (Cambridge, 1972).

_____ , *Reform and Renewal* (Cambridge, 1973).

_____ , Review of J. McConica's "English Humanists and Reformation Politics", *Historical Journal*, Mar. 1967.

_____ , *Studies in Tudor and Stuart Politics and Government*, 2 vols. (Cambridge, 1974).

The English Reformation Revised [ed. C. Haigh] (Cambridge, 1987).

Evennet, Outram, *The Spirit of the Counter-Reformation* (Cambridge, 1968).

Fenlon, Dermott, *Heresy and Obedience in Tridentine Italy: Cardinal Pole and the Counter-Reformation* (Cambridge, 1972).

Froude, James A., *The History of England from the Fall of Wolsey to the Defeat of the Spanish Armada*, 12 vols. (London, 1898-1901).

Gairdner, James, *Lollardy and the Reformation in England*, 4 vols. (London, 1908).

Guy, J.A., *The Public Career of Sir Thomas More* (New Haven, 1980).

_____ , *Tudor England* (Oxford, 1990).

Hughes, Philip, *The Reformation in England*, 3 vols. (New York, 1963).

Janelle, Pierre, *L'Angleterre Catholique à la vielle du Schisme* (Paris, 1935).

Jedin, Hubert, *A History of the Council of Trent*, vol. i (St. Louis, 1957).

Jordan, W. K., *Edward VI; The Young King* (Cambridge, Mass., 1968).

_____ , *Edward VI: The Threshold of Power* (Cambridge, Mass., 1970).

Knowles, Dom M.D., *The Religious Orders in England: The Tudor Age*, vol. iii (Cambridge, 1961).

Leff, Gordon, *Heresy in the Later Middle Ages*, 2 vols. (New York, 1967).

Lehmberg, S. E., *The Reformation Parliament 1529-1536* (Cambridge, 1970).

_____ , *The Later Parliaments of Henry VIII* (Cambridge, 1977).

Le Van Baumer, Franklin, *The Early Tudor Theory of Kingship* (New York, 1966).

Loach, Jennifer, "The Marian establishment and the Printing Press" *English Historical Review*. (Jan. 1986).

Maclear, G. F. and Williams, W. W., *An Introduction to the Articles of the Church of England (London*, 1895).

Marius, Richard, *Thomas More*, (New York, 1985).

Mayer, Thomas F. "Faction and Ideology: Thomas Starkey's Dialogue". *The Historical Journal* (I. 1985).

_____ , "Starkey and Melancthon on Adiaphora: A Critique of W. Gordon Zeeveld, *Sixteenth Century Journal* (I. 1980).

McConica, James K., *English Humanists and Reformation Politics* (Oxford, 1965).

Morrall, John, *John Gerson and the Great Schism* (Manchester, 1960).

Muller, James *Stephen Gardiner and the Tudor Reaction* (Cambridge, 1926).

The New Cambridge Modern History, vol. iii, *The Counter-Reformation and the Price Revolution*, ed. R. B. Wernham (Cambridge, 1968).

Oakley, Francis, "Edward Foxe, Matthew Paris and the Royal Potestas Ordinis," *Sixteenth Century Journal* (III. 1987).

Parker, T. M., *The English Reformation to 1558* (Oxford, 1950).

_____ , "Was Thomas Cromwell a Machiavellian?", *Journal of Ecclesiastical History* i (1950).

Pickthorn, Kenneth, *Early Tudor Government*, 2 vols. (Cambridge, 1934).

Redworth, Glyn "A Study in the Formulation of Policy: The Genesis and Evolution of the Act of Six Articles", *Journal of Ecclesiastical History*, i. (1986).

Ridley, Jasper, *Thomas Cranmer* (Oxford, 1962).

Sawada, P. A., "Two Anonymous Tudor Treatises on the General Council", *Journal of Ecclesiastical History* (Oct. 1961).

Scarsbrick, J. J., *Henry VIII* (Berkeley, 1968).

_____ , *The Reformation and the English People* (Worcester, 1984).

Slavin, Arthur J., *Humanism, Reform and Reformation in England* (New York, 1969).

Smith, H. Maynard, *Henry VIII and the Reformation* (London, 1962).

Smith, John Holland, *The Great Schism 1378: the Disintegration of the Papacy* (New York, 1970).

Smith, Lacey Baldwin, *Henry VIII: the Mask of Royalty* (London, 1973).

_____ , "Henry VIII and the Protestant Triumph", *American Historical Review(July, 1966).*

_____ , *Tudor Politics and Prelates* (Princeton, 1953).

Surtz, Edward, S. J., *The Works and Days of John Fisher* (Cambridge, Mass., 1967).

Taylor, Jeremy, *Tracts on the Points at Issue between the Churches of England and Rome* (Oxford, 1853).

Tjernagel, N.S., *Henry VIII and the Lutherans* (St. Louis, 1965).

Warnicke, Retha M. *The Rise and Fall of Anne Boleyn,* Cambridge, 1989).

Whiting, Robert, "Abominable Idols: Images and Image-breaking under Henry VIII" *Journal of Ecclesiastical History* (Jan. 1982).

Wood, Antony A., *Athenae Oxoniensis*, ed. P. Bliss (London, 1809).

Zeeveld, W. Gordon, *Foundations of Tudor Policy* (Cambridge, Mass., 1948).

Zell, Michael L., "The Prebendaries' Plot of 1543: A Reconsideration, *Journal of Ecclesiastical History*, (July, 1976).

Notes, Introduction

[1]But in certain dioceses such as Lincoln and Ely, or counties like Lancashire and Sussex, we are learning much more thanks to the work of local historians whose efforts comprise the backbone of new "revisionist" view of the Henrician Reformation. See, e.g. M. Bowker, The Henrician Reformation: *The Diocese of Lincoln under John Longland, 1521-1547* (Cambridge 1981), hereafter, *Bowker*; and C. Haigh, *Reformation and Resistance in Tudor Lancashire* (Cambridge 1973). Some tentative generalizations are reached in *The English Reformation Revised*, ed. C. Haigh (Cambridge, 1987), and J.J. Scarisbreck, *The Reformation and the English People* (Blackwell, Oxford, 1984).

Broadly speaking, the new Revisionists offer a more generous interpretation of Henrician Catholicism among the parish clergy and laity, and are less quick to condemn the motives of the Catholic leaders out of hand. But there has been little attempt to come to grips with the 'ideology' of conforming Catholicism.

[2]See M. Bowker *op.cit.*, pp. 71-74; 78.

Notes, Chapter 1

[1]J.J. Scarisbrick, *Henry VIII*, (Berkeley, 1970), p. 399, a work to which this book is heavily indebted since the author discusses theological aspects of the reign with rare acumen.

[2]*Calendar of State Papers, Spanish*, ed. Bergenroth, Gayangos and Hume, (London, 1862), IV, p. 349. (Hereafter, *Sp. Cal.*)

[3]*Letters and Papers, Domestic and Foreign, of the Reign of Henry VIII*, ed. Brewer, Gairdner and Brodie, (London, 1862-1910), IV, 5415. Letter of Campeggio to Sagna, 3 April 1529. (Hereafter known as *L & P*)

[4]J. Strype, *Ecclesiastical Memorials* . . . , (Oxford, 1822), I, i, p. 172. (Hereafter, Strype, *EM*). According to John Foxe, the government, notwithstanding, continued to persecute those caught with the book. In 1531, bishop Stokesley of London had 12 persons deleted to him for possession of forbidden books, the most frequently named being the Tyndale *New Testament*, but one Michael Lobley, for owning the *Obedience of a Christian Man*. See J. Foxe, *Acts and Monuments* . . . (New York, 1965), V, pp. 24-38. (Hereafter, *Foxe*).

[5]The tale of Anne's presenting Henry with the book no doubt is owed to the "reminiscences" of archdeacon Louthe, who made Foxe a present of this and other anecdotes. See, *Narratives of the Reformation*, ed. J.G. Nichols, Camden Society Old Series (New York, 1968) pp. 52-56. Foxe utilized some of this material, and Strype, other sections. The tale is patently hearsay, since at the time of its occurence, the future archdeacon was only ten years old. Its author, a violent anti-papist, was beneficed under Queen Elizabeth, and several other of his anecdotes do not exactly bear the strain of verification. Yet the essence of this one—that before the breach with Rome, Henry could turn a fair eye to Protestant writings—is borne out by a letter of bishop Nyx of Norwich to archbishop Warham. Nyx complains of the impossibility of dealing with "arronious books in Englesh" and goes on to add that "dyverse saith openly . . . that the Kings grace wolde that they shelde have the said arronious boks, and so mayntayneth themself of the king." The letter is dated 14 May 1530. See J. Strype, *Memorials of . . . Thomas Cranmer*, (Oxford, 1840), II, pp. 694-96.

[6]*L&P*, XI, 117. After Anne's execution it was revealed that Latimer and Shaxton owed the Queen bonds of £200 each. No Catholic ecclesiastics were similarly in her debt. Cranmer's

connection with the Boleyn household is, of course, well known.

[7]*L&P*, X, 797. This was (and is) a patently Catholic devotional practice; much objected to by the Reformers. It is of some interest in this connection that, while awaiting execution, Anne asked for the ministrations of her chaplain, Dr. Skip, who, but a few weeks before her fall had been summoned before the Council for a sermon defending the old practices of the Church, and for warning against all but necessary innovations. See, *ibid.*, X, 615.

[8]*Foxe*, V, pp. 60-61, for a paean of Anne's virtues and piety, somewhat difficult to square with most contemporary accounts. For a more positive appraisal of Anne as a patroness of reform see M. Dowling "Anne Boleyn and Reform", *Journal of Ecclesiastical History* (January 1984) pp. 30-47.

[9]W.G. Zeeveld, *Foundations of Tudor Policy*, (Cambridge, Mass. 1948) for an account of Pole's household and Cromwell's recruitment of scholars therefrom. More recently, Dr. Elton has refined our notions of this recruitment, pointing out that several of the more prominent Henrician publicists such as Starkey and Morison, sought out employment. Their services were not utilized until 1536. See, G.R. Elton, *Reform & Renewal* (Cambridge, 1973), pp. 38-65. (Hereafter, Elton, *R & R*.) Perhaps the aggressive aspect of this recruitment is best illustrated in the prodding of conservatives like Gardiner and Stokesley.

[10]G.R. Elton, *Policy and Police*, (Cambridge, 1972), p. 424. "Contrary to all appearances and recent tradition, Thomas Cromwell really was a genuine sort of Protestant ... " which remark hardly does justice to Professor A.G. Dickens who has been advocating this same thesis these last forty years. I do not myself doubt Cromwell's inclination toward the Reformed religion, especially in his last years. What is less certain is the degree of his commitment. It should be noted too, that piety does not necessarily entail theological interest or competence, and my point is that Cromwell's correspondence yields little evidence of either. Dr. Elton's attempts to suggest otherwise are not, to my mind, entirely convincing. His evidence is drawn largely from avid place seekers like Starkey, or conservatives, like Oliver, anxious to assure the minister of their sincere change of heart. Lacking the confirmation of Cromwell's writing, they must remain suspect as hyperbole. The value of some of these conservative avowals may be judged from the example of Owen Oglethorpe, who wrote to Cromwell seeking preferment on 11 November 1539. In the letter he assured the minister that he was no longer an "addicte" to canon law and schoolmen's phantasies (*L&P*, XIV, 498). Several months later the seventeen part questionaire finds him among the extreme Catholics. Oglethorpe ended as Marian bishop of Carlisle.

[11]G. Burnet, *The History of the Reformation ...* , ed. N. Pocock, (Oxford, 1865), IV, pp. 443-96, and VI, pp. 241-48. (Hereafter given as *Burnet*.) Volumes IV-VI of this work consist of original source material. In volume IV, Burnet has arranged the replies so as to give the individual responses to the questionnaire. The original papers are to be found in *Lambeth MSS, 1108*. Folios 69-70 comprise the questionnaire itself; 71-140, the individual replies of the bishops and theologians, 141-43, a summary of the responses. The questionnaire was set out sometime after April 1540, and the King's comments on a somewhat revised set of responses are to be found in *B.M., Cleo., E VI*, fol. 42. The questionnaire and responses are of great interest, allowing us to make specific inferences as to the theological opinions of the King, his bishops and theologians, at a specific time. Moreover, they are certain proof that the Reformation was not curtailed by the Six Articles. It is also clear that Henry's comments fall considerably to the left of most of his spiritual advisors, particularly in the matter of the sacrament of orders.

[12]*Foxe*, V. pp. 562-64. Henry's proposal was made in Cranmer's presence, and the latter reported it to his secretary, Morice. Foxe names Morice as his source. Interestingly, this was the year that Cranmer was converted by Ridley to a denial of a "physical" presence in the eucharist.

[13]For the diplomatic complications preceding the Council, see H. Jedin, *A History of the Council of Trent*, (St. Louis, 1957), I,pp. 490-554.

[14]Gardiner, then Henry's ambassador to Charles V, pointedly warned the King that any further religious innovations would endanger the Anglo-Imperial alliance; *L&P*. XXI, 109.

[15]Scarisbrick, *op. cit.*, pp. 414-17.

[16]*Burnet*, IV, p. 475.

[17]*ibid.,* p. 477.

[18]*ibid.,* p. 475.

[19]Scarisbrick, *op. cit.,* 253.

[20]Quoted in S.L. Greenslade, *The Cambridge History of the Bible,* (Cambridge, 1963), III, p. 150. The source of this is surely a book of Alexander Aless (or Alesius), *Of the auctoritie of the word of god agaynst the bisshop of London,* (Leipsig? 1538?), fol. Avi. According to Aless, Cromwell, addressing the assembled clergy, told them that it was the King's will that they "conclude all things by the word of god without all brauling or scolding neither will his magesty suffer the scripture to be wrested & defaced by any glossys, any papistical lawes or by auctoryte of doctors or councels and moch less will be admit any articles of doctrine not conteyned in the scripture, but approved only by cetynuance of tyme and olde custome and by unwritten verytes as ye were want to doo." Aless, a Scottish Lutheran, was introduced into this meeting by Cromwell, and made an inpromptu speech much resented by a Catholic majority already discomfited by the Vicar-General's remarks. Aless' tract, published in 1538 at the latest, does not make clear what assembly he is reporting. He does tell us that the events took place the year previously. Is that 1536 or 1537? There was no convocation in the latter year, but certain bishops and theologians did meet to hammer out the details of the so-called "Bishops' Book". C. Wriothesley, *Wriothesley's Chronicle,* Camden Society Old Series, (London, 1885), I, p. 65, mentions a "synod" held in February of that year. Nevertheless, Foxe (*Foxe,* V. p. 378) puts the date at 1536, at convocation prior to the making of the ten articles. This has a basis in Aless' book since he tells us that Bishop Fox of Hereford had just returned from Germany, where he had been engaged in conferences with the Lutheran theologians. This would fix the date at July 1536. James Gairdner, *Lollardy and the Reformation in England, (London, 1908), II, p. 279,* revises Foxe's and his own earlier surmise to 1537, arguing that the Ten Articles—which he interprets as orthodox—"could not have occasioned much, if any controversy." But later analysis has shown how deeply the new theology made inroads into the articles. The matter must still be regarded as unresolved.

[21]For this letter, see *Burnet,* IV, pp. 298-99.

[22]By 1536, the primate's inclinations toward *sola fide* were overt. Aless (*op. cit.,* fol Avii) at the above "synod" has Cranmer posing the question "whether we receyve our iustificacyon thorow fayth". See also *L&P,* XI, 361 (26 August 1536) letter of Cranmer to Henry, where in a rather offhand way, the former reports preaching that our sins are remitted by Christ's death, and that it is an injury to that sacrifice to impute any remission to laws and ceremonies. For the entire letter, see Strype, *Memorials of ... Cranmer,* II, pp. 696-701.

[23]Scarisbrick, *op. cit.,* pp. 406-07.

[24]*ibid.,* p. 408.

[25]Stephen Gardiner, *de vera obedientia,* in *Obedience in Church and State,* ed. P. Janelle. (Cambridge, 1930) p. 117. See also, Edward Fox, *Opus eximium de vera differentia,* (Berthelet, 1538) fol. 78-79. this is the second edition of Fox's work. The first edition, which preceded Gardiner's efforts, was published in 1534.

[26]*L&P,* VII, 690.

[27]Pole's judgment appears in a letter to Contarini: *L&P,* XIV, pt. 2, 54 (16 August 1539). And a similar judgment by a very different man, Dr. Layton, Cromwell's earthy visitor of the monasteries: "if he (Tunstall) would write a book on it (the popes' usurped power) all the kings of Christendom would follow in our master's steps, so great is his learning and reputation." *L&P,* X, 183, letter to Cromwell, 26 January 1536.

[28]*B.M., Cleo., EV,* fol 125; text also given in *Burnet,* IV, pp. 400-04.

[29]*ibid.,* pp. 405-07. For a discussion of the royal contretemps with Bishop Tunstall see G. Redworth. "A study in the Formulation of Policy: The Genesis and Evolution of the Act of Six Articles," *Journal of Ecclesiastical History* (Jan. 1986) pp. 61-62. Hereafter *Redworth, op. cit.*

[30]For Catholic expectations after Anne's fall, see *L&P*, X 752, 881, 992, 947, 956, 1043, 1077. But an interesting letter of this time from Pole to Contarini cautions the latter against high expectations. See, *ibid.*, 1197, Venice, 24 June 1536.

[31]"His Highnes, sumtyme of necessite, sum tyme of policie, hath wisely used them. . ." See, *Letters of Stephen Gardiner*, ed. J.A. Muller, (Cambridge, 1930), p. 162, letter to Paget, Brugge, 5 November 1545. (Hereafter, Gardiner, *Letters*.)

[32]*ibid.*, pp. 300-05. See particularly letters 124 and 125, where Gardiner rebuts Cranmer's charge that Henry was "seduced" into authorizing the "King's Book". Cranmer's letters in the exchange are lost, but there can be no question that Gardiner accurately represents the thrust of Cranmer's argument.

[33]*L&P*, X, 570.

[34]*ibid.*, 975: a precis of Pole's *de Unitate Ecclesiastica*.

[35]And then certainly not at the time his *Opus eximium de vera differentia* was published (see note 25, this chapter.) This work with its appeal to the pope to compose his differences with Henry was published 1534. Fox maintained a reputation for orthodoxy right through the German mission of 1535-36. In 1535, Barnes expressed hope of Fox's conversion (*L&P*, IX, 1030), but as late as the following March, Melanchthon and others found Heath far more sympathetic than Fox (*L&P*, X, 112, 265, 266, 289, 447). But after Fox's return at the end of June, he appears at the forefront of the reforming bishops.

[36]Gardiner, *Letters*, pp. 67-68.

[37]Simon Mathew, *A Sermon made in the cathedrall churche of Saynt Paul at London . . .* (Berthelet, 1535), fol. Cvii-viii. It is possible that Mathew, a canon of S. Paul's, made the sermon at Stokesley's instigation, to counter what the Bishop regarded as rank heresy being preached from the pulpit. But its emphatic Catholicism must have commended it to the government since it was in print a month and three days after its delivery. (See note [39] below)

[38]*L&P*, VIII, 527.

[39]*ibid.*, 1054. The bad blood between Cromwell and the bishop is already evident here. Stokesley's letter seethes with resentment: having refused to produce the sermon, he goes on to complain of "pernicious" doctrines being preached at Paul's Cross, and particularly to the appointment of George Brown, a notorious reformer soon to be made archbishop of Dublin. A year or so later, the Vicar-General will single out Stokesley "by name for defending of unwritten verities." See Aless, *op. cit.*, fol. Avii.

[40]*L&P*, VIII, 600. A letter of John Whalley to Cromwell suggests the government would make more headway with the recusant monks there if they would send men of the "popish sor". A certain Mr. Rastall (More's cousin?) was too advanced in his views and the inmates greeted his efforts with derision. Whalley suggests Cromwell dispatch men such as Edward Lee, Gardiner, Tunstall, Clerk, Longland, Stokesley and the vicar of Croydon. Apparently Cromwell heeded this advice. The letter itself, of April 1535, is clear evidence of the split already existing in the new establishment. Not only does Whalley charge the conforming Catholics with "popery"—though all have renounced the pope—but his list is an accurate one of the leading Catholic partisans in the struggles of the next five years.

[41]H. Ellis (ed.), *Original Letters Illustrative of English History*, (London, 1825), series III, II, pp. 85-86.

[42]*State Papers during the Reign of Henry VIII*, (London, 1830-1852), I, pt. 2, p. 453. (Hereafter given as *St. P.*). Lee protests to Cromwell the King's doubts about the Archbishop's sincere acceptance of the Supremacy.

[43]*L&P*, VIII, 859 for the questions put to Fisher. For the continued harrassment of archbishop Lee see *ibid.*, 869, 870.

[44]This hope proved a vain one, but it is possible Tunstall did hesitate during the early months of the settlement.

[45]J.A. Muller, *Stephen Gardiner and the Tudor Reaction*, (New York, 1926), p. 65.

[46]Gardiner, *Letters*, pp. 328-29. This is a likely interpretation of the somewhat cryptic remark in a letter to Cranmer written from the Fleet: "Wriothesley was not ignorant how you had been disposed toward me before ... and what you had done against me, concerning letters from Germany."

[47]H.M. Smith, *Henry VIII and the Reformation*, (London, 1962), p. 185.

[48]*L&P*, VII, 690: Chapuys reports Edward Lee, Tunstall and Stokesley less than ardent in their defense of the new order. For Tunstall's remark, see *L&P*, VIII, 1082, where the bishop of Durham, like the archbishop of York before him, was invited to defend the sincerity of his submission. Kite's treason is reported in *L&P*, X, 908, Chapuys to Charles V, 19 May 1536. But as far as we can tell, Kite did nothing to abet the Northern rising late in the year. It may be that he was ill: he died February 1537.

[49]This was Kitchin of Llandaff.

[50]*St. P.*, I, pt. 2, p. 428 for the full text of this letter in which the archbishop of York gives his rationale for a Catholic submission to the Supremacy. Edward Lee's obstreperousness toward the 'new order' is discussed in Joseph Block, "Thomas Cromwell's Patronage of Preaching," *Sixteenth Century Journal (April 1977)* pp. 37-50.

[51]*Starkey's Life and Letters, England in the Reign of Henry VIII*, ed., S. Herrtage, Early English Text Society (Oxford, 1878), p. xvii. (Hereafter, Starkey, *Life and Letters*.)

[52]Stephen Gardiner, *si sedes illa*, in *Obedience in Church and State*, p. 37.

[53]*L&P*, XI, 72, 13 July 1536.

[54]Though the "Bishops' Book" attempts to maintain it. The believer is enjoined to "abhorre and deteste all heresies and schismes, wherby the true interpretation and sence of scriptures is or maye be peruerted...." He is also required to believe "that the sayde churche of Rome with all thother partycular churches in the worlde, compacted and unyted togyther, do make and constitute but one catholyque churche or body" which monetheless attains only a "mere spirituall unitie." See, *The Institution of a Christen Man...*, (Berthelet, 1537), fol. 15.

Notes, Chapter 2

[1]In Professor Clebsch's judgment " ... every known Protestant writer owed life and career to Wolsey's gentleness and good humor in dealing with accused heretics ... under him, abjuration and self-exile were the rule, execution the very rare exception. The elevation of Thomas More to the Chancellorship swiftly changed all that ... " See, William A. Clebsch, *England's Earliest Protestants*, (New Haven, 1964), p. 277. The harsher policy however, can not be wholly thrust on More's shoulders, for the executions did not cease upon his resignation from the chancellorship in May 1532. Foxe gives the details of three trials and burnings in 1533, including that of the notable Frith. See, *Foxe*, V, pp. 15-18.

[2]Scarisbrick, *op. cit .*, pp. 265-70

[3]For Fr. Hughes "the question at issue is not whether it was then believed that the pope is ... the earthly head of the Church of Christ, but whether Catholics then believed that he is its head by divine appointment; whether, for them, the papal authority over the Church was a thing divinely ordained. And the first point to be noted is that in 1529 *in the belief of all*, except the people universally reprobated as heretics—Lollards, Hussites, Lutherans, Zwinglians and the like—the divine character of that authority was part of the Christian tradition". See, Philip Hughes, *The Reformation in England*, (New York, 1936), I, p. 199.

It is a key principle of this book that the above quotation does not do justice to the variety of opinion among Catholics on the eve of the Reformation. The previous two hundred years of history had undermined certainty of the divine ordination of the papacy among many informed Catholics. Both Conciliarism and recent investigation into patristics had served to challenge papal claims. It was apparent, for instance, "that whatever Petrine authority amounted to..." in antiquity, it was quite different in magnitude from the full-blown claims of the high medieval papacy. Nor was there yet a theory of "development" to account for the discrepancies. In the minds of pre-Reformation Catholic theologians, the question may be broken down thus: if the papacy was divinely ordained, was this an immediate or mediated grant? And if the latter, was it given by the apostles, or by later Councils? And if the latter, was it granted by the Councils *in perpetuo* and under the guideline of the Holy Spirit (as Thomas More seems to suggest)? Or was it a mere expediency, to be bestowed or taken away as necessity might decree? Certainly those who attempted to defend any but the first propostion were *not* "universally reprobated as heretics". As I will attempt to show, other opinions were well within accepted Catholic tradition.

[4]*Correspondence of Thomas More*, ed. E.F. Rogers, (Princeton, 1947), p. 498.

[5]*L&P*, XI, 73. Starkey to Thomas Cromwell. Starkey, an intimate of Pole's, was convinced the latter was uncertain on the subject of the primacy until the executions of Fisher, More and Reynolds impelled him to rethink his position.

[6]For examples of the use to which some Henrician Catholics could put Cyprian, see *A Letter written by Cuthbert Tunstall late Byshop of Duresme and John Stokesley sometime Byshop of London, sent unto Reginalde Pole . . .* (Reginald Woulie, London, 1560), fol. Bv-vi; and Richard Sampson, *Oratio . . .*, printed in Styrpe, *EM*, I, pt. ii. p. 171. For Cyprian's opinion of the primacy, see, H. Burn-Murdoch, *The Development of the Papacy*, (London, n.d.), pp. 129-34.

[7]For the precedent offered by the French schism, see P. Hughes, *op. cit.*, I, pp. 204-05

[8]Stephen Gardiner, *de vera obedientia*, in *Obedience in Church and State*, p. 125.

[9]Richard Smith, *A brief treatyse settynge forth diuers truthes . . .*, (Thomas Petit, Oxford, 1547), fol. Cvi. (Hereafter, Smith, *A brief treatyse . . .*)

[10]More, *Correspondence*, p. 499.

[11]For Catholic resistance to the papal claims, see H. Jedin, A *History of the Council of Trent*, (Saint Louis, 1957), I, pp. 191-92: a volume to which this chapter is heavily indebted, particularly for the continental background of Henry's Conciliar policy. (Hereafter, Jedin, *op. cit.*)

[12]Quoted in J. Holland Smith, *The Great Schism*, (New York, 1970), p. 205.

[13]Jedin, *op. cit.*, p. 7.

[14]*ibid.*, p. 9.

[15]*ibid.*,p. 10, n. 2. For a more detailed and qualified view of Ockham's role, see Gordon Leff, *Heresy in the Later Middle Ages,* (Manchester, 1967), II, pp. 422-34. Professor Leff shows that though Ockham considered a General Council superior to a pope, he cannot in the strict sense be called a Conciliarist since he did not grant infallibility to Councils, but to the entire Church.

[16]John Morall, *Gerson and the Great Schism*, (Manchester, 1960), p. 82.

[17]*ibid.*, p. 34.

[18]The particular use to which this distinction was put was to deny that the papacy was founded upon divine law, or that the canon law was divine law. So Thomas Starkey explicitly asserts that the Roman primacy is not founded on the "law of God", but arose as a thing "conuenyent to the conseruatyon of the chrystyan vnyte". See, Starkey, *Life and Letters. . .*, p. xix. So too, Richard Sampson, in one of the two earliest apologias for the settlement, could contend that the bishop of Rome's power is founded on "man law". See Strype,*EM*, I, pt. i, p. 241.

[19]Morall, *op. cit.*, p. 47.

[20]*ibid.*, p. 48.

[21]*ibid.*, p. 49. Compare with Starkey's "this I haue euer rekenyed, that dyersyte of opynyon in such thyngys wych perteyne not of necessyte to mannys saluatyon, shold neuer brek loue and amyte betwyx them . . ." See, Starkey, *Life and Letters*, p. xxxiv.

[22]Morall, *op. cit.*, pp. 88-89.

[23]Thomas Starkey, *An exhortation to the people instructynge theym to unitie and obedience*, (Berthelet, London, ?1536), fol. Ri. (Hereafter, Starkey, *Exhortation*)

[24]*Burnet*, VI, p. 182.

[25]*ibid.*, p. 181. The work Tunstall refers to was written while its author was a firm Conciliarist. Later, Nicholas defected to the papal cause and ended his career as Cardinal-bishop of Brixen.

[26]*L&P*, XI, 80. Chapuys to Charles V (14 July 1536).

[27]*ibid.*, XIV, 1003, 1015. The bitter disputes among the bishops which had marked the convocation of 1536, and the preparations for the "Bishops' Book" the following year, were renewed again in 1539, and by any showing, there was far more doctrinal unity among the laity: when the Six Articles were submitted to Parliament, it served to break the doctrinal deadlock among the clergy. (The matter is treated more fully in Chapter 5, this book.)

[28]*Burnet*, VI, pp. 41-46.

[29]Scarisbrick, *op. cit*, pp. 245-50.

[30]It is no intention of mine to enter into the "King of Minister" debate save to note that it is largely irrelevant to the subject of this book. Our real concern is those theological ideas which were used as a platform for the new religious settlement, and here —barring new evidence —it seems unlikely that either the King or Cromwell was originally responsible for them. At the moment, all we can say is that the King was turning them over before the ascendancy of Cromwell. But who *was* responsible for them? This indeed is the mystery, and perhaps the best guess we can hazard at the present is that Cranmer's suggestion to canvass the universities may have turned up more than had been anticipated. For the above debate, see G.R. Elton, *Studies in Tudor and Stuart Politics and Government*, 2 vols., (Cambridge, 1974), I, 173-88, and Scarisbrick, *op. cit.*, pp. 317-397.

[31]*L&P*, VII, 1.

[32]*ibid.*, 690.

[33]*ibid*, X, 133 (19 Jan 1536).

[34]*ibid*, 112. Anthony Musa to Stephen Rothe (Jan 1536). Musa remarks that the King's reformation is entirely contingent upon the divorce. So little had the mission of Fox and Heath impressed the Lutheran divines!

[35]*ibid.*, VIII, 948. Chapuys to Charles V (30 Jun 1535). For Charles' refusal to convoke a Council on his own authority, see Jedin, *op. cit.*, p. 239.

[36]*ibid*, 1105. Chapuys to Charles V (25 July 1535).

[37]*ibid*, 823. Edward Fox to Cromwell (4 June 1535).

[38]*ibid.*, IX, 213. (Sept 1535)

[39]Strype, *EM*, I, pt. 2, pp. 234-35.

[40]Edward Fox's role in the making of the Ten Articles and the "Bishops' Book" is stressed by all contemporary reports. He is mentioned as a leader in the convocation of 1536 (*L&P*, XI, 124), an opinion confirmed by Aless' account of the disputes which took place then, or in the informal meetings of the following February.

[41]It is difficult to believe that the omission of the four sacraments was not deliberate, since it not only left the door open to further negotiations with the Germans, but also —since holy orders was among the four—left open the question of a sacerdotal monarchy, so frequently mooted now in England. Still another memorandum of this time notes certain difficult texts in John and Acts upon which the Catholic stalwarts based the authority of bishops. The memorandum looks to get around these passages, and so eliminate the scriptural foundation of an autonomous clerical order. This is the meaning of the argument for "appointment" rather than "ordination". (*L&P*, XI, 83).

[42]*ibid.*, IX, 704.

[43]*ibid.*, 725.

[44]For the judgment, see *Burnet*, IV, pp. 300-02. According to Wriothesley, the 1536 convocation subscribed to an "act" voiding any summons to a General Council by Pope or Emperor because "this realme is a whole monarchie and an emperiall sea of itself". *Wriothesley's Chronicle*, I, pp. 52-53.

The convocations' judgment plainly grew out of an equally difficult attempt of four of their number to compose an agreement. This is found in *Lambeth MSS* 1107, fol. 163, and begins "for the generall counsaill . . . "Certain of its phrases and arguments did find their way into the official document as when it is asserted that since "now . . . the empire of Rome and the monarchy of the same hath no . . . generall dominion, but many princes haue absolute power in ther owne realms and ay hole and entire monarchie, no one prince may by hys authoritie call any generall counsaille". The document was the work of Cranmer, Clerk, Tunstall and Goodrich, whose signatures are appended. It was no doubt Tunstall and Clerk who added the monitory note which concludes the paper—and which did *not* find its way into the final declaration—that " . . . in all auncient counsailles of the churche in matters of faith and interpretacy of scripture no man may make . . . but busshopes and prestes as the declaration of the worde of god perteynyth to them." This last should be taken as a Catholic retort, the first of several, to the encroachments suggested in note 41 above.

[45]A rather full redaction of the first of these manuscripts is given in *Burnet*, I, pp. 285-88. The second, apparently unknown to Burnet, was published by Burthelet in 1538, and a rare copy is extant in the Lambeth Library. James Gairdner dates these manuscripts 1534 in *L&P*, but this is probably incorrect for the first, and certainly so for the last. The latter, published under the title *A Treatise Concernyngegenerall councilles, the Byshoppes of Rome, and the Clergy*, has the blurred date "1534" on the title page, but the colophon gives "ANNO M.D. XXXVIII . . . Bertheleti" while the anonymous author refers to to General Councils "of late summoned" (Aiii) which could only mean Mantua and Vicenza. Both these manuscripts are discussed by P.A. Sawada. *Two Anonymous Tudor Treatises on the General Council* in *The Journal of Ecclesiastical History*, vol. 12, no. 2, Oct. 1961, pp. 197-214.

[46]J. Gairdner pointed out the handwriting of both manuscripts was not that of Cranmer or his secretaries. In the case of the first manuscript, one might wonder as well if the argument is not too Catholic for the Archbishop's household, e.g., the author admits that a pope may summon a General Council, but not override it by a negative vote. Moreover, the references in the work are purely Conciliar: Gerson's principle of *epikeia* is utilized since "new diseases require new remedies", (*L&P*, VII, 691). Sawada, *op. cit.*, p. 210, suggests Henry Cole as the probable author, and his arguments are persuasive; but if so, then Cole's views had undergone considerable modification when, a quarter of a century later, he undertook to defend the old faith from the challenge of Jewel, and from the point of view of a Conciliarist.

[47]*Burnet*, I, pp. 287-88.

[48][anon.] *A Treatise Concernynge generall councilles, the Byshoppes of Rome, and the Clergy*, (Berthelet, London, 1538), fol. Ai. The work is imperfectly paginated.

[49]ibid., fol. Aii.

[50]*ibid*, fol. Avi.

[51]*ibid*, fol. Bvii.

[52]*ibid.*, fol. Cvi-vii.

[53]Remarkably in this tract, there is no harping on the distinctively Lutheran doctrine of *sola fide* but the anonymous author continually puts forth Lollard or Donatist notions. In the second chapter we are told that "as for the putting away of synne, no prist maye doo it, neyther by the lawe of god, ne by the law of man, for god onely of his mercye, through contricion, which is the very trewe penaunce, putteth away synne . . . " (Avii). In the third chapter, ordination is said to depend upon the spirit of the ordinand: "if they that do it be in grace, it maye doo good, and elles it will do lytel good". Benedictions and hallowings too are said to do good or harm depending on whether the minister is in a state of grace (Aviii). The author roundly condemns the opinion that a minister's "euyll lyfe . . . hurteth not his consecrations & absolutions" (Bi), though he has said earlier of shriving that "no prist mayde doo it".

In the opinion of P.A. Sawada, *op. cit.*, pp. 210-11, Aless is the probable author of this work. On internal evidence, I would question this. Aless, a Scot, was a strong Lutheran; the author of the *Treatise* is more inclined to Lollardy. The style of Aless' tract, *Of the Authority of the Word of God* . . . written at the same time as the *Treatise* is lucid, tight and vehement; that of the *Treatise* is flacid, meandering and uncertain. Aless, fresh from a quarrel with the bishops, is not likely to have included an encomium to the English episcopate which appears in the *Treatise*. (All quotations in the above paragraph are from the *Treatise*.)

[54] *L&P*, VII, 1383. J. Gairdner dates this memorandum 1534, and Elton somewhat hesitantly concurs *R&R*, p. 76) "because it fits the situation much better". The document envisions a strong Protestant program, i.e., no mediator but Christ, denial of purgatory, intercession of the saints, and veneration of images. It also directs inquiry into the meaning of John 20:21 and Acts 20:28 —two key tests upon which the clergy rested an autonomous authority. The "secret" inquiry into the authority of Councils has a similar import: the intent of the document is patently to pave the way for a purely Erastian settlement. In light of the last two concerns, 1536 seems amore likely date, especially since Councils were hardly a major issue in Clement VII's lifetime.

[55] Jedin, *op. cit.*, p. 335, and note 7. The work is *A Protestation made for the most highly and redoubted kynge of England & his hole counsel and the clergie. . .* (Berthelet, London, 1537).

[56] *ibid*, fol. Aiii.

[57] *ibid*, fol. Avi-Avii.

[58] *ibid.*, fol. Aviii.

[59] *ibid.*, fol. Bii-Biv.

[60] *ibid*, fol. Cv-Cvi.

[61] *An Epistle of Henry the Eighth to the emperor, Christian princes and all true Christen men.* . . , (Berthelet, London, 1538).

[62] *ibid.*, fol. Aiii. After putting forth the now familiar claim that no Christian prince more avidly desires a Council, the King goes on to amplify his hesitations: " . . . as our forefathers invented nothynge more holyer than generalle councilles, used as they ought to be, so there is almost noo thyng that may do more hurt to the Chrystan common welthe, to the faith, to our religion . . . if they be abused to luker, to to gaynes, to the establishment of errours". This is nothing but a bare paraphrase of the bishops' judgment on General Councils. (See p. 44, this chapter).

[63] *ibid*, fol. Avii.

[64] D. Wilkins, *Concilia Magnae Britanniae et Hiberniae* 4 vols., (London 1737), iii, p. 825 (hereafter, Wilkins, *Concilia*); *L&P*, XI, 1110.

[65] This is not simply a value judgment of the author: the leading representatives of both parties expressed grave reservations about the book. For Stephen Gardiner, who was away in France when it was made, and who resented having his signature appended to it, the "Bishop' Book" was "a common storehouse whereevery man laid up . . . such ware as he liked". Returning to England, he learned that the book was the tattered compromise obtained after "much stoutnes had been" between Fox and Stokesley. (see, Gardiner, tters p. 345.) Latimer, too, was unhappy with the book for the opposite reason, but thought it was the best that could be had granted the "freylte and grosse capacite" of the majority. (See, *St. P*, I, pt. ii. pp. 563-64.)

[66] *The Institution of a Christen Man* ____, *(Berthelet, London, 1537), fol. Aiii-Aiv.*

[67] For an account of Henry's exercise of the magisterium, see *Scarisbrick, op. cit*, pp. 498-547.

[68] John Standish, *A discourse wherein is debated whether the Scripture should be in English for al men to reade that wyle.* (Caly, London, 1554) fol. Kvii.

[69] *Burnet*, IV, p. 298.

[70] *The Loci Communes of Philip Melanchton* ed. C.L. Hill, (Boston, 1944), pp. 131-35.

[71] *ibid*, p. 141.

[72] *A letter written by Cuthbert Tunstall . . . and John Stokesley,* fol. Dv.

[73] *ibid.*, fol. Bvii.

[74] *L&P* VI, 414.

[75]Starkey, *Life and Letters*, pp. lxii-lxiii.

[76]*ibid.*, p. lx.

*(p. 23) These were Liberius and Zossiums who flourished in the patristic age, and John XIII, who was charged with heresy at Constance in 1414.

*(p. 24) It may be argued that "ultramontanism" found no general acceptance outside Italy until the Napoleonic era. There was still lively resistance to it up to and including the first Vatican Council of 1870.

*(p. 30) The exception to the rule was Osiander of Nuremberg, Cranmer's familiar and uncle-in-law.

*(p. 34) In southern convocation: Cranmer (Canterbury), Goodrich (Ely) , Latimer (Worcester), Shaxton (Salisbury), Fox (Hereford), Barlow (S. David's) and Hilsey (Rochester).

Notes, Chapter 3

[1]See P. Janelle, *L'Angleterre Catholique a la Veille du Schisme*, (Paris,1935) (and hereafter, Janelle, *L'Angleterre Catholique*), and the same author's introduction to *Obedience in Church and State*, three early tracts by Stephen Gardiner, already quoted in this work, and the first two discussed in this chapter.

[2]A.G. Dickens, *The English Reformation*, (London, 1964), p. 158.

[3]*English Historical Documents,*ed., C.H. Williams, (Oxford, 1967), V. p. 738.

[4]K. Pickthorn, *Early Tudor Government*, (Cambridge, 1934), II, p. 201.

[5]See P. Hughes, *op. cit.*, I. pp. 33-41: F. Le Van Baumer, *The Early Tudor Theory of Kingship, (New Haven, 1940), pp. 3-54; Zeeveld, op cit*, pp. 129-35; Dickens, *op. cit.*, pp. 123-25.

[6]Edward Fox, *Opus Eximium de Vera Differentia*, (Berthelet, London, 1535), fols. 45v & 10 respectively. Fox's (Latin) work was reprinted again in 1538, then translated into English as *The True Differences of Foxe* (Copeland, London, 1548) by Henry Lord Stafford. Stafford, an in-law of Pole's, but a strong Reformer, was prodded to his work by Richard Morison.

[7]Even the rigidly orthodox John Fisher held Ockham in high repute. See E. Surtz S.J.,*The Works and Days of John Fisher*, (Cambridge, Mass., 1967), p. 164.

[8]For Marshall's Protestant views see *L & P*, VII, 308; XI, 325. Marshall's "heresies" and "works" were among those that the Northern Pilgrims wished Henry to suppress. *ibid.*, XI, 1246. Maria Dowling in "Anne Boleyn and Reform" *Journal of Ecclesiastical History* (Jan. 1984) p. 41 argues that Marshall was more the Queen's protege' than Cromwell's, but fails to note that Marshall pressed the minister, not Anne, for the Loan.

[9]*ibid.*, VII, 422, 423. But as early as 3 January 1534, Chapuys in a letter to Charles V claimed to be cognizant of this English translation; see *ibid*, VII, 14.

[10]*ibid.*, XI, 1355. Cromwell's factotum Gostwick was pressing Marshall for the debt.

[11]Unlike the works of Fox, Sampson, Gardiner and Simon Mathew, there does not appear to have been any haste to publish to English version of the *Defensor*. Again, one observes the speed with which Mathew's sermon in particular was published, and Cromwell's efforts to press Stokesley into print, and compares them with Marshall's redaction and the year or more wait before its publication. It is difficult not in infer from this—and the fact that the English *Defensor* was *not* published by Berthelet—that Cromwell felt the matter was of small importance. All of which is somewhat odd if Marsiglianism was the guiding genius behind the (1533) Statute in Restraint of Appeals.

[12]Starkey, *Life and Letters*, p. xxv.

[13]Alan Gewirth, *Marsilius of Padua, The Defender of the Peace*, 2 vols., (New York, 1951, 1956), II, pp. 426-30. The second volume of this work is Dr. Gewirth's translation of the *Defensor Pacis* (Hereafter, *Defensor*)

[14]*Defensor*, p. 246.

[15]*ibid.*, p. 271.

[16]*ibid.*, p. 273.

[17]*ibid.*, p. 115.

[18]*ibid.*, pp. 119-21.

[19]*ibid.*, p. 140.

[20]Including S. Thomas, Ockham, Gregory of Rimini and Gerson. For citations of the doctrine of "scriptural sufficiency" see Yves Congar, *Tradition and Traditions*, (New York, 1957), pp. 113-16. In principle, Marsiglio certainly does not go beyond the radical simplicity of S. Bonaventure's dictum, "Omnis veritas salutaris vel in scriptura est, vel ad ipsa emenat, vel ad eam reducitur."

[21]*Defensor*, p. 246.

[22]ibid., p. 290. According to Zeeveld, *Foundations*, pp. 130-31, Starkey's opinion of General Councils follows that of Melanchthon. So far as I have been able to discover, there is no proof that Starkey had read or been impressed by Melanchthon, while it is a fact that he followed Marsiglio. In the matter of summoning Councils and the implementation of their decrees, Starkey is patently a Marsiglian.

[23]*Defensor*, p. 152.

[24]*ibid.*, p. 103.

[25]Quoted in P. Hughes, *op. cit.*, I, p. 332, note 2.

[26]*Defensor*, p. 280.

[27]For a consideration of Starkey's *Dialogue*, and his notion of elective monarchy, see G.R. Elton, *Studies of Tudor and Stuart Politics and Government*, 2 volumes, (Cambridge, 1974), II, p. 240.

[28]"La marche du raisonment est tout a fait la meme que dans le Defensor Pacis". Janelle, *L'Angleterre Catholique*, p. 275. Without denying the essential truth of Janelle's remark, I would attributer considerable influence to the Conciliarists, and the new "historical" humanism.

[29]For a coherent account of Henrician legislation, both in Parliament and Convocation, see S. Lehmberg, *The Reformation Parliament 1529-1536* (Cambridge, 1970) and *The Later Parliaments of Henry VIII* (Cambridge, 1977).

[30]The tract indeed concludes with an appeal to "your holiness" to conclude his difficulties with the King. *Edward Fox, Opus Eximium de Vera Differentia*, fol. (Hereafter, *De Vera Differentia*).

[31]For Fox's diplomatic career, and his work as Henry's agent at the English and continental universities prior to the schism, see Scarisbrick, *op. cit.*, pp. 274-78.

[32]As has been noted, by 1536 Fox was the active leader of the Reformers in convocation. His death in April 1538 was a grave loss to the Protestant faction, as none of his coreligionists commanded his unique blend of worldly acumen, suavity and tact: Latimer, Shaxton and Barlow were too abrasive; Cranmer, too hesitant and timid.

Both Janelle (*Obedience in Church and State*, p. xxiv) and L.B. Smith, *Tudor Prelates and Politics* (Princeton, 1953), p. 305, identify Fox with the "conservatives", while Elton (*P&P*, p. 182) places him by implication with the Reformers at the time of writing *De Vera Differentia*. In fact, Fox was unquestionably of the old school until early 1536: see references in this book, Chapter 1, note 35. While on his mission in Germany, Fox impressed the Lutherans far less than his cohort, Nicholas Heath (subsequently the Marian archbishop of York!). But upon Fox's return home, he led the drive to bring the English Church into conformity with Wittenberg. The testimony of Aless and Gardiner is one at this point.

Francis Oakley in his essay "Edward Foxe, Matthew Paris, and the Royal Potstas Ordinis," (*Sixteenth Centuru Journal* XVIII, No. 3, 1987 pp. 346-353) shows that Henry, Lord Stafford, in his English version of De vera differentia 'Protestantized' Fox's Latin. obscuring the difference between potestas ordinis and potestas jurisdictions, and so implying the Supremacy entailed the power to 'consecrate' bishops. Fox did not suggest this in 1534, but after 1536, everything we know of the Bishop suggests he is a leader of the Lutheran party-which denied that orders were a sacrament.

[33]"Tandem vero succurrebat, huius ambiguitatis certuisimam dissolutionem ex scripturis petendam, in quibus uiget etiam hodie et spirat ille doceret omnem veritatem. Nam aliqui hominum traditionibus, res admodum varia ac diversa habita est." (*De Vera Differentia*, fol. 5). At the synod reported by Aless, Fox took the same line in repudiating Stokesley's defense of "unwrytten verityes". "The doctors and schole writers ... are contrary to themselves also almost in eyery article ... (and) there is no hope of any concorde to be made if we must leane to their judgementes in these matters of controuersy." See A. Aless, *On the auctorite of the Word of God*, fol. Bvii. This little tract offers a vivid picture of Cromwell, Cranmer and Fox.

[34]*De Vera Differentia*, fols. 9→-11. Fox explicitly attacks this Pope whose bull *Exercribilis* prohibited appeals from a papal decision to a future General Council. This is plainly related to the government's policies of 1533 which were still overtly Conciliarist.

[35]ibid., fol. 10.

[36]ibid., fol. 15.

[37]ibid., fol. 17.

[38]ibid., fol. 21.

[39]ibid., fol. 30.

[40]ibid., fol. 32→.

[41]Janelle, *L'Angleterre Catholique*, p. 275.

[42]*De Vera Differentia*, fol. 37. If the right of Kings to execute priests has at this date any contemporary significance, it must be to the contemplated prosecution of the Nun of Kent and her clerical cohorts. But Sampson, as we shall see, makes a similar reference.

[43]*ibid.*, fol. 42.

[44]See the King's own comments in his correction of the "Bishop's Book" in *Miscellaneous Writings and Letters of Thomas Cranmer*, ed. J. Cox, (London, 1846), p. 97; and the implications of question 9 of the 17 questions on the sacraments, *Burnet*, IV, p. 467.

[45]*De Vera Differentia*, fol. 47→.

[46]Janelle, *L'Angleterre Catholique*, p. 272.

[47]Strype, *EM*, I, pt. 1, p. 128. But see p. 203, this book, for the Edwardian development of Sampson's theology.

[48]The original work was published (in Latin) by Berthelet in 1534, and is most readily available in Strype, *EM*, I, pt. 2, no. XLII. For this book, I have used Strype's redaction of Thomas Becon's translation.

[49]*L&P*, VIII, 1062, 1106: IX, 143, 848: X, 7.

[50]*ibid.*, VIII, 603, 604.

[51]Strype, *EM*, pt. 1, pp. 236-37.

[52]*ibid.*, p. 237, and compare with note 42 this chapter. It is perhaps more than coincidental that Sampson repeats Fox here, but almost certainly we should read this as a justification of the executions of the Nun of Kent and her advisors, rather than an attempt to prepare public opinion for the trials of the following summer.

[53]*ibid.*, p. 238.

[54]*ibid.*, p. 239.

[55]*ibid.*, p. 240.

[56]*ibid.*, p. 241.

[57]*ibid.*, p. 243. The division between "divine" and "man law" we have already noted as an essential teaching of Gerson (chapter 2, this book). It is to be found no less in Ockham, Marsiglio and, indeed, Aquinas. It is quite clearly the foundation of "adiaphorism". Sampson is writing this

before Melanchthon's *Loci Communes* was received in England. But in fact, Sampson is merely reiterating the point already made by Fox, who in his turn quoted Innocent III as his authority! (See note 40, this chapter.)

[58]*ibid*, p. 244.

[59]"The matchless, and indispensable leader of the conservative party", so W.K. Jordan, *Edward VI: the Young King*, (Cambridge, Mass., 1968), p. 47, in what may be taken as a representative assessment. After 1540, the judgment cannot be faulted.

[60]In letters written in 1547 to Cranmer and Somerset, Gardiner specifically discharged himself from any role in the making of either the "Bishops' Book" or the "King's Book"—the two "definitive" formulae of a most indefinite settlement. See Gardiner, *Letters*, 302, 345, 365. We must be wary of the attempt, begun in the early 1540's, to bloat Gardiner's importance in the Henrician Catholic faction. It is largely the work of his enemies who increasingly came to see the Bishop as the evil genius of Henry VIII. Most of these wrote after the deaths of Stokesley and Clerk, and after business or ageing had removed Edward Lee, Tunstall, Longland and Sampson from playing the active role they had earlier. In the 1530's Gardiner was not nearly so eminent. I find the above view confirmed—at least by implication-in Redforth *op. cit.*, p. 42. Speaking of Gardiner's putative responsibility for the Six Articles, he writes: "All of the allusions to Gardiner's involvement come from hostile sources, and most of these ascriptions are vague and lacking in circumstantial detail."

[61]See *Obedience in Church and State*, ed. P. Janelle, (Cambridge, 1930), pp. 69-73. (Hereafter, reference will be to Gardiner, and the specific tract.)

[62]For the full text of this letter, see Ellis, *Original Letters*, II, pt. ii, pp. 85-86.

[63]*L&P* VIII, 592.

[64]*ibid*, XI, 213. Fox was dispatched to Germany with books by Cranmer, Melanchthon [sic], and two by Gardiner. One of these was certainly *De Vera Obedientia*, published by Berthelet; the other—nearly as certainly—were manuscript copies of *Si Sedes Illa*.

[65]*ibid.*, XI, 403 (21 Sept. 1535). The precise import of this letter is obscure, but its tone is ironic and slightly deprecating. Was this merely the professional jealousy of a writer who had addressed himself to the same subject, and had been surpassed? Or another manifestation of the rapidly developing division within the settlement. Though a former friend and companion of Gardiner's, Fox manages to hint that the former's "oath" (of Supremacy?) was insincere.

[66]*ibid*, XI, 443.

[67]The brief is given in Janelle, *Obedience in Church and State* pp. 12-19.

[68]Gardiner, *Si sedes illa* p. 27.

[69]*ibid.*, p. 29.

[70]*ibid.*, p. 47.

[71]G.R. Elton, *P&P*, pp. 407-08. Dr. Elton suggests that the Pope's decision to make Fisher a cardinal (the news of which reached England at the end of May 1535) determined Henry to proceed to extremes. Unlike Gardiner, he does not imply the gesture was made in the hope of producing a martyr. It is more likely the Pope had the intention of protecting the imprisoned Bishop from further harm. The probability of this is enhanced by the earlier proceedings against the Nun of Kent, and the executions of the Carthusian priors and Fr. Reynolds which took place on 4 May. With the smaller fry anyway, Henry and Cromwell did not require Papal defiance to exact the ultimate penalty. For the persecution of the last see M.D. Knowles, *The Religious Orders in England, III: The Tudor Age*, (Cambridge, 1959), pp. 182-94, 212-40.

[72]*L&P* VIII, 725 (17 May 1535).

[73]Gardiner, *Si sedes illa*, p. 37.

[74]Janelle, *Obedience in Church and State*, p. lv. However, I would not subscribe to the author's further comment that this work is "permeated with Protestant biblicism". The recourse of Catholic polemicists to the Bible is anything but infrequent, and the particular subject Gardiner

had chosen, obedience, pretty well constrained him to scriptural reference. Moreover, as noted before, the subject of the divorce, still the utmost concern of the government, turned on an appeal to the text of the Old Testament. As we shall see, Gardiner was not slow to turn this to Catholic advantage.

⁷⁵By Janelle himself in his introduction to this work, and again, in *L'Angleterre Catholique* P. Hughes offers a thorough discussion in op. cit., I, pp. 337-41, and Professor Dickens a sharp, comprehensive outline in his *English Reformation*, pp. 241-43.

⁷⁶Janelle, *Obedience in Church and State*, p. xxviii.

⁷⁷For Bonner's preface, see *Foxe*, V, pp. 78-79.

⁷⁸Gardiner, *De Vera Obedientia*, p. 73. (*De Vera Obedientia* comprises pp. 69-159 of Janelle's *Obedience in Church and State*: the left hand pages are the original Berthelet Latin text of 1535, the right hand, the anonymous English translation of 1553.) Here the English words "puddles" and "qualimyres" though representing an accurate option, are a bit stronger than the original Latin. Gardiner's point, one perfectly consonant with his Catholicism, is that Scripture's clear injunction is to be preferred to men's opinions.

⁷⁹"Nihil asse aliud puto uere obedire, quam obedire veritati", *ibid.*, p. 72.

⁸⁰*ibid.*, p. 75.

⁸¹*ibid*, p. 79.

⁸²*ibid.*, p. 83.

⁸³*ibid*, p. 87.

⁸⁴*ibid.*, p. 85.

⁸⁵Many of Gardiner's interventions were made from abroad, and the arguments he advanced were invariably of the *politique* sort. That this powerful polemicist seldom resorts to theological arguments to persuade the King throws an interesting light, not, as is usually assumed, upon the Bishop's theology, but upon the King's "Catholicism". If Henry and Gardiner really shared the same theological views, the Bishop's contentions in these letters would appear to be singularly superfluous. If Gardiner appealed to what Dr. L.B. Smith calls the "new sophistry of human prudence", this was not because *his* views were grounded on such, but rather that he knew that this was the argument which, alone, would carry the cause with Henry.

Early in 1536, Gardiner wrote from France to advise Henry not to accept the draft of an agreement with the German Lutherans. He pointed out that the prospective compact with the German princes would limit Henry's freedom of movement. Furthermore, the King ought not to demean himself by dealing as an equal with those of "lower degrees"—it would undermine his position for these inferiors were technically in rebellion against *their* sovereign, Charles V). If, writes Gardiner, Henry does enter into a compact with the Germans, it must be as their chief. (Text in Strype, *EM*, I, pt. ii, pp. 236-39).

In 1539, Bucer wrote Philip of Hesse that Gardiner had dissuaded Henry from further reformation on the grounds that it would incite the lords of England to insurrection. This, by the way, *after* the passage of the "definitive" Six Articles. (See L.B. Smith, *Tudor Prelates and Politics*, p. 221.)

Seven years later, we find Gardiner again throwing an impediment against further innovations. Then writing from the court of Charles V, he would warn Henry that certain reforms contemplated by the King would imperil the Imperial alliance. (*Foxe*, V, p. 562).

⁸⁶Gardiner, *De Vera Obedientia*, p. 91.

⁸⁷Gardiner, *Si sedes illa*, p. 30, where the bishop describes Fisher's crime as denying that Henry was "principi dei vicario".

⁸⁸Gardiner, *de Vera Obedientia*, p. 95.

⁸⁹P. Hughes, *op. cit.*, I, p. 339.

⁹⁰*Burnet*, IV, pp. 298-99. It is important to note here that the attitude of Catholics and official

Reformers toward the Supremacy was not the same. The second expected considerably more doctrinal initiative from the King.

[91]Gardiner, *De Vera Obedientia*, p.117. This is the now famous formula in English. But, in fact, Gardiner's Latin reads, "Justiniani ... qui leges *aedidit* de summa trinitate, et de fide catholica, de episcopis, de clericis, de haereticis, et caetaris id genus" (italics mine). One notes firstly that the preferred translation of "aedidit" is "put forth", which is somewhat different from "make". I would suggest Gardiner's meaning is Justinian put forth "coercively" those canons already made by churchmen. The reader may recognize that Gardiner's words are scarcely more than a repetition of those of Fox. (See note 45, this chapter.)

[92]*ibid*, p. 129.

[93]*ibid*, p. 135.

[94]*ibid*, p. 137.

[95]*ibid.*, p. 139.

[96]Strype, *EM*, I, pt. i, p. 239.

[97]The reference to Justinian is followed by a number of ancient precedents of emperors who summoned Councils and issued decrees. These are all "orthodox", though Gardiner was surely aware that he had a generous option of Arian emperors, their Councils and their decrees to fall back on. Pondered in this light, the Bishop's examples would indicate that he views the magistrate as an enforcer of orthodox canons made by a visible Church. In short, the ultimate *magisterium* is still the Church. One cannot therefore wholly agree with Professor Dickens' judgment (*The English Reformation*, p. 241) that Gardiner "and his associates were as good as Henricians as their opponents, and intellectually ... stood even closer to the King's conventional mind". The Catholics grudged Henry's right to order religious matters as the Reformers did not. The much referred to "seventeen questions" of 1540 clinches the matter.

[98]Gardiner, *De Vera Obedientia*, pp. 97-103.

[99]Tunstall, *Sermon ... 1539*, fol. Bvii.

[100]For ample evidence of Papist restiveness under the new laws, see Elton, *P&P*, pp. 1-170, passim, an ample and absorbing survey of "Papists muttering in corners".

[101]But see L.B. Smith, *Tudor Prelates and Politics*, p. 204, where the "Bishops' Book" is said to be "a clear expression of their (the Catholics) social philosophy".

[102]Simon Mathew, *Sermon*, fols. Avii, Di. We have quoted Gardiner's dictum (note 73, this chapter). In 1536, Stokesley and Tunstall were assuring Pole that "the Kynges highnes taking upon him ... Supreame heads of the Churche ... dothe nethe make innoacion in the Churche, nor yet trowble the ordre therof ..." (*A letter written by Cuthbert Tunstall __ and John Stokesley ...*, fol. Div. Thomas Starkey, too, somewhat inconstantly it must be admitted, denies "that the defection frome it [Roman authority] ... shulde induce suspition of heresye or schisme..." (Starkey, *Exhortation,* fol Zi).

The argument that the English Church is not in schism appears in certain "official" documents as well, e.g., in the protest against the summons to a Council, a document whose purpose, among others, is to assure Charles V and Francis I that England has not slipped from Catholic Verity (see *A Protestation made for the ... kynge of England*, fol. Avi); and in the *Bishops' Book*, where the English people are adjured to "abhorre and deteste all heresies and schismes..." (*The Institution of a Christen Man*), fol. 15.

[103]So Cranmer in a sermon of 6 Feb. 1536. See, Wriothesley, *Chronicle*, I, pp. 33-34; and *L&P*, X, 283, Chapuys to Granvella (10 Feb. 1536), where the Imperial ambassador has some scathing words for the "notable and good Catholic archbishop of Canterbury" who offered his hearers texts from scripture to prove the Pope is "Antichrist".

[104]Gardiner, *De Vera Obedientia*, p. 147.

[105]Tunstall, *Sermon ... 1539*, fol. Bvii.

*(p. 47) I have not dealt on this book with the polemics of the common-lawyer, Christopher St. Germain since his duel with thomas More preceeded the breach with Rome.

Notes, Chapter 4

[1]These are too numerous to cite in detail, but include the works of Zeeveld, A.G. Dickens, H. Maynard Smith, L.B. Smith and M.D. Knowles. One book however merits special mention: J.K. McConica, *English Humanists and Reformation Politics* (Oxford, 1965) gives a detailed account of Erasmian scholarship in England. Dr. McConica pins down Erasmus' influence to specific writings, and gives an exact account of the facts concerning patronage.

[2]G.R. Elton in his review of McConica, *op. cit.*, in *Historical Journal* vol. X, No. 1, (March 1967), pp. 137-38.

[3]*Tudor Royal Proclamations*, ed. P.L. Hughes & J.F. Larkin (New Haven 1964) I, 287, Proclamation of 1 Edward VI, 31 July 1547.

[4]Scarisbrick, *Reformation and the English People*, p. 47 notes that Erasmus' great influence was among Catholics: "His best friends in England in 1529 were the archbishop of Canterbury ..., the bishop of Rochester, the bishop of London ... and Thomas More." Gardiner and Longland should be added to the list. For a brief account of Lee's controversy with Erasmus see L.B. Smith, *Tudor Prelates and Politics*, pp. 54-55.

[5]Erasmus seems to have held Gerson in unusually high regard. Bainton holds that the Dutch humanist derived his educational theory in part from the Parisian eclectic. See R. Bainton, *Erasmus of Christendom* (New York, 1969), p. 29. See also the reference to Gerson as an "outstanding theologian" in *The Colloquies of Erasmus*, ed. and trans. by Craig Thompson (Chicago, 1965), p. 348. The subject under discussion is exemption from Papal laws. (Hereafter, Erasmus, *Colloquies*)

[6]In the opinion of Dickens (*English Reformation*, p. 230) "the conservatives ... so often trained in the laws and occupied by official duties, lacked both the time and the intellectual background to become worthy exponents and regenerators of Catholic theology". The judgment of P. Hughes, *op. cit.*, I, pp. 72-90 is more detailed and severe.

[7]The phrase "new learning" has a patently Erasmian ring, but I have refrained from using it frequently in this book, since it was utilized indifferently by both Catholics and Reformers at this time. Cranmer, for instance, observes in a discourse on celibacy that "not only men of the newe lerning as they be called but also the very papisticall authors ... hold ... that by the woord of god, priests be not forbidden to marry". Clearly the Archbishop here uses the phrase to characterize those of the Reformed persuasion. See *B.M.*, MSS Cleo, EV, fol. 56 (new pagination).

[8]Numerous letters of Erasmus rebut the charge "I laid the egg; Luther hatched it". On one occasion he replied, "What I laid was a hen's egg; what Luther hatched was altogether different". *See, Erasmus and His Age: Selected Letters of Desiderius Erasmus*, ed. Hans Hillerbrand (New York, 1970), p. 183. (Hereafter, Erasmus, *Selected Letters*)

[9]*ibid.*, p. 31. Letter of October, 1499.

[10]Quoted in *the Essential Erasmus*, trans. J. Dolan, (New York, 1964) p. 208. Letter to John Slechta, November 1519.

[11]Erasmus, *Selected Letters*, pp. 283-84. For other endorsements of "adiaphorism" see pp. 162, 164, 185, 204, 214. A full program of this sort is set out for Charles V's chief minister in the Netherlands on pp. 166-68.

[12]Zeeveld, *Foundation*, p. 141; and Dickens, *English Reformation*, pp. 117, 251.

[13]For Erasmus' attitude to scholasticism and theology in general, see M.D. Knowles, *The Religious Orders in England*, III, pp. 141-56, a masterpiece of descriptive criticism. The accumulation of canon laws, when seen through the lens of S. Vincent's formula, could only be viewed in the light of a burdensome accretion of "man law": it was Ockham and Gerson who first suggested the insidious comparison of the canon law with the law of the Pharisees. But Augustine himself had distinguished between beliefs necessary to salvation and expedient practices.

Erasmus' own list of adiaphora may be most conveniently found in his *Liber de sarcienda Ecclesiae Concordia*. This tract, written in 1533, may be instructively compared to the Henrician polemics of the 1530's, and particularly Starkey's *Exhortation*. The relative freedom of Erasmus from political restraint no doubt accounts for the genuine air of liberalism and impartiality which pervades his work. Reprinted and translated in Dolan, *The Essential Erasmus*, pp. 327-88.

[14]*ibid.*, pp. 384-85,

[15]Strype, *EM*, I, pt. ii, p. 242.

[16]Gardiner, *Letters,* pp. 2-4; 383-85.

[17]Stephen Gardiner, *A declaration of Such True Articles as George Ioye hath gone about to confute as false,* (Johannes Herford, London, 1546), fol. iii. (Hereafter, Gardiner, *A Declaration*).

[18]Gardiner, *Letters*, p. 334.

[19]Gardiner, *A Declaration,* fol. vi.

[20]Gardiner, *Letters*, p. 313.

[21]Erasmus, *Colloquies*, pp. 296-97.

[22]*Burnet*, IV, pp. 447, 452, 458, 461, 469, 475, 486, 488.

[23]Dickens, *English Reformation*, p. 342.

[24]Some Protestant historians exempted Tunstall from their regular condemnation of the Catholic leadership: "Tunstall ... a man of good learning and an unblemished life, these virtues produced one of their ordinary effects in him, great moderation, that was so eminent in him, that at no time did he dip his hands in blood". So *Burnet*, I, p. 70.

[25]Elton, *P&P*, pp. 160-62. Dr. Elton remarks that Stokesley "was in a manner the leader of the conservative hierarchy" and gives an account of the government's attempt to break him by charging him with *praemunire.* This was done, though shortly thereafter the Bishop was pardoned. However Elton's conclusion that the "trick worked" and that in the last year of his life Stokesley "ceased to champion the cause nearest his heart" is wide of the mark. According to Melanchthon, it was Stokesley who was the moving spirit behind the introduction of the Six Articles in Parliament in the spring of 1539 (L&P, XIV, pt. i, 631), an opinion confirmed by Burckhardt who gives Stokesley and Gardiner as the prime movers behind the act (*ibid.*, XIV, pt, ii, 423). Burckhardt, the Saxon emissary, sat on a theological commission to negotiate an agreement with the English Church in 1538. Stokesley, the chief opponent of the agreement, sat with the English team even as he received his pardon from Henry (9 July 1538). Gardiner , at this time, was in France.

[26]The very title of Aless' previously quoted tract gives the "bisshop of London" as the chief adversary of reform. It is Stokesley who is singled out "for defending of unwritten verities" (fol. Avii) by the "lord crumwell". But in spite of the rebuke, Stokesley, quoting S. John and S. Paul, insisted we must "obserue and kepe certe unwritten tradicyons and ceremonys" (fol. Bvi), and defended the "word of god unwritten" (fol. Bvii). We are told the Reformed party smirked at this, but the Bishop must have shown considerable pluck and wit both to defy the Vicar-General and to quote scripture in support of tradition. See, Ales, *Of the auctoritie of the word of god agaynst the bisshop of London.*

[27]E. Hall, *Chronicle,* (New York, 1965), p..319.

[28]*The Earliest English Life of John Fisher,* ed. P. Hughes, (London, 1935), p. 160.

[29]*L&P*, III, 394. The Protestant chronicler Wriothesley reporting the Bishop's obsequies in September 1539 remarks that "he was counted of that sect to be a great papist in his heart", but also describes him generously as "the greatest divine that was counted in this realm of Englande, and also counted for one of the most famous clearkes in Christendome". The funeral sermon was preached by a certain Dr. Hodges who stressed Stokesley's "steadfastnes . . . in all the scysme and division tyme, and the upholding of all the sacramentes and holie ceremonies of the church . . . which he had alwies holden with by his great knowledge of learning". See Wriothesley, *Chronicle*, I. pp. 105-07.

[30]Longland seems to have remained a correspondent of Erasmus until the latter's death. There is a draft of a letter to the Bishop in *Erasmi Epistolae,* ed. H.M. Allen, XII vols., (Oxford, 1096-58), xi, 3108, 16 March 1536. Erasmus' last recorded letter to Tunstall was written in 1530, see *ibid.*, viii, 2263.

[31]See L. B. Smith, *Tudor Prelates and Politics*, pp. 173-74.

[32]*Documents illustrative of the Continental Reformation*, ed. B.J. Kidd, (Oxford, 1911), pp. 314-15. (Hereafter, Kidd, *Documents*).

[33]The documents speaks of "abusus magnus et perniciosus in gymnasticus . . . inquibus multi philosophae professores impietam docent, imo in templis fiunt disputationes impiissimae: et se quae sunt piae, tractantur in eis res divine coram populo valde irreverenter". *ibid.*, p. 315. Gardiner gives an amusing example of just such a disputation: see Gardiner, *Letters*, p. 407.

[34]Wyllyam Peryn, *Thre godlye and notable Sermons of the moost honorable and blessed Sacrament of the Aulter,* (John Herforde, London, n.d.). Peryn, a former Dominican, has occasional recourse to Aquinas, and the the arguments of the 3rd sermon are modeled on the questiones disputatiae.

[35]Quoted in F. Clark, *Eucharistic Sacrifice and the Reformation*, (Oxford, 1967), p. 136.

[36]The Ten Articles made no mention of four sacraments while the *Bishops' Book* notes that particular churches "do moche dyffre and be discreptant . . . not onely in the dyersite of nations and excellencye of certayne suche gyftes of the holy goost . . . but also in the dyuerse usynge . . . of such outwards rytes, ceremonies, traditions, and ordynaunces, as be instituted by theyr gouernours . . . " *The Institution of a Christen Man*, fol. 15.

[37]Starkey does not figure in contemporary accounts of the reign such as Wriothesley or Hall, or the polemics of Aless, Bale, Turner, Joye, Gardiner, Tunstall or Standish. He is not discussed in the narratives of Foxe, and only once, and that incorrectly, by Burnet, who singles him out (mistakenly) as one of the King's advisors in the divorce; see *Burnet*, I. p. 279. Strype alone mentions Starkey as a "very learned man" and gives two abstracts of the *Exhortation*, but never once refers to his doctrine of the "mean", much less mention Starkey as a source of the *via media*. Strype's abstracts are concerned with the repudiation of the primacy. See Strype, *EM*, I, pt. i, pp. 266-67, 514-18.

[38]". . . adiaphorism . . . became through Starkey, the direct ideological forebear of the Anglican polity . . . it was through him that it became anglicized in the form in which it appeared in the Thirty nine Articles . . . in Hooker . . . and in Laud". Zeeveld, *Foundations*, p. 129.

[39]". . . it was he who introduced Melanchthon's doctrine of *adiaphora* or things indifferent to a permanent place in the Anglican scheme". Dickens, *English Reformation*, p. 251. "Starkey . . . stands at the beginning of the long line of writers on the middle way (*via media*) . . . "See, *Humanism, Reform & Reformation*, ed. A.J. Slavin, (New York, 1969), p. 121, . . . with justice he has been seen as the first specific advocate of the Anglican *via media*". See Elton, *P&P*, p. 193. But Prof. Elton has his suspicions, and later he attributes the *via media* to Cromwell's inspiration of Starkey. See Elton, R&R, p. 52.

[40]Starkey, *Life and Letters*, p. x.

[41]Starkey remained on confidential terms with the Pole family in England (see *ibid.*, p. lxv) while his will remembered Pole's brother, Lord Montague (Zeeveld *Foundations*, p. 227). Even as Starkey was dying, the government struck at the family, and Lord Montague was executed in December 1538. Richard Morison, a polemicist as poisonous as Bale, but without the saving grace of the latter's transcendent convictions, wrote a book justifying the executions. Of the Poles he writes that they would "putte any theyr seruantes out of seruyce, yf they were spyed with anew testamente in theyr handes" and he conjectures whether Cardinal Pole put this notion in their heads or whether they were inspired by their "chaplayns accordyng to theyr heartes, menne desyrefulle to kepe them . . . from the knowledge of theyr duties, fromm the light of god, his word, whyche they hated, aboue all thynges". One wonders if Starkey was one of those whom Morison had in mind. True, they had been friends, and Starkey had once furthered Morison's cause with Cromwell, but Pole, too, had been a benefactor of Morison's. See Richarde Morisyne, *An Inuective Ayenste the great and detestable vice of treason* (Berthelet, London, 1539), fol. xxviii.

[42]The *Dialogue* is the concluding section of Starkey, *Life and Letters*. It is discussed in P. Hughes, op. cit, I, pp. 28-31. For the dating of the Dialogue see Thomas F. Mayer, "Faction and ideology: Thomas Starkey's dialogue" *The Historical Journal* (I. 1985) pp. 1-25.

[43]See G. R. Elton, *R&R*, pp. 38-65 for a masterly and precise evalua on of Cromwell's role as a patron of scholarship and reform. My only qualification of Elton's judgment is that the writings published were too narrowly honed by circumstantial utility and —in Starkey's case certainly —by intimidation. Of Starkey's works, only the *Exhortation* was published, and that, on Dr. Elton's own demonstration, after he was made to conform his thought to Cromwell's direction. A comparison less flattering to the minister might be made between the careers of Starkey and Morison. The last grew from strength to strength under Cromwell's aegis, and published no less than five books in four years. Of the two, Morison was much the more lively, serviceable and malleable writer, but a far less distinguished thinker.

[44]*L&P*, VIII, 575.

[45]Starkey, *Exhortation,* fol. Mi-Tiv. (Though paginated as well in Roman numerals, these are confused in the publication.)

[46]Elton, *R&R*, p. 51.

[47]While Frith awaited the trial that was to lead to his execution in 1533, Tyndale wrote him two letters of advice. The first described the doctrine of the Real Presence as an "indifferent thing until the matter can be discussed at leisure" and warned him not to "engage in doubtful matters". The second repeated the advice to "stick at necessary things". (L&P, VI, 403, 458). Frith maintained this position though it did not save him. Earlier, Latimer had written Warham in defense of his position "I owe it is lawful to make use of images, to go on pilgrimages, to pray to saints, to be mindful of purgatory. But these things are voluntary, and are to be moderated by God's commands of necesary obligation on which I stand fixed". (*ibid.*, V, 859, March, 1532). In these Protestant examples, there is no mention of Melanchthon, though we know these men went through an Erasmian phase prior to their conversion to the Reformation. We do indeed find Melanchthon mentioned in a latter of Edward Lee, who appealed to the German doctor's principle of finding a consensus among the Church fathers. But to confuse matters, Lee is plainly one of the most unbending Catholics among the bishops (see *L&P*, IX, 704). Simon Mathew too, in a sermon noteworthy for its uncompromising Catholicism refers to the "dapnable techynges . . . which haue caused men to leaue the commandementes of god undone for the humane traditions". See, Mathew, *Sermon*, fol. Bii.

[48]Zeeveld, *Foundations*, p. 152, note 69.

[49]In the autumn of 1535, Fox was sent as the president of a high-powered embassy to reach an accord with the Protestant princes. His instructions mention keeping to a mean between the Papists on one hand, and the Sacramentaries and Anabaptists on the other: see *L&P*, IX, 213. Agreement was scuttled by German insistence on the acceptance of the Augsburg Confession *in toto,* and by Gardiner's aforementioned counsel to Henry, exposing the disadvantages of English submission.

[50]Elton, *R&R*, p. 51.

[51]I have been unable to find evidence that Starkey had the smallest influence upon Cranmer, Ridley, Hooper or Jewel, nor, more surprisingly, upon Hooker, Andrewes or Taylor. Admittedly, Edwardian and Elizabethan Anglicanism were notoriously "low" but one might expect reference to Starkey among the founders of the Jacobean and Caroline revival. In *Tracts ascribed to Richard Bancroft*, ed. A. Peel (Cambridge, 1953), the anonymous author, almost certainly Elizabeth's last Archbishop of Canterbury, undertakes the defense of the remaining ceremonies, rites and vestments of the Church against the "precisions". The author calls to his defense the weighty authority of Calvin, but also Bucer, Gualter, Bullinger, Peter Martyr, Beza and Jewel. There is no recourse to Melanchthon—or for that matter any Lutheran theologian—much less say Starkey.

[52]Starkey, *Exhortation,* fol. Fiv. G.R. Elton's assertion that Starkey denied purgatory is mistaken (Elton, *P&P*, p. 194). What Starkey rejects (like Simon Mathew before him), is the "new fashion" of purgatory which led to the popes' "pardons and reseruations" (fol. Riii) but he explicitly defends the notion, insisting that the "ancient maysters of Christis doctrine . . . say & affirme such a place to be, where in mans sowle shall be purged from alle spottes of worldly affection . . . " (fol. Wiv). Indeed, Starkey's later letter to the King makes clear that, like Mathew

and Longland, he was uncomfortable with the governments' line on purgatory; see, Starkey, *Life and Letters*, p. liv.

[53]Starkey, *Exhortation*, fol. Giv.

[54]*ibid..,*, fol. xii.

[55]*ibid.,.,* fol. Ci.

[56]*ibid..,*, fol. Tii.

[57]*ibid.,* fol. Hi. "If there is one consistent strand on Starkey's thought conciliarism is it" asserts Mayer, *op. cit.,*, p. 17, n. 94. Dr. Mayer has also argued to the extreme unlikelihood of Melancthon's influence on Starkey; see T. Mayer, "Starkey and Melancthon on Adiaphora", *Sixteenth Century Journal* (XI, no. 1, 1980) pp. 39-49. The tenor of these two articles is similar to mine, though Dr. Mayer concentrates largely on Starkeys political theory. His chronology is meticulous, and he is able to resolve certain problems that have previously bedevilled the Starkey enigma. I have not been able to avail myself of Dr. Mayer's unpublished doctrine thesis.

[58]*ibid.,* Yii.

[59]Jewel, whose *Apologia* was the classic defense of the 1559 settlement, had a difficult time defending the few outward relics—such as linen surplices-retained by the Church. Yet with respect to doctrine, he was able to reassure a Swiss colleague that "we have pared every thing away to the very quick". Quoted in N.M. Southgate, *John Jewel and the Problem of Doctrinal Authority* (Cambridge, Mass., 1962), p. 96.

[60]Starkey, *Exhortation*, fol. Ri.

[61]Modern historians who have asserted Starkey's influence on the settlement have hardly taken into account this charge of popery and its significance. (See *L&P*, XI, 157, 169, 170).

[62]Most of this letter is given in Starkey, *Life and Letters*, pp. xlviii-lxi. There is an illuminating discussion of it in Elton, *R&R*, pp. 52-55.

[63]Starkey, *Life and Letters*, p. li.

[64]*ibid.,* p. xlix.

[65]*ibid.,* p. l.

[66]*ibid.,* p. li.

[67]Mary's final submission to the King was made in late June, 1536; see *L&P*, X, 1021. Her reservations were well known, and Starkey's outspoken praise of her is another bit of evidence of his theological alignment.

[68]Starkey, *Life and Letters,* p. lii.

[69]*ibid.*

[70]See Erasmus' pragmatic defense of the old order in *Liber de Sarcienda Ecclesiae Concordia*, printed in J. Dolan, *The Essential Erasmus*, especially pp. 378-88.

[71]Starkey, *Life and Letters*, p. liii.

[72]*ibid.*

[73]*ibid.,* p. liv. The word "releuyd" certainly implies a traditional and Catholic notion of purgatory. See also note 52, this chapter.

[74]*ibid.,* p. lv.

[75]*ibid.,* pp. lv-lvi.

[76]*ibid.,* p. lvi.

[77]*ibid.,* p. lviii. Starkey is the *only* Henrician Catholic who favored a married clergy. It is important to grasp that this does not point to a more 'Protestant' tendency—the Orthodox parish clergy permitted marriage, as did the Latins until the eleventh century. In other matters, as we shall see, he is more 'Catholic' than his comperes.

[78]*ibid.* Compare the sentiments of Stephen Gardiner, *Letters*, p. 218, where the Bishop pleads

that St. Cross, a hospitaliers establishment, be spared and goes on to lament the decay of other fine monastic buildings. St. Cross is still one of the most handsome edifices in the British Isles.

[79] Starkey, *Life and Letters*, p. lix.

[80]*ibid.*

[81]*ibid.*, p. lxi. These words repeat a contrast already made in the *Exhortation.*

[82]*ibid.*

[83]*ibid.*, p. lxii. Starkey here echoes a commonplace of the Henrician Catholic polemic against the Reformers. Tunstall's position is examined in the following chapter.

[84]This is Zeeveld's opinion and it is followed with greater reservations by Professor Dickens. Its danger lies in failing to discriminate between theological and political liberalism. Starkey, like Erasmus, is certainly an exemplar of the first, but hardly the second. Whatever his private reservations about the executions of More, Fisher and Reynolds, expressed in the letter to Henry, he publicly supported the government in the *Exhortation* (fol. Gii-iii). In a paper on preaching,, Starkey contends that those who stray from the long-received tradition of the Church, where this is not repugnant to God's word or the Royal prerogative, should be taken as seditious, and their goods and bodies put at the King's disposal (L&P, IX, 1160). It is important to understand that for Starkey, adiaphora may be determined by the King and the common council: to flout this determination is "damnable", and the miscreant should be punished. This position is Marsiglian, not liberal.

[85]See P. Hughes, *op. cit.*, III, p. 70-71. Through use of the Zurich correspondence, Hughes shows that Jewel, Grindal and Horne greatly feared a Lutheran settlement in England. Gualter cautioned the English Reformers against the Lutherans whose doctrines seem to be "carnal judgment to full of moderation, and especially adopted to the promotion of concord". In truth, writes Gualter, they contain the "seed of popery". In the situation of 1559, it is plain that, in the eyes of the new leadership, Lutheranism was the mean or fulcrum between Catholicism and the Reformed religion.

[86]Calvin described these as "tolerabiles ineptiae". See T. M. Parker, *Protestantism and Confessional Strife* in *The New Cambridge Modern History*, III, e. R.B. Wernham (Cambridge, 1968), pp. 72-125. The above quotation is found on p. 78, and there is a terse consideration of the theology of the Marian exiles and their relationship to the new Elizabethan settlement on pp. 106-10.

*(p. 72) I have not forgotten the so-called "commonwealth men". But these, even the earliest, were Protestants, as Erasmus—and Starkey—were not.

Notes, Chapter 5

[1]One exception to this generalization is a lost book of Stephen Gardiner's, *The Examination of the Hunter*, which has been reconstructed by J. A. Muller from William Turner's surviving rebuttal of it. See, Gardiner, *Letters*, pp. 480-92.

[2]See *L&P*, VIII, 1054 (July, 1535). It is probably no coincidence that a few days after Mathew's sermon which explicitly bids his congregation to pray for the dead (see note 10 below), Stokesley wrote a highly indignant letter to Cromwell complaining of the appointment of George Browne to the roster of preachers at Paul's Cross. He particularly fears that Browne will "maintain his indiscreet fashion of remembrance of the souls departed" and set forth some "pernicious" doctrine.

[3]Simon Mathew, *A Sermon made in the cathedrall churche of Saynt Paul at London . . .* , (Berthelet, 1535), fols. Bii, Cvii.

[4]*Ibid.*, fol. Avi.

[5]*Ibid.*, fol. Avii.

[6]*Ibid.*, fol. Aviii.

[7]*Ibid.* This notion appears to have been a commonplace of the Tunstall-Stokesley circle.

[8] *Ibid.*, fol. Bii.

[9] *Ibid.*, fol. Di.

[10] *Ibid.*, fols. Avi-Avii.

[11] *A Sermod Spoken before the Kynge his maiestie at Grenwiche Vppon good fryday, 1536* (no publisher's colophon), hereafter referred to as Longland, *1536*; and *A Sermonde made before the Kynge his maiestie at grenewiche vpon good frydaye*, (Thomas Petit, 1538), hereafter: Longland, *1538*

[12] For treatment of these devotional writings, see Dickens, *English Reformation*, pp. 18-40, and McConica, *English Humanists and Reformation Politics*. But a more detailed study of this aspect of the Catholic decline remains to be written.

[13] A story widely believed but denied by More's early biographer, William Roper. See *Lives of Saint Thomas More*, ed. E.E. Reynolds, London, 1963, p. 76. According to Roper, Longland's confessor and chaplain, Dr. Draycott, heard of the rumor and broached it to the Bishop. Longland insisted that the reverse was true, that the King had raised the matter to him and never ceased to harp upon it until the Bishop had given his consent, which he afterward bitterly repented. Margaret Bowker, the historian of the diocese of Lincoln under Longland's rule, holds that Longland "was entirely in agreement with the King over the dissolution of the Marriage", but does not take account of Roper's assertion. See, Margaret Bowker, *The Henrician Reformation, The Diocese of Lincoln Under John Longland, 1521-1547*, (Cambtridge, 1981) p. 14.

[14] *LP*, XI, 714.

[15] *Ibid.*, 705.

[16] See, Aless, *Of the Auctoritie of the Word of God ...* , fol. Avii, where Aless numbers Longland among the supporters of "unwritten verities"; and *LP*, VIII, 600; IX, 20, 611, X, 804.

[17] *LP*, X, 891; XI, 136, 137, 138; and G.H. Cook. (ed.), *Letters to Thomas Cromwell and Others on the Suppression of the Monasteries*, (London, 1965), p. 76.

[18] Foxe, *V*, p. 454.

[19] *Ibid.*

[20] For Longland's career, see Anthony Wood, *Athenae Oxoniensis*, ed. P. Bliss, (New York, 1967), I, 161, and Bowker, *The Henrician Reformation*, passim, but especially pp. 8-15.

[21] *LP*, XVI, 449 (12 Jan 1541) where Marillac reports Longland's arrest and the seizure of his papers. But apparently nothing compromising was discovered for the Bishop was on hand in his cathedral city to receive the King during the latter's progress in the North in the summer of 1541.

[22] *Burnet*, VI, p. 103; *St. P.*, I, p. 411. Note particularly item three.

[23] Longland, *Sermon, 1536*, fol. Aii-iii.

[24] *Ibid.*, fol. Bi.

[25] *Ibid.*, fol. Di.

[26] *Ibid.*, fol. Fiv. To Prof. Brendan Bradshaw I owe the interesting suggestion that Longland's remarks look backward to Henry's complications with his first wife, and this is a possibility, though I think a remote one. Longland's sermon was delivered on April 14; twelve days later, Chapuys is telling Charles V that Stokesley has already been consulted by the King with a view to dissolving the second marriage, the obvious ground being Henry's previous cohabitation with Anne's sister. Stokesley had told Chapuys that he had been wary of giving his opinion, but clearly the Bishop was pleased by the difficulties of Anne and her cohorts. It is difficult to imagine that a Catholic like Longland was not aware of the opportunities opened to their faction by the weakening of Anne's position. On the other hand, since Catherine had died the previous January, a reference to *that* incestuous complication would seem somewhat gratuitous. (See, *LP*, X, 752.)

[27] Longland, *Sermon, 1536*. fol. Giv.

[28] *Ibid.*, fol. Hii.

[29] *Ibid.*, fol. Hiv.

[30] *Ibid.*, fol. Lv.

[31] But the publisher is Thomas Petyt, not Berthelet, the usual "official" printer.

[32] Longland, *Sermon, 1538*, fol. Bii.

[33] *Ibid.*, fol. Ci-ii.

[34] *Ibid.*, fol., Diii. There is an excellent possibility that the Bishop's derogation of human merit owed nothing either to Lutheran or government influences. it is perhaps suggestive that the Bishop's nephew, Richard Pate, became, along with Pole, the most outspoken of the solefidians at the Council of Trent. After his flight from Henry's service, Pate retired to Pole's household, and in 1543, was created bishop of Worcester by Paul III. He returned to assume his diocesan duties during the reign of Mary. For Pate's career in Italy, see D. Fenlon, *Heresy and Obedience in Tridentine italy, Cardinal Pole and the Counter Reformation*, (Cambridge, 1972), pp. 144-60.

[35] Longland, *Sermon, 1538*, fol. Diii.

[36] *Ibid.*, fols. Eii-iii.

[37] Longland's Catholic puritanism is evident in his tendency to blend the terms "flesh" and "sin". In Henrician literature, it is the Catholics who regularly uphold an attitude of censorious puritanism.

[38] *Burnet*, IV, P.341.

[39] Longland, *Sermon, 1538*, fol. Gii. See also the comments of M. Bowker, in *The English Reformation Revised* (Cambridge, 1987) pp. 86-87.

[40] *Ibid.*, fol Hiv.

[41] *Ibid.*, fol. Gii.

[42] *Ibid.*, fol. Ki.

[43] Elton, *P&P*, pp. 189-90.

[44] Tunstall, *Sermon, 1539*, fol. Bv.

[45] *Ibid.*, fol. Bvii.

[46] *Ibid.*, fol. Bvi.

[47] *Ibid.*, fol. Bvii.

[48] *Ibid.*, fol. Ci.

[49] *LP*, X, 183.

[50] Tunstall, *Sermon, 1539*, fol. Eii.

[51] *Ibid.*, fol. Ei.

[52] See Richard Morison, *An Inuective Ayenste the great and detestable vice, treason ...* , (Berthelet, London, 1539), fol. xxv, where Pole is apostrophied thus: "all men must hate the,yea thy mother her selfe shall thynke her selfe worthy deth if she not hate the aboue all creatures." This harping upon ingratitude comes strangely from one who, as a self-confessed starveling, found refuge in Pole's household, In light of Cromwell's recently elevated status as a patron of learning and humanism, it is worth comparing the careers of Morison and Starkey and their respective attitudes toward their former patron, Pole.

[53] Tunstall, *Sermon, 1539*, fols. Evii-viii.

[54] *Ibid.*, fol. Eviii.

[55] *Ibid.*, fol. Fi.

[56] *Ibid.*, fol Eviii.

[57] For the texts of Tunstall's letter and the King's reply (the latter incorrectly postdated by two years), see Wilkins, *Concilia*, iii, pp. 742, 762-65.

[58] Tunstall, *Sermon, 1539*, fols. Cv-vi.

[59] Tunstall's letter and Henry's reply are printed in *Burnet*, IV, pp. 400-07. The Bishop's

trenchant commentary on Matt. 18 is "Remittere autem aut solvere nemo potest id quod ignorat; occulta autem peccata nemo praeter peccantem novit nisi solus Deus; quare nisi peccata aperiantur sacerdoti, nec earligare nec solvere posset". (*Ibid.*,p. 401) We have already noted that the tone of the King's reply did not encourage further discussion. It should be added that the King aligned himself explicitly with Cranmer in this controversy (*Ibid.*, p. 405). Henry's letter speaks of the discussion taking place "in our house"—which suggests the debates preceding the fomulation of the Six Articles.

⁶⁰Tunstall, *Sermon, 1539*, fol. Fii.

⁶¹*Ibid.*, fol. Cvi.

⁶²*Ibid.*, fol. Ciii.

⁶³*Ibid.*, fol. Dvii.

⁶⁴The following account of the Six Articles owes much to J. Ridley, *Thomas Cranmer* (Oxford, 1962) pp. 178-79; S. Lehmberg, *The Later Parliments of Henry VIII* (Cambridge, 1977) pp.58-74; and G. Redworth, *op.cit*, passim. The last gives detailed emphasis to the potentially dangerous détente between France and the Empire in inclining Henry toward the appearances of orthodoxy. But all three writers incline to the view that the Articles express in the words of Redworth, "The King's traditionalist frame of mind at the time" (*op.cit*, p. 46). Thougout this book I have tried to argue that Henry grew increasingly opportunistic in religious matters. Certainly the King was active in the emasculation of the Articles, and already shortly after they were passed. See this book. pp. 143-46.

⁶⁵*LP*, XIV,pt. 2, 423. Burckdardt had been present in England for the abortive negotiations with the Lutherans in 1538. In these, Tunstall and Stokesley took a prominent, if unaccommodating part.

⁶⁶We have already noted the King's views on auricular confession. Not infrequently historians have adduced Henry's continuing attachment to the old faith from his unswerving support of clerical celibacy. But in fact, the King seems less motivated by theological than secular considerations. In 1541, Henry took umbrage with the concord reached at Ratisbon in which the Catholics conceded the point of celibacy as well as utraquism. He gave as a reason for his pique that the clergy through marriage, and the possibility of hereditary benefices, would build up wealth and power equivalent to that of the secular princes (*LP*, 733, 737).

This suggestion is reinforced by an attack on celibacy written by an exile, and published in 1541. Norfolk, the author tells us, gave a "pollitike reason in the parlement" for advancing celibacy, for "scripture knoweth the non". The Duke is reported as saying that the clergy would marry daughters of gentlefolk and so increase their power beyond measure.

The reference is likely to the debates accompanying the adoption of the Six Articles, and serves to support the notion that the peer was acting as a stalking-horse for the government, and that in good part, the impetus behind the Articles was political. See James Sawtry, *The defence of the Mariage of Preistes Agenst Gardiner and Repps*, (Jan Troost, Auryk? 1541), fol. Cii.

⁶⁷*LP*, XIV, pt. 2, 186 (Bucer to Philip of Hesse, 16 September 1539).

⁶⁸*Burnet*, VI, pp. 243-45. A copy of a set of answers with Henry's annotations in the margin.

⁶⁹*LP*, XIV, pt. 2, 423.

⁷⁰*Ibid.*, 430. For Bonner's role in the publication of the "Great Bible" see H.M. Smith, *Henry VIII and the Reformation*, pp. 336-337; and Dickens, *English Reformation*, pp. 189-90.

⁷¹*LP*, XIV, pt. 2 477.

⁷²*Ibid.*, 543.

⁷³*Ibid.*, 498.

⁷⁴*Ibid.*, 601. This is the same Crome whose attack on "masses satisfactory" will be discussed in the following chapter.

⁷⁵*Ibid.*, 750.

⁷⁶*Ibid.*, 736, 737. Marillac to Francis I and Montmorency, 1 June 1540. For Sampson's earlier

difficulties with Cromwell, see Strype, *EM*, pt. 2, pp. 378-80.

[77]Scarisbrick, *op.cit.*, pp. 380-83.

[78]For a discussion of Barnes' theology, see W. Clebsch, *England's Earliest Protestants*, pp. 58-77.

[79]There is a precis of Barnes' *Protestation* in *Foxe*, V, pp. 434-36. An edition of the work appeared in Wittenberg with a preface by Luther.

[80]John Standish, *A Little Treatise Against the Prestation of R. Barnes*, (Redman, London, 1540), fol. Av. There are two editions of this work, both published in 1540. I have used the second, slightly expanded version.

[81]*Ibid.*, fol. Avi. Standish claims to have heard Barnes preach words to that effect two years previously at Barking. Curiously, the charge repelled by Barnes, of preaching that Our Lady was no better than a saffron bag, had surfaced before as one of the propositions condemned by the lower house of Convocation in 1536. It appears to have been of Lollard, not Lutheran inspiration. See Strype, *EM*, I, pt. 2, p. 261. This protest of the lower clergy is known as the "mala dogmata".

[82]*Ibid.*, fol. Aiiii-v.

[83]*Ibid.*, fols. Aviii-Bv.

[84]*Ibid.*, fol. Dvii. Standish's argument reappears in Richard Smith's confutation of Cranmer's book on the eucharist, and in the writing of the Marian author, James Brooke.

[85]*Ibid.*, fols. Dvii-viii.

[86]*Ibid.*, fol. Eiii.

[87]*Ibid.*, fols. Avii-viii.

[88]*Ibid.*, fol. Av.

[89]*Ibid.*, Gardiner repeats the charge that the Reformers have inverted the order of the Lord's Prayer in his 1546 polemic against George Joye.

[90]*Ibid.*, fol. Fv.

[91]*Ibid.*

[92]*Ibid.*, fol. Gi. These words lend veracity to Gardiner's later depiction of his relations with Barnes.

[93]*Ibid.*, fol. Gii.

[94]See Anthony a Wood, *Anthenae Oxoniensis*, ed. P. Bliss, (New York, 1967), 235. The relative neglect of Standish may have its root in his biography: the consistency of his thought was not equalled by the consistency of his life. He apparently conformed and married under Edward, but greeted the accession of Mary with loud hosannahs. Under Elizabeth he was deprived of his archdeaconry, but retained his prebendary, which suggests a second conformity to the national Church. Neither party has been anxious to claim him as their own. Nevertheless his writings, this tract, and two later works written during the reign of Mary, identify him as a Catholic: though he died in 1570, there is no indication that he published a line in favor of the Reformed doctrines.

[95]Standish, *A Little Treatise*, fol. Ciii.

[96]*Ibid.* Among the devotional practices upheld are the veneration of the Blessed Virgin (Avi), intercession and the communion of the saints (Diiii, Eiii, Evii), fasting and other ascetical practices (Biv).

[97]*Ibid.*, fol. Fv.

[98]Standish, the boldest of the Henrician Catholics until now (1540) in his defence of the visible Church, still qualifies this lamely: "Christes Churche, that is to saye, in this region y kynges maiesty with his learned councell"! But what if the King and his Council ordain something less than orthodoxy? Standish does not even consider the question. For the above quotation, *Ibid.*, fol. Ev.

*(p. 90) Not even with Tunstall himself. Much of the sermon is a mere rehash of the letter

written jointly with Stokesley to Pole in 1536. But the letter was not published until 1560. (See chapter 2, note 6)

Notes, Chapter 6

[1] *L&P*, XVI, 45. See also Wilkins, *Concilia*, iii, pp. 860-61 for a list of Latin terms Gardiner wished to have reinserted in the official bible. The orginal annotations of Gardiner are in *Lambeth MS*, no. 140.

[2] For an account of Cranmer's activities during the last years of the reign see J. Ridley, *Cranmer*, pp. 246-57. 1543 was also the year of the so-called Prebendaries Plot which Henry adjudicated entirely to the Catholics' disadvantage. *L&P* XVIII, pt. 2, 546, devotes 88 pages to this affair. Alone it is quite sufficient to raise doubts about the unmitigated prevalence of Catholicism in the years subsequent to Cromwell's fall. For a detailed discussion of the local ramifications of the "plot" see M.L. Zell "The Prebendaries Plot of 1543; a Reconsideration" *Journal of Ecclesiastrical History* (July 1976) pp. 241-53.

[3] The testimony on this point is somewhat confusing. According to Gardiner's letter to the Privy Council written at the end of August 1547, the chief makers of the book were Heath, Day and Thirlby. He explicitly disavows any role for himself, and as for Cranmer, if the Archbishop had had any part in the book, Gardiner would have been only too glad to have taxed him with it, for it was at this time that he was charging Cranmer with going back on his original subscription. See, Gardiner, *Letters*, p. 365. The convocation record also makes mention of Thirlby, Heath, Salcot and Skip, and (somewhat ambiguously) Cranmer. I am inclined to believe Gardiner rather than what is possibly a dressed-up official record. It is inconceivable he would have misrepresented a matter to which he was an intimate witness, and where moreover, there was no advantage to a lie which might be so easily detected. For convocation's record, see *L&P*, XVIII, pt. 1, 365.

[4] But note the qualifications of this orthodoxy in Scarisbrick, *Henry VIII*, pp. 534, 540, 543.

[5] *Burnet*, IV, pp. 443-96.

[6] Only Bonner, however, remained steadfast into the next reign, and was early imprisoned and then deprived. Skip voted regularly against the major innovations in Edward's time, but must have been prepared to support them once enacted, for he retained his doicese down to his death in 1552. Salcot voted for the first act of Uniformity in 1549, but was absent from the voting on the new ordinal (1550) and the Second Prayer Book (1552). But he submitted to Mary and retained his diocese down to his death in 1557. See P. Hughes, *Reformation in England*, II, pp. 106, 113-14, 123. Some nine years after Salcot's death, he was described by Thomas Harding as "soft, sensual and loth to displease the Prince" but also as a known Catholic, see Thomas Harding, *A Detection of Sundrie foule errours* . . ., (Louvain, 1568), fols. 242-43.

[7] After his detention in the Tower (May, 1540), Sampson was made to relinquish his promotion to Westminster. But in 1543, restored to favor, he was translated to Coventry & Lichfield to replace the recently deceased Rowland Lee. Like his predecessor he assumed with his diocese the Presidency of the Council of Wales, an absorbing task which left him scant time for theological ruminations. In this decade, his theological conservatism became somewhat loosened. He abandoned the straightforward doctrine of transubstantiation by 1548 (see, *Burnet*, V, p. 202) and voted for the first act of Uniformity. Absent from later votes on the ordinal and the Second Prayer Book, he, too kept his diocese during the most radical years of Edward, only to turn again at the accession of Mary. He died in retention of his diocese in 1554.

Tunstall, who also had played a major role in the theological controversaries of the 1530's, was wholly absorbed in the business of the Council of the North in the next decade. In 1547, Gardiner voiced suspicion of him, proof, anyway, of the lack of coordination among the catholic leadership, for Tunstall voted *only* for the bill ordaining communion in both kinds (1548) and against the ordinal and the first Act of Uniformity. He does however, appear to have been ready to carry out these reforms once they were instituted by law. In 1551, he was imprisoned and deprived. During his incarceration he wrote two brief but beautifully reasoned Latin tracts, one in support of the Mass, the other against the absolute predestinarians.

⁸For Longland's arrest, see *L&P*, XVI, 449, Marillac to Francis I (12 Jan 1541) . More indicative, no mention is made tht he played any role in the apprehension of Anne Askew, though that obstreperous lady had made Lincoln cathedral an early theatre of her activities. See *Foxe*, V, p. 541.

⁹For the careers of the prelates appointed after 1540, see L.B. Smith, *Tudor Prelates and Politics*. With the singular exception of George Day, none of these played any role in resisting the Edwardian innovations. To a man they were undistinguished theologically, favoring neither one side nor the other. Typical of their number were Wakeman, Holgate, Knight and Kitchin.

¹⁰*L&P*, XXI, 109, 110; for Henry's letter to Cranmer, see *Burnet*, V, 355-56, for the legislation concerning Chantries collegiate endowments and religious fraternities see Lehmberg, *Later Parliaments*, pp. 221-222; and Scarisbrick, *Reformation and the English People*, passim, but especially pp. 65-67.

¹¹For Crome's arrest, see *Foxe*, V, p. 537. There is a lengthy discussion of Crome's sermon and the subsequent purge in J. Gardiner, *Lollardy and the Reformation*, II, pp. 434-61.

¹²*Foxe* V, p. 692.

¹³For a discussion of the King's orthodoxy, see the article of L.B. Smith, "Henry VIII and the Protestant Triumph", *The American Historical Review*, LXXI, No. 4 (July 1966), pp. 1237-64. In Dr. Smith's opinion, Henry's exclusion of Gardiner and his appointment of a largely Protestant regency council is explained by the King's greater fear of restoration of Popery, not by any interest in furthering reform as such. Dr. Smith's interpretation cannot be lightly dismissed: there is evidence both for and against it. For Dr. Smith, as for Dr. McConica before him, Queen Catherine Parr's circle and the tutors of the young Prince Edward are primarily scholars and Erasmian humanists. This view is more than a little dubious, especially in light of Anne Askew's interrogation. Moreover, Dr. Smith is perhaps a little mellow about Richard Cox, whose orthodoxy he vouches for (until 1547) by the latter's association with the *King's Book*. But, Cox, after all, was heavily outnumbered, and his responses to the seventeen questions some three years earlier reveal him well to the left of the others save Cranmer and Barlow. One cannot help but wonder that Henry did not find more Catholic tutors for the young Prince.

Nor, I think, can one grant Dr. Smith's premise that because certain men gave outward conformity to the official formulae, they can be regarded as moderates. True, the King insisted on good form being observed, but that either Henry or others at the court were deceived by this, I cannot believe. As early as 1535, as we have noted, there seems to have been little doubt as to where this or that particular person stood with regard to the Reformation. We might, I think, dissipate some of this confusion if we begin by assuming that Henry, for politic reasons, insisted upon conformity and not orthodoxy. Like his daughter, he was not prepared "to make windows into mens' souls".

¹⁴The literature of Cranmer's eucharistic beliefs is enormous. There is an excellent account, unmarred by special pleading, in Dom Gregory Dix, *The Shape of the Liturgy*, (Westminster, 1964), pp. 640-74.

¹⁵Roger Edgeworth, *Sermons, conflated in 1557*, (n.p., 1557) I have not been able to avail myself of a copy of Edgeworth's *Sermons* of the 1540 edition, but apparently this work was reissued with little, if any, editing in Queen Mary's time. Several times the author implies that Henry was a good Catholic, once actually mentioning him as the author of the *Assertio*, but not the schism! (see fol. iv). The author argues to the existence of purgatory (fol. xxi), and mentions his troubles with Latimer in Bristol and with Barlow at Wells. Another argument anticipates that of Smith and James Brooke when the author confesses that the scriptures "hath not the sayd word Purgatory", but goes on to note that in the same scriptures "wee reade not this word TRINITAS, or thys worde CONSUBSTANCIALIS, yet God forbid that we should denye the Blessed Trinitie in the Godhead or the sonne to be ... of one substance with the father ..." (fol. xxi).

¹⁶Among the most famous exiles were Tyndale, John Rogers, Bale, George Joye, William Roy and Coverdale. Since most followed Frith's views on the eucharist, the possibility of accommodation with the settlement was slender indeed. The exiles were voluminous writers, often the only source for certain biographical details of the lives of the Catholic leadership. It is from Joye,

for instance (under a pseudonym) that we learn that Norfolk gave "politike" reasons for his support of celibacy in Parliament, but also that Bishop Repps (Rugge) of Norwich was a "dronke blak monke", and that Stokesley remarked that it is better for a priest "to live alone yea to have an C whores then to be maryed". Needless to say, these details must be taken with a grain of salt, but are valuable nonetheless. The first assertion seems very likely, in that it tallies with the King's later sentiments about the (abortive) agreement reached at Ratisbon. From statements such as the second we may deduce, not that the bishop of Norwich was a dypsomaniac, but a strong Catholic persecutor. James Sawtry, *The defence of the Mariage of Priestes* ... , fol.. Cii, Av, Aiii, in order of quotation.

[17]John Bale, *The Epistle exhortatorye of an Englyshe Christiane agaynste the pompouse popyshe Bysshoppes* ..., pseydonym: Henry Stalbrydge (Basle, 1544), fol. ii.

[18]*Ibid.*, fol. ix.. Germane Gardiner, the Bishop's secretary, and possibly a nephew, was executed for popery in 1544. Foxe, reporting a conversation of Suffolk and Cranmer, gives the incident as a cause of Henry's increasing distrust of the Bishop.

[19]*Ibid.*, fol. xxiiii.

[20]*Ibid.*, fol. viii. We must remind ourselves that Bonner is not yet Marian bishop of London. Bale is castigating him for his part in the trial of Richard Mekyns in 1541.

[21]*Ibid.*, fol. xiiii. Edward Lee was dead in 1544; his successor, Robert Holgate would not be installed until the following year. It is doubtful if Bale had received news of Lee's death prior to publication. Holgate, then a moderate, had no reputation as an ardent Catholic or a persecutor. In the following reign he would conform himself nicely to the Reformation. Yet "without wytte" seems a much more accurate characterization of Holgate, a political bishop and a trimmer, than Lee who was both a renown theologian and a generous patron of learning (oddly, the archbishop was Ascham's patron.) Lee, however, was a firm Catholic and a Thomist which could easily explain Bale's phrase.

[22]*Ibid.*, fol. xviii.

[23]William Chedsey, *A Sermon Preached at Paules Cross* ...(J. Herford, London 1545), fol. Ciii. Chedsey preached this sermon on 16 Nov 1543. It is bound with Cuthbert Scot's sermon preached the following year, and the publishing date given as 1545. I have used the Lambeth Library copy of this little known work.

[24]See J. Strype, *The Life and Acts of Matthew Parker*, 3 vols., (Oxford, 1821), vol. II, pp. 20-30. The correspondence consists of six letters between Gardiner and Parker and one final missive from the Council. One cannot but admire the vice-chancellor's skill in protecting the culprits, and Gardiner's pertinacity in getting to the root of the matter.

[25]Cuthbert Scot, *Here begynneth Master Scottes sermon* ..., (see note 51 above: Scot's sermon begins at fol. Fiv), fol. Fviii-Gii.

[26]*Ibid.*, fols. Giii-iv.

[27]*Ibid.*, fols. Hii-iv.

[28]*Ibid.*, fols. Hvii-viii.

[29]See A. G. Dickens, *Thomas Cromwell and the English Reformation*, p. 23 for the services rendered by the London clothing merchants to the financing of Tynedale's New Testament.

[30]Scot, *Sermon*, fols. Iii-iii.

[31]*Ibid.*, fols. Jvi-vii.

[32]In the sneering words of George Joye: "seldon are these popyshe lawers good dyuines ... "See Gardiner, *A Declaration of Such True Articles* ..., fol. lii.

[33]The phrase appears to have originated with Bale in the work quoted above (see note 17). For the most recent use see Redworth *op. cit.*, p. 45. Mr. Redworth's use is ironic in an article pointing out that Gardiner was either out of favor or out of England as the Six Articles were being prepared.

[34]See Gardiner, *Letters*, p. 316. Dr. Muller's edition of the Bishop's correspondence contains

numerous examples of his wit, e.g., the marvelous passages on preaching, as true today as when they were written (pp. 311-314), a caustic dismissal of Cranmer's (somewhat ingenuous) explanation of his change of heart on the eucharist (p..448), observations on the morals of the clergy of Lancashire (p. 386), his revelling in an absurd scholastic conundrum (p. 407), or his droll comments on Nicholas Udall's translation of Erasmus' *Paraphrases*: "In a longe work ... a slumbre is pardonable, but this translator was a sleep when he began." (p. 418).

[35] *DNB*, vol. VII, pp. 863-64.

[36] These later works, written in Latin, centered on the question of celibacy. All were published in Louvain, and are listed in the bibliographic appendix (II) of James Muller, *Stephen Gardiner and the Tudor Reaction*, (New York, 1926), pp. 309-18.

[37] Gardiner, *Obedience in Church and State*, pp. 175, 177.

[38] Gardiner, *Letters*, pp. 408-92. There appears to be no surviving copy of the work itself.

[39] *Ibid.*, p. 482.

[40] *Ibid.*, pp. 485-86.

[41] *Ibid.*, p. 487. Here again is the insistence that the Orthodox Church has kept Catholicism intact without papalism.

[42] Gardiner, *Letters*, p. 163.

[43] Clebsch, *England's Earliest Protestants*, pp. 44-48, for the details of Barnes' early career. I cannot agree with Professor Clebsch's opinion that "the entire proceeding mystified Barnes". Barnes, if you like, was the Tyll Eulenspiegel of the English Reformation: his protestations of innocence must be taken with a grain of salt. Moreover, he had already evinced a talent for putting his opponents in the wrong. Of course, I do not intend to deny the courage or conviction of the man.

[44] L.B. Smith, *Tudor Prelates and Politics*, p. 36.

[45] Gardiner, *A Declaration of Such True Articles* ..., fol. v. Gardiner does add that his chancellor "thoughte it better to disapoynte Barnes on the morowe, then some catholique man, appointed on other sondayes".

[46] *Ibid.*

[47] *Ibid.*, fol. viii.

[48] *Ibid.*, fol. ix. In the course of their brief reconciliation, Gardiner offered Barnes a benefice worth v 40 a year.

[49] But not before an admirer of Barnes "had written to a friend at court how gaily they had all handled the matter, both to satisfy the recantation and also in the same sermons to utter out the truth.... "This letter by "negligence" came into the hands of the Council (to which Gardiner had not yet been readmitted), and it was the Council that consigned Barnes, Jerome and Garrett to the Tower on April 3rd.

In light of the above, it is difficult to understand the insistence of Dr. Scarisbrick that "Gardiner—though he later denied this—somehow contrived to have the three quickly transported to the Tower". I cannot see any evidence either that Gardiner was in fact behind it, or, for that matter, that the case entailed much contrivance. Scarisbrick gives *Foxe*, V, pp. 430-34 as his source, but a check of this passage reveals that Foxe follows Gardiner's account of the incident almost verbatim. Foxe does allege (incorrectly) that Gardiner says the letter fell into Cromwell's hands, and commenting on the Bishop's insistence that he was not party to their incarceration, adds that the "said Gardiner cannot persuade us to the contrary". With no evidence at all, Foxe suggests privy sessions with the King and secret whisperings at Court as the Bishop's devices. Granting Foxe's loathing of Gardiner, the vagueness of his charges, and the fact that Gardiner seems his only source for the incident, this seems very slender evidence indeed for the indictment. A far more likely interpretation is that Barnes' *volte-face* during the recantation, and the unfortunate letter posed an intolerable affront to the government's authority.

See J. Muller, *Stephen Gardiner and the Tudor Reaction*, pp. 87-89; and Scarisbrick, *Henry VIII*, pp. 378-82.

50Gardiner, *A Declaration* . . . , fol. x.

51*Ibid.*, fol. xii.

52*Ibid.*, fol. xvi.

53*Ibid.*, fol. ssii. In connection with this, and very shrewdly, Joye and the reformers are convicted of "idolatry"—or words. See,*Ibid.*, fol. xxxiv.

54*Ibid.*, fols. xxviii-xxix.

55*Ibid.*, fol. xxx.

56*Ibid.*, fol. xxxii.

57*Ibid.*, fols. xxxii-xxxiii.

58*Ibid.*, fol. xli.

59Aside from the replies to Bucer already noted, Gardiner wrote two ripostes to Cranmer on the eucharist in the following reign. Indeed, while in prison, Gardiner wrote continual polemics against Cranmer, Bucer, Peter Martyr, Hooper and Oecalampadius. See, J. Muller, *Stephen Gardiner and the Tudor Reaction,*pp. 313-14.

60The mixture of pomp and straightforwardness in Gardiner's demeanor recalls that of his first patron. But I cannot subscribe to the judgment of Professor Dickens: "In this field of court intrigue he proved himself an even subtler schemer; the memory of his humble origins certainly failed to soften a proud and ambitious spirit. Unlike Cranmer he was every inch a man of affairs, a committee-leader and negotiator who never achieved the rank of a statesman" (*English Reformation*, p. 241).

It does not seem irrelevant that this subtle schemer failed thrice to maintain his preeminence at court: in 1534, 1539, and most disastrously, in 1546. He seems in fact to have been outfoxed by Cromwell, Wriothesley, Paget, Seymour, and—yes—Cranmer; his frequent diplomatic missions kept him precariously away from the center of things. The Archbishop too, was a man of affairs, and (in my judgment) a much finer committee-leader and negotiator than Gardiner. And while I would agree with Professor Dickens that the Bishop evinced no "marked spiritual endowments" (he did, however, suffer close imprisonment for his faith), I would suggest that these were not too evident in Cranmer's career either. The widest gap between the two men was one of temperment: Gardiner was bumptious: Cranmer, reserved and calm. We still tend to look at Gardiner through the lens ground by Bale and Foxe.

61See William Peryn, *Thre godlye and notable Sermons, of the moost honorable and blessed sacrament of the Aulter*, (John Herforde, London, n.d.), fol. Aii (hereafter, Peryn, *Thre Sermons*).

62*L&P*, XXI, pt. 2, 710. Feckenham, the future Marian Abbot of Westminster, would be prominent among the disputants for the old faith in the first months of Elizabeth's reign. At this sermon, on 16 January 1547 (new style), Bonner was in attendance, a fact the Council thought noteworthy. For Feckenham's defense of the old religion—and that of Nicholas Health, archbishop of York, and Cuthbert Scot, bishop of Chester—consult *Proceedings of the Parliaments of Elizabeth I*, [ed. T.E. Hartley] (Lelcester-Wilmington, 1981), pp. 7-32. All three men were prominent Henricians.

63Stephen Gardiner, *A Detection of the Devils Sophistrie, wherewith he robbeth the unlearned people of the true byleaf, in the most blessed Sacrament of the aulter*, (John Herforde, London, 1546), fol. ii. (Hereafter, Gardiner, *A Detection*).

64*Ibid*, fols. vi-viii. The above arguments offer striking examples of Gardiner's use of *reductio ad absurdam.*

65*Ibid*, fol. ix. Gardiner appears to have been one of the first Catholic theologians to have detected the drift toward spiritualism in the new doctrines, particularly those of Zwinglian origin. He retaliated with an insistence that the Christian economy of salvation finds its paradigm in the Incarnation: as Christ took flesh, so in the eucharist He is body and blood, soul and divinity. The same principle is applied to the justification of sensuous worship.

The above argument recalls the point made against Turner, that Christ used such homely things as spittle and his garment to work miracles. Gardiner will strike the same note again in a letter to Ridley, where he makes the point that, on the latter's axioms, we might well condemn the printing of the Bible since it gives us graven images of a world beyond. (See Gardiner, *Letters*, p. 258.)

In spite of the weakness of his ecclesiology (as compared to Smith or Peryn) Gardiner's perception of how the Incarnation might be utilized to justify the Catholic paraphernalia of worship, his imaginative style, and his insight into his opponents' inadequacies, made him the most dangerous of the Catholic polemicists.

⁶⁶Gardiner, *A Detection*, fol. xviii.

⁶⁷*Ibid.*, fols. xxxvii-lix.

⁶⁸*Ibid.*, fols. lxvi-lxvii.

⁶⁹*Ibid.*, fol. lxxxiv.

⁷⁰*Ibid.*, fol. cxl.

⁷¹*Ibid.*, fol. cliii.

⁷²Gardiner, *A Declaration*, fol. lv.

*(p. 103) Crome, as far as we can tell, a Lutheran, did not deny the real Presence, but only that the mass was a sacrifice to be applied to the benefit of the quick and the dead.

*(p. 105) These are Edmund Bonner, John Longland, Cuthbert Tunstall, Edward Lee (but see footnote 21), George Day and John Salcot. Wilson, only a priest, had one time shared imprisonment with More and Fisher, but had later conformed. He was still a firm Catholic.

*(p. 114) It was incumbent on Gardiner to use the word "some" since Catholics, like their adversaries, accepted the efficacy of infant baptism. There are then, some of mankind, who do not cooperate in their own salvation.

Notes: Chapter 7—Concluding Remarks

¹See Strype, *EM*, pt. II, pp. 260-66; Wilkins, *Concilia, iii, pp. 804-07.* These are an interesting melange of Lollard, Lutheran and Anabaptist opinion.

²Wilkins, *Concilia*, III, 762-73.

³*The Institution of a Christen Man*, preface by Edward Fox, (Berthelet, London, 1537), fol. Aiii-iv, where Fox, speaking for the bishops, writes, "we do most humbly submyt it to the most excellent wysdome & exact judgment of your maiestie, to be recognised, oversene, *and corrected, if your grace that finde any worde or sentence in it were to be changed, qualified or further expounded ... whereunto we shall in that case conforme our selfes, as to our most bounded duties to god* and to your highnes apperteineth." (italics mine)

⁴Ed. J.E. Cox, *The works of Thomas Cranmer, Archbishop of Canterbury, Martyr, 1556,* (Cambridge, 1844), p. 98.

⁵*Ibid*, p. 97.

⁶*The Institution of a Christen Man*, fol. 15.

⁷Richard Smith, *A Defence of the sacrifice of the Masse*, (Wyllyam Myddlton, 1547), fol. xlii. Smith himself dates the preface of this book September, 1546. (Hereafter, Smith, *A Defence.*)

⁸Richard Smith, *The Assertion and Defence of the sacramente of the aulter* (J. Herford, London, 1546), fol. 56. (Hereafter Richard Smith, *The Assertion ...*).

⁹Richard Smith, *A brief treatyse settynge forth diuers truthes necessary both to be belieued of chrysten people & kept also, whiche are not expressed in the scripture but left to y church by the apostles traditio,* (London, 1547, preface. Unpaginated. (Hereafter, Richard Smith, *A brief treatyse ...*).

¹⁰Longland, *Sermon.... 1536,* fol. Aiv; for Aldrich's reference to Thomas Walden (or Netter) see *Burnet*, IV, p. 447.

[11]Richard Smith, *A Defence* ..., fol. xix; and again in his *A Confutation of a certen book, called a defence of the true and Catholike doctrine of the sacramet* ..., (Caly, Rouen, 1550), fol. 13. (Hereafter, Richard Smith, *A confutation* ...).

[12]Gardiner, *Letters*, pp. 291-94.

[13]This was Richard Smith, *A godly and faythfull retraction made and published at Paules Cross*, (London, 1547), (Hereafter, Richard Smith, *A Retraction* ...).

[14]Cuthbert Tunstall, *De Veritate Corporis et Sanguinis Domini Nostri Jesu Christi in Eucharistia*, (Paris, 1554?) and *Contra Impios Blasphematores Dei Praedestinationis*, (Antwerp, 1555). There is a copy of this second work, beautifully written and handsomely published, in the Folger library. As an example of its serene argument, I quote this lovely passage: " ... Omnia quaecunque veluit dominus, fecit in coelo & in terra in mari & in omnibus abyssis, id quod nemo negabit, nisi omnino impius & dignior qui inter bestias numeretur quam inter homines. Itaque qui homini subtrahit liberum arbitrium, in deum blasphemes reperitur, ad cuius imagine homo creatus est, a quo sicut ab homine nimis impie liberum tellit arbirtrum."

[15]There had been sharp contention between the two men when Bonner had been sent to replace the bishop as emissary to the court of Francis I. For Bonner's complaint to Cromwell, see *Foxe*, V, pp. 150-61.

[16]For the 1548 questionnaire, see *Burnet* V, pp. 197-217. The key question was the third, and Cranmer's reply to it is a rather ambiguous repudiation of the Real Presence.

[17]Such was the opinion of Cranmer himself. See *Cranmer's Works*, II, p. 459, 468, and the interesting discussion of the theology of the 1549 Prayer Book in Dix, *The Shape of the Liturgy*, pp. 640-55.

[18]For the voting of the bishops on the various Edwardian reforms, see P. Hughes, *Reformation in England*, II, pp. 106, 113-114, 123.

[19]See the index to L. B. Smith, *Tudor Prelates and Politics*, which gives a list of the bishops and the dates of their appointments to the various dioceses. Of the men appointed after 1540, only George Day (Chichester from 1543) was to be distinguished for a stand of any kind in the religious changes which followed.

[20]See *Burnet*, V, p. 202, where Sampson's answer to the third question is shaky indeed.

[21]Gardiner, *Letters, p. 300.*

[22]*Ibid.*, p. 336.

[23]*Ibid.*, pp. 301-02.

[24]*Ibid.*, p. 321.

[25]*Ibid.*, p. 303.

[26]Smith's career is somewhat obscure. He was the object of Protestant animus, first as a Catholic polemicist, later as the preacher of a brutal sermon at the execution of Latimer and Ridley. The details of his recantations as given by Strype, *EM*, pt. 1, p. 61, and *Burnet*, II p. 281 are misleading. Both retractions made in May and July 1547 are extraordinarily equivocal, and should be read in light of his previous writings. They are discussed in more detail below, and in note 28, this chapter. In 1560, bishop Jewel reported that "smith was married, and that, being hated and despised by all sides, he was forced to keep a public house." Quoted in *Burnet*, III, p. 493.

[27]Richard Smith, *The Assertion* ... fol. 2.

[28]In *A Retraction*, a rendition of the same at Paul's Cross in May 1547, Smith withdrew the opinion that the clergy could make laws and ordinances without the approval of the prince. This being found unsatisfactory he authored *A Playne Declaration made at OXforde the 24 daye of July*, (London, 1547). Some of this is the purest nonsense, as when he declares that he did not intend to make a sacrificing priest equal with Christ (fol. Ci). But in his previous *Defence of the Sacrifice of the masse*, Smith indeed had rejected this view explicitly as a Protestant parody. The priest, he had rejoined, does not sacrifice Christ anew, but offers "the selfe same sacrifice whiche

Christ *ones for euer* offered by deathe and bloode shedynge on the crosse." (fol. liiii). (Italics mine.) In short, Smith was made to recant a view he never held.

²⁹*Burnet*, II, p. 195.

³⁰Richard Smith, *The Assertion* ... , fol. 3.

³¹*Ibid.*, fol. 12. It was the last that drew the attention of the Council and Cranmer.

³²*Ibid.*, fol. 83 ff for a refutation of Berengar. This eleventh century heretic was a favorite of sacramentaries in search of a hallowed tradition; fol. 89 ff for Wycliffe; fol. 91 for Frith.

³³Richard Smith, *A Defence* ..., fol. xv. Smith appears to have been aware of his stylistic inadequacies, and the work is prefaced by a quotation from Theophilius warning of the "vayne-glorye" induced by eloquence.

³⁴*Ibid.*, fol. cxx.

³⁵*Ibid.*, fol. xiii. Smith is, of course, referring to the ancient heretic's peremptory dismissal of the entire Old Testament, and Luther's cavalier treatment of the epistle of James.

³⁶*Ibid.*, fol. lxix.

³⁷*Ibid.*, fol. cxxxix. The author repeated this argument in his *Confutation* ..., fol. 27.

³⁸Richard Smith, *A Defence* ..., fol. xlv.

³⁹*Ibid.*, fol. lxxi.

⁴⁰*Ibid.*, fol. 1. In his 1550 *Confutation* of Cranmer, Smith develops this argument into its logical conciliar outcome. Since bishops are the successors of the apostles, it is they who have rule of the Church through General Councils.

⁴¹Richard Smith, *A brief treatyse* ..., fol. Ai.

⁴²*Ibid.*, fol. Bviii.

⁴³*Ibid.*, fol. Dvii. A major portion of Smith's writing is directed to the defense of accumulated Catholic practices, e.g., the mixture of water with wine in the chalice. I neglect these since they are not directly pertinent to our theme, but they offer interesting examples of Smith's scholarship, and his ability to find precedents in the ancient fathers and canons for Catholic practices with no basis in scripture.

⁴⁴Thomas Cranmer, *A Defense of the true and Catholike doctrine of the sacrament of the body and bloud of our saviour Christ*, (London, 1550). This book was attacked by Smith in *A Confutation* ...and by Stephen Gardiner, *An explicatio and assertion of the true Catholique fayth, touchyng the moost blessed Sacrament of the aulter*, (Rouen, 1551?). Smith's book was being circulated inLondon by March 1551 where it caused considerable alarm to the Council, see W.K. Jordan, *Edward VI: The Threshold of Power* (Cambridge, Mass., 1970), p. 249.

⁴⁵Richard Smith, *A Confutation* ...fol. 37, for his treatment of the Lateran Council; fol. 23, 162 for mention of the "bishop of Rome"—the traditional, indeed the only permissible Henrician appellation of the pope. On fol. 23, Smith repeats that the bishop of Rome did not devise the mass.

⁴⁶*Ibid.*, fol. 17.

⁴⁷Dr. N. S. Tjernagel, *Henry VIII and the Luthrans*, (St. Louis, 1965), p. 247, speaks of Stephen Gardiner in 1546 as a "Roman Catholic bishop" while W. K. Jordan, *Edward VI: The Young King*, (Cambridge, Mass., 1968), p. 219 speaks of Roman Catholic dissent in the years 1547-49.

⁴⁸Richard Smith, *A Confutation* ... , fol. 4.

⁴⁹*Ibid.*, fol. 10. In a curious way, Smith's use of the adjective "whollie" harkens back to *A defence* where, in 1546, he argued that the Councils never "erred in any wyghte matter belongynge to oure faythe" (fol. lxxii). He was made to retract this view, which in fact, he reiterated in his retraction. His views then in 1546, 1547 and 1550 were remarkably consistent, since he never said that General Councils were "whollie" free from error, but only infallible in matters essential. It is another example of Smith being made to retract an opinion he never held. In light of this, it is

perhaps a little hard to accuse the man of bad faith when his opponents humiliated him by forcing him to recant a parody of his own tenets.

[50]Richard Smith, *A Confutation* . . . , fol. 19.

[51]*Ibid.*, fol. 20.

[52]James Brokes, *A sermon very notable, fruicteful, and Godlie, made as Paules crosse* . . . , (Caly, Rouen, 1554).

[53]*Ibid.*, fol. Aviii.

[54]*Ibid.*, fol. Biii.

[55]*Ibid.*, fol. Ci.

[56]*Ibid.*, fol. Ciii.

Acknowledgements

I would like to record my thanks to institutions and persons for help generously given. Dr. Gerald Strake and his wife, Lois, I owe a great debt for their encouragement and continued friendship; and to Professors A.G. Dickens and Brendan Bradshaw for helpful suggestions. I am also happy to acknowledge the long and encouraging friendship of my colleague, Dr. H. James Burgwyn of West Chester State University, West Chester, Pennsylvania.

I must record my gratitude to the friendly staffs of Lambeth Place Library, the British Museum, the Folger Shakespeare Library, West Chester State University, and especially during my two visits to St. Louis, to the wonderfully helpful people at the Eden-Webster Library. In the history department of Webster University, St. Louis, I would like to thank my friends and colleagues, Dr. Alice Cochran, Sr. Mary Mangan and Sr. Barbara Ann Barbato for their patient reading of the text.

Author Index

Author Index

Subject Index

Subject Index